The philosophy and mechanical principles of osteopathy

A T. 1828-1917 Still

Henry Phelps Whitcomb D.O.
Burlington Vt
Feby 29 1904

THE PHILOSOPHY and MECHANICAL PRINCIPLES of OSTEOPATHY.

By

ANDREW TAYLOR STILL,

Discoverer of the Science of Osteopathy;
Founder and President of the American School of Osteopathy,
Kirksville, Adair County, Missouri.

1902.
HUDSON-KIMBERLY PUB. CO.
KANSAS CITY, MO.

Preface.

In taking up a pen at my age, and assuming the responsibility of writing a book on the causes and treatment of diseases, philosophically and in a comprehensible manner, with words and forms to meet the demands of this enlightened age, I feel it is a very great undertaking, and ask that the world give me its friendly criticism. Read and adopt, or reject, as you may feel disposed when you have perused what I may write. I start out on this journey alone, with no compass except my reason, and if I fail, no one will suffer for the trip excepting myself.

A. T. S.

JANUARY 1, 1902.

[illegible] it is a ver[illegible] the wo[illegible]

[illegible], or reject, as

[illegible]

CONTENTS.

Introduction.

My Authorities.

I quote no authors but God and experience. Books compiled by medical authors can be of little use to us, and it would be very foolish of us to look to them for advice and instruction on a science of which they know nothing. They are not able to give an intelligent explanation of their own composite theories, and they have never been asked to advise us. I am free to say that only a few persons who have been pupils of my school have tried to get wisdom from medical writers and apply it to any part of osteopathy's philosophy or practice. The student of any philosophy succeeds best by the more simple methods of reasoning. We reason for necessary knowledge only, and should try to start out with as many known facts and as few false theories as possible.

Anatomy is taught in our school more thoroughly than in any other school, because we want the student to carry a living picture of all or any part of the body in his mind, as an artist carries the mental picture of the face, scenery, beast, or anything that he wishes to represent by his brush. I constantly urge my students to keep their minds full of pictures of the normal body.

Age of Osteopathy.

In answer to the question, "How long have you been teaching this discovery?" I will say: I began to give reasons for my faith in the laws of life as given to men, worlds, and beings by the God of Nature, in April, 1855. I thought the swords and cannons of Nature were pointed and trained upon our systems of drug doctoring. Among others, I asked Dr. J. M. Neal, of Edinburgh, Scotland, for some information that I needed badly. He was a medical doctor, a man of keen mental abilities, who would give his opinions freely and to the point. The only thing that made me doubt that he was a Scotchman was that he loved whisky, and I had been told that the Scotch were a sensible people. John M. Neal said that drugs were bait for fools; that the practice of medicine was no science, and the system of drugs was only a trade, followed by the doctor for the money that could be obtained by it from the ignorant sick. He believed that Nature was a law capable of vindicating its power to cure.

I will not worry your patience with a list of the names of authors that have written upon the subject of drugs as remedial agents. I will use the word that the theologian often uses when asked for whom Christ died: the answer universally is, *"All."* I began to realize the power of Nature to cure after a skillful correction of conditions causing abnormalities had been accomplished so as to bring forth pure and healthy blood, the greatest known germicide. With this faith and by this method of reasoning, I began to treat diseases by osteopathy as an experiment; and notwithstanding I obtained good results in all diseases, I hesitated for years to proclaim my discovery. But at last I took my stand on this rock, where I have stood and fought the battles and taken the enemy's flag in every engagement for the last twenty-nine years.

Columbus had to navigate much and long, and meet many storms, because he had not the written experience of other travelers to guide him. He had only a few bits of driftwood, not common to his native country, to cause him to move as he did. But there was the fact, a bit of wood that did not grow on his home soil. He reasoned that it must be from some land amid the sea, whose shores were not known to his race. With these facts and his powerful mind of reason, he met all opposition, and moved alone, just as all men do who have no use for theories as a compass to guide them through the storms. This opposition a mental explorer must meet. I felt that I must anchor my boat to living truths and follow them wheresoever they might drift. Thus I launched my boat many years ago on the open seas, and have never found a wave of scorn nor abuse that truth could not ride and overcome.

Demand for Progress.

The twentieth century demands that advance in the healing arts should be one of the leading objects of the day and generation, because of the truth that the advancement in that profession has not been in line with other professions. The present schools of medicine are injurious schools of drunken systems that are creating morphine, whisky, and other drug-taking habits, to the shame and disgrace of the advancement and intelligence of the age. A wisely formulated substitute should be given before it is everlastingly too late. The people become diseased now as in other days, and to heal them successfully without making opium fiends and whisky sots for life should call for and get the best attention that the mind of man can give.

This work is written for the student of osteopathy; written to assist him to think before he acts, to reason for and hunt the cause in all cases before he treats; for on his ability to find the cause depends his success in relieving and curing the afflicted.

With the posted osteopath all the old systems of treating diseases are relegated to the waste-basket and marked "Obsolete." He must remember that the American School of Osteopathy does not teach him to cure by drugs, but to adjust deranged systems from a false condition to the truly normal, that blood may reach the affected parts and relieve by the powers that belong to pure blood. The osteopath must remember that his first lesson is anatomy, his last lesson is anatomy, and all his lessons are anatomy.

LIKE THE APPRENTICE.

He is like an apprentice who wishes to learn the trade of a carpenter. The carpenter's first instruction or his first lesson begins with the framework of the house. His instructor begins at the foundation, and he is positive and emphatic that it must be very solid, it must be perfectly square and level. Then his instructor, after having finished the foundation, tells him that his next lesson will be lectures and demonstrations on the sills, which have to be long enough to reach the whole length of the foundation walls. He saws off, splits and laps, and completes one corner of the building, and then proceeds to finish in like manner the remaining three corners, having fastened together and squared them by the mathematical rule of 6, 8, and 10, well known to builders as the rule for obtaining a perfect square. At this time the instructor begins to teach the apprentice the importance of a good foundation. After finishing this instructive lecture, he tells the apprentice to observe the rule that must be followed to prepare this sill for the studding or ribs that are to stand firmly fixed and fastened to the sill upon the foundations. These ribs are intended to hold up the first and overhead floors, which are supported by joists extending from side to side of the building The apprentice soon finds or is told that there must be a sill or wall-plate at the upper extremity of the studding, to receive rafters and roof with all weights thereunto belonging. Still the young man is not a carpenter, which he will observe when directed to put on the siding in a workmanlike manner. Instruction is equally important at this stage of construction. He will find that his first and many other boards that he puts on according to his own judgment are condemned and ordered pulled off by the master mechanic, because they do not meet the requirements of the plans and specifications. On his next examination the siding looks and shows well, and the young man smiles with the thought that he has pleased the old man once, and exclaims, "How will that do, boss?" which is answered by, "Did you forget to countersink the nails?" The young fellow says, "Oh, I did forget that." At this time the boss says to the apprentice, "Notify the painter that one side of the house is ready for him." The boss is now ready to give instruction in reference to the windows, which are to be raised and lowered both from above and below by ropes and pulleys. He assists the apprentice with a few of them, as this is a very important part of the work. Then he instructs and trusts the apprentice to proceed with the balance of the windows, and orders him to report when he has finished one. On inspection the boss says, "O. K.; go on." He opens the plans and specifications and says, "We will now lay the permanent floors," gives a few instructions, adjusts a few boards, and tells the apprentice to go on with the work. After a time, the boss workman brings in the plans and specifications to ascertain whether the work is proceeding according to the plans, which read that the floors in all joints, both side and end, shall be keyed and squared to a perfect fit. He says to the apprentice. "There is a crack one-eighth of an inch all along this side of this board; and several boards do not meet at the ends because they have not been cut to the square. They will not be received nor paid for, because they have not been laid according to the plans and specifications; we will have to tear them up, and lose time, lumber, and nails." At this time the boss gives instruction in the use of the tri-square and saw, with these words, "I want you to pay special attention and make all boards fit both at side and end." As we wish to stop further detailing, we will say that this rigidity in following the plans and specifications must be kept up until the last nail is driven, and as the house approaches closer to the finish there is a still greater demand for exactness, and the penalty is greater for omissions. There is just the same perfection of work demanded of the plumber, electrician, and plasterer as there was of the apprentice in the laying of the foundation and adjusting the framework. I have given this homely, well-known, everyday illustration in order to rivet on the mind of the student the working hypothesis that he is also an inspector, and, as an osteopath, he is to judge and adjust all defects or variations from the abnormal to the normal, as found in the plans and specifications for the healthy human body. The student begins this study with the bony framework of the house in which life dwells. He has found that the foundation and all parts have been wisely planned and definitely specified, when he thinks of that phrase found in Holy Writ which reads, "Let us make man." That, to the student and operator, should mean, "Let us study man, who was made after wonderful plans and specifications, and when completed was pronounced not only good, but very good, by that scrutinizing Inspector who makes all and omits nothing." In man's construction we have another cogent illustration of the truth that perfection in all parts can only be accepted as good. This hasty comparison I hope will assist the student when he goes forth to give health and harmony to the afflicted.

This work, which is designated as a guide- or text-book for both student and operator, will be written with the purpose on the part of the author to assist the beginners and the more advanced in their efforts to obtain good results by accommodating Nature to do its own mending and restoring. The doctor of osteopathy, as foreman, can only preside over a shop of repairs; and, in order that he may wisely proceed and make his investigations thoroughly, we think it best to divide the human body into a number of divisions, beginning with the head and neck and including such diseases as belong to that division, then the upper spine, chest, and its organs to the diaphragm, and from the diaphragm to the sacrum, and from the sacrum to the coccyx. All diseases common to the human race will be classified and presented in the plainest and most forcible words at my command, to enable the reader to fully comprehend the meaning of this philosophy, which is written to simplify a knowledge of the cause and cure of all curable diseases to which the human race is subject.

Truth Is Truth.

We often speak of truth. We say "great truths," and use many other qualifying expressions. But no one truth is greater than any other truth Each has a sphere of usefulness peculiar to itself. Thus we should treat with respect and reverence all truths, great and small. A truth is the complete work of Nature, which can only be demonstrated by the vital principle belonging to that class of truths. Each truth or division, as we see it, can only be made known to us by the self-evident fact which this truth is able to demonstrate by its action.

If we take man as the object on which to base the beginning of our reason, we find the association of many elements, which differ in kind to suit the purpose for which they were designed. To us they act, to us they are wisely formed and located for the purpose for which they were designed. Through our five senses we deal with the material body. It has action. That we observe by vision, which connects the mind to reason. High above the five senses on the subject of cause or causes of action, is motion. By the testimony of the witness, the mind is connected in a manner by which it can reason on solidity and size. By smell, taste, and sound we make other connections between the chambers of reason and the object we desire to reason upon; and thus we get the foundation on which all five witnesses are arrayed to the superior principle, which is mind.

Man Is Triune.

After seeing a human being complete in form, self-moving, with power to stop or go on at will, to us he seems to obey some commander. He seems to go so far and stop; he lies down and gets up; he turns round and faces the objects that are traveling in the same direction that he is. Possibly he faces the object by his own action. Then, by about-facing, he sees one coming with greater velocity, sees he cannot escape by his own speed, so he steps aside and lets that body pass on, as though he moved in obedience to some order. The bystander would ask the question, "How did he know such a dangerous body was approaching?" He finds, on the most crucial examination, that the sense of hearing is wholly without reason. The same is true with all the five senses pertaining to man, beast, or bird. This being the condition of the five physical senses, we are forced by reason to conclude there is a superior being who conducts the material man, sustains, supports, and guards him against danger; and after all our explorations, we have to decide that man is triune when complete.

First, there is the material body; second, the spiritual being; third, a being of mind which is far superior to all vital motions and material forms, whose duty is to wisely manage this great engine of life. This great principle, known as mind, must depend for all evidences on the five senses, and on this testimony all mental conclusions are based, and all orders are issued from this mental court to move to any point or stop at any place. To obtain good results, we must blend ourselves with and travel in harmony with Nature's truths. When this great machine, man, ceases to move in all its parts, which we call death, the explorer's knife discovers no mind, no motion. He simply finds formulated matter, with no motor to move it, with no mind to direct it. He can trace the channels through which the fluids have circulated, and he can find the relation of parts to other parts; in fact, by the knife he can expose to view the whole machinery that once was wisely active. Suppose the explorer is able to add the one principle motion; at once we would see an action, but it would be a confused action. Still he is not the man desired. There is one addition that is indispensable to control this active body, or machine, and that is mind. With that added, the whole machinery then works as man. The three, when united in full action, are able to exhibit the thing desired—complete.

Trash.

We must remember that when we write or talk, we have asked the reader or listener to stop all pursuits to read our story or listen to it. We must be kind enough to give him something in exchange for his precious time. We must remember that time to an American is too valuable to be given for hours to a long story that does not benefit him. We care but little for what queens, kings, and professors have said; it is what you know that we want. Man's life is too short and useful to be spent reading any undigested literature that amounts to nothing. Suppose that a farmer should write on stock- or grain-raising, and his book informed the student just how Professor So-and-So planted, bred, and failed, and gave no lesson that did not close with a "However," or "I would remark, as stated before," and so on. Of what use would it be to the young agriculturist who read it, and if he had no other instruction, what would he amount to as a farmer? You know he would be a total failure in the profession until he learned to be governed by known truths. His success depends on what he knows, and not on being able to recite what someone had failed to accomplish.

OSTEOPATHY.

What is osteopathy? It is a scientific knowledge of anatomy and physiology in the hands of a person of intelligence and skill, who can apply that knowledge to the use of man when sick or wounded by strains, shocks, falls, or mechanical derangement or injury of any kind to the body. An up-to-date osteopath must have a masterful knowledge of anatomy and physiology. He must have brains in osteopathic surgery, osteopathic obstetrics, and osteopathic practice, curing diseases by skillful readjustment of the parts of the body that have been deranged by strains, falls, or any other cause that may have removed even a minute nerve from the normal, although not more than the thousandth of an inch. He sees cause in a slight anatomical deviation for the beginning of disease. Osteopathy means a knowledge of the anatomy of the head, face, neck, thorax, abdomen, pelvis, and limbs, and a knowledge why health prevails in all cases of perfect normality of all parts of the body. Osteopathy means a studious application of the best mental talents at the command of the man or woman that would hold a place in the profession. Osteopathy has no time to throw away in beer-drinking, nor has it time to wear out shoe-leather carrying a cue around the pool- or billiard-table. It belongs to men of sober brains, men who never tire of anatomy and physiology or of hunting the cause of disease. An osteopath answers questions by his learning. He proves what he says by what he does. An osteopath knows that to the day of the coming in of osteopathy, the whole medical world was almost a total blank in knowledge of the machinery and functions of the abdomen of the human body. The medical man to-day, if we judge his knowledge by what he does, is perfectly at sea as soon as he enters the abdomen. He combats bowel disease by methods handed down to him by symptomatology. Beginning with chronic constipations, he reasons not on the causes. His one idea is to fall onto a successful purgative drug, which never should be used excepting with great caution. When the most active purgatives fail, with the aid of injections, to effect a movement; the bowels filling up and packing the abdominal cavity so full and tight that no organ below the diaphragm can act and all motion is lost, even to the blockage of arterial and venous circulation of the blood; with the stomach crowded with food, then on to vomiting of fecal matter and the vitality low all over the body; what is left for the medical doctor but surgical interference? And he proceeds with his instrumental skill with hope and doubt. The osteopath gets his success with such diseases through adjustment of the abdominal viscera, with the view of relieving the bowels of bulks of fecal matter, either hard or soft, that are laboring to pass away from the body through the natural channels, but meet mechanical obstructions that are caused by kinks, folds, twists, and knots of the bowels, the result of heavy strains, lifts, and falls that have forced the bowels to abnormal positions in the abdomen, deranging the mesentery at various points. The osteopath feels that he is not justified in administering purgatives, nor even injections into the bowels, until he has straightened out the viscera so that no resisting obstruction is liable to block the passing fecal matter. He proceeds as a mechanic.

A Question of Intelligence.

Osteopathy is not so much a question of books as it is of intelligence. A successful osteopath is in all cases, or should be, a person of individuality, with a mechanical eye behind all motions or efforts to readjust any part of the body to its original normality, because unguided force is dangerous, often doing harm and failing in giving the relief that should be the reward of well-directed skill. A knowledge of anatomy is only a dead weight if we do not know how to apply that knowledge with successful skill. That is all there is to the question why our knowledge of anatomy should be more perfect than it is with any other school of the healing art. The osteopath should be thoroughly educated by books and by drill, and in my reference to books I mean those that are essential to a complete knowledge of anatomy.

For fear that the student will not comprehend what I mean by the books pertaining to a complete knowledge of anatomy, I will give something of an approximate list, as follows: Descriptive anatomy, by the very best and latest authors; demonstrative anatomy, human physiology, histology, and chemistry. A thorough knowledge obtained in the branches named, pertaining to the one subject, anatomy, is the qualification necessary for the student. He must receive instruction why and how to apply this knowledge of anatomy to useful purposes, with anatomical exactness, for the purpose of giving vent to suspended fluid circulation either to the parts of or from the body, locally or generally.

With a correct knowledge of the form and functions of

the body and all its parts, we are then prepared to know what is meant by a variation in a bone, muscle, ligament, or fibre or any part of the body, from the least atom to the greatest bone or muscle. By our mechanical skill, preceded by our intelligence in anatomy, we can detect and adjust both hard and soft substances of the system. By our knowledge of physiology we can comprehend the requirements of the circulation of the fluids of the body as to time, speed, and quantity, in harmony with the demands of normal life. We think that osteopathy has proven that it is a short, true, and powerful science, strictly under natural law.

Osteopathy an Independent System.

It does not now ask nor has it ever asked help of allopathy, homeopathy, eclecticism, or any other system of healing. It claims independence from all of them, and ability to steer its way in the future as in the past. All systems depend on sending guns of wisdom into the camps of sickness with orders to kill disease, but not to hurt the sick man, woman, or child. No difference how deadly the poison the bullets contain, the gun must shoot and kill diseases and leave the patient well of all maladies. Some cure by wise looks and words to suit their snapping fingers. Then water cure, prayer, and so on through the list, come in. None has a foundation in a well-regulated system to insure good health and long life. Osteopathy proclaims and proves that success in cures comes when all joints in the body move as Nature ordered. We do not reason that Nature would turn out imperfect or inferior goods, for the market of this or any other world. Questions like the following must have a negative answer, with substantial proofs, before a drug doctor is able to argue intelligently for the demand or need of adding drugs to a sick man's blood: "Has Nature's God an abundance of skill to do good work in the workshops of Nature?"

Nature Is Health.

In Nature we look for good machines in form and action. We have learned to know that Nature does no imperfect work, but, on the other hand, does its work to perfection, and perfection is its watchword in all its parts and functions. The wise man has long since learned that no suggestions he can offer can do any good, but, as a rule, are vastly harmful. He often kills or ruins the machine to such a degree that it fails in part or in whole to do its work. He finds his supposed helps have disabled his man or woman even to death. The drug-giver is not satisfied that God has quite the wisdom necessary to make a machine that will do the work that all daily demands require. He hopes to do something to have life do better work. He sees only one thing in which to begin and end all his labors, "drugs."

Does a chemist get results desired by accident? Are your accidents more likely to get good results than his? Do order and success demand thought and cool-headed reason? If we wish to be governed by reason, we must take a position that is founded on truth and capable of presenting facts to prove the validity of the truths we present. All Nature is kind enough to exhibit specimens of its work as witnesses of its ability to prove its assertions by its work. Without that tangible proof, Nature would belong to the gods of chance, and the laws of mother, conception, growth, and birth, from atoms to worlds, would be a failure, a universe without a head to direct. But as the beautiful works of Nature stand, giving us the evidence that all beings, great and small, come by the law of cause and effect, are we not bound to work by the laws of cause if we wish an effect?

Our Relation to Other Systems.

We hope to get the first premium of respect from the whole world for attending to our own business. We expect

are free Americans. We do
ools and we will not be lorded
be trampled upon or taken
rs. We expect to educate
aration, and to use all the
ion in surgery, obstetrics,
e to the qualified student
o or four years, but when
edge of anatomy, physiology, chem-
urgery, obstetrics, and of all the principles taught in the American School of Osteopathy. We have no time to spend with any doubtful theory. It is quality, not quantity, that we want. Other systems may take quantity; we take quality, attend to our own business, and hope that other systems will attend to theirs. Our school was not created for a time-killer. Brevity should be our object. Qualified merit is the best thing a man can possibly possess. We want a full share of that. If we can get it in two years, by putting in every day and night in hard study and thorough drills, and can stand the severest tests of our knowledge and prove to the world that we know what we claim, then we want to be treated civilly while we pursue our profession. Our legislatures are friends to progress and will give us what we merit. They are all Americans, believe in fair fighting, will clear the ring, and see the best man win. A just verdict is all we ask. We have used no drugs to give children the lockjaw, and don't intend to, but if the members of the medical trust do not leave us alone, we will ask the legislature to give them a little anti-toxin to lock their meddlesome jaws, or have "cow-rot" injected into them and retire them to Hot Springs to get the cow syphilitic tetanus boiled out. I mean vaccine rot, that cursed filth that is taken from cows afflicted with mad itch, cows with all the venereal diseases of man and brute.

Old Systems Hard to Throw Off.

All old systems of education that have been adopted by the people are very hard to throw off, because of the habits of professors who have been made teachers and have taken the places of their preceptors as instructors. They follow the old system without a murmur, for several reasons. First, the young teacher can teach that which he has been taught more easily than what he may feel should be taught. At this time the young man or woman feels that he must have a living before he can make a move or suggestion to change old methods of instruction for new. To lose his place and salary would nonplus him and turn him adrift in the world with the name of a fault-finder. As bread and meat are first with him, he decides to be silent for a year, then next and next year rolls around and his living holds him into silence, until it becomes second nature to him. He has lost all hope of reformation, and then concludes to be a popular author. He begins to quote and clip and finally gets out a "new book," with no friction with other writers. His hair now begins to grow thin with suppressed ambition, and in a few years his hair all falls out and hope is forever gone. He has learned rote teaching and how to compile innocently from other old theories. Another and another generation follows this old system that has not given a single new thought for ages. Thus our people are dragged through centuries because the fear of losing bread and meat has kept the teachers in the narrow paths of the most ignorant days of any age known to history. I want volunteers to push this medical revolution. We must conquer before our hair falls out or we will never succeed. I have just read a text-book on gynecology that gives a list of three hundred and fifty-seven other books quoted by the author. The book has only seven hundred pages and there are three hundred and fifty-seven authors quoted. If there is a single hair on your heads, that one hair will give you sense enough to know that that man is only a clipper, an author by quotations. He is not the kind of an author that will ever be arrested, tried, and found guilty of leading a revolution and shot by court-martial. Our school has declared itself progressive. We try to fear the command, "Thou shalt not lie." Let us live up to our proclamations.

CHAPTER I.

Important Studies.

ANATOMY.

In early life I began the study of anatomy, believing it to be the "alpha and omega," the beginning and the end, of all forms and the laws that give forms, by selection and the association of the elements, kinds and quantities, to the human body. The human form indicates an object. In the first place, it is constructed as a hieroglyphical representation of all beings and principles interested physically or mentally in the production of worlds, with their material forms, their living motions, and their mental governments. Man represents the mind and wisdom of God to the degree of his endowments. This is shown by his display of knowledge, and ability to increase that knowledge to the degree of fullness attainable by his allotted mental perception, and by his accumulation and association of facts to the degree of able conclusions. He reasons because of the lack of that amount of mental ability known as knowledge absolute. He can fill all the limits in his sphere, and no more. The fish can swim up to the surface of the water; it can dive to the bottom; it can swim the length and width of rivers and oceans in which it is prepared to dwell and explore—in obedience to that command, "Thus far shalt thou go, and no farther." The high-sailing birds are only the fish of the atmospheric ocean. They can touch the upper surface of this great ocean; they can descend to the lower surface; their limits of life are between the superior and lower limits above cited. They can live, flourish, and enjoy themselves in the field of usefulness for which they were created. The same of the fish. The same law is equally applicable to the human being. If the fish should change place with the bird, it would surely die and become extinct. The same law would be applicable to the bird That element that sustains animal life belonging to each is abundantly supplied and dwells in its peculiar environment. The same law of extinction would be equally forcible should the bird try to dwell in the waters of the seas. Let us make the application of this crude base of our philosophy, and make a few changes for the convenience of reason. Suppose we should move the heart up to the cranial cavity and the brain down to the place now occupied by the liver, and the liver to the position of the lungs, and place the lungs on the sacrum; what would you expect but death to both fowl and fish? Thus the practical osteopath must be very exacting in adjusting the system. He must know that he has done his work right in all particulars, in that the forms, great and small, all through the body, must be infinitely correct, with the object in view, that the necessary fuel and nutriment of life that is now in the hands of Deity may be adjusted to the degree of perfection that it was when it received the first breath of individualized life.

Osteopathy is built upon the principle of debtor and creditor. We must willingly credit Nature with having done its work to perfection in all the machinery and functions of animal life, and that the after-results are good or bad according to centers and variations. If we observe any variations from the normal center, our work is never complete nor the reward due us until by adjustment we have reached the normal. We know our responsibility, and should labor to render a just account, and willingly submit our work to the anatomical critic.

PHYSIOLOGY.

Works on physiology at the present date are compilations of many theories and a few facts. In animal physiology we all know that a babe is not as big as a man, but that it may in time grow to man's size. To get large, man must be builded of material to suit his form. Each piece must be so shaped that in union with all other pieces a complete running engine will be made, not by chance, but by the rule of animal engine-making. When complete, he is a self-acting, individualized, separate personage, endowed with the power to move, and mind to direct in locomotion, with a care for comfort and a thought for his continued existence in the preparation and consumption of food to keep him in size and form to suit the duties he may have to perform.

So far, we are only able to see man in his completed form. We know but little of how he obtained his shape, size, and action. At this point we mentally ask, How is all this work done? We soon learn that the book of Nature is the only true source from which we can get such knowledge, and if we are to know the whys and hows of the wonderful work, we must enter the shops of Nature, observe, and reason from effect to cause. We know that if we ever know the whole, we must first know the parts. We take the dead man to the table and open all parts to view. We begin our book of knowledge under the wise teaching of experience. Here we launch out on the sea of anatomy. We cut away the skin that encases or covers the whole body. As soon as we pass through and remove the skin, we enter the fascia. In it we find cells, glands, blood- and other vessels, with nerves running to and from every part. Here we could spend an eternity with our present mental capacity, before we could comprehend even a superficial knowledge of the powers and uses of the fascia in the laboratory of animal life. From the fascia we journey on to the muscles, ligaments, and bones, all in forms and conditions to suit Nature's great design of the living machine. By the knife we expose organs, glands, and blood-vessels.

Let us treat "Physiology" with due respect and credit old theories with all the light they give and all the good they have done, but do not be afraid of their wisdom. So far, they have only seen with the microscope that which appears in dead flesh and in chemical analyses of the dead compounds. They have tried to learn something. They say, "Possibly," "However," "Doubted by So-and-So," and "As we remarked before in our last lecture, that there was great differences of opinions on the subject of bacteria, microbes, and various other theories on the physiological action or blood-changes in croup, diphtheria, and all diseases of the throat, trachea, tonsils, and glandular system during the rage of such epidemics." At about this time the student is told that in all diseases of the throat and lungs a wonderfully new remedy, antitoxin, in full and frequent doses, has been very favorably reported upon, and that less than 50 per cent of the cases of diphtheria had died under the antitoxin method of treating the disease. What I want to say to the student is about this: I think that at the very time a young doctor needs knowledge on the cause of diseases he is pushed into the idea that he must look over the recipe papers till he finds "Good for Croup" on a prescription-sheet. Then a copy is sent in haste to the drug store to be filled. The good but wise druggist does not have quite all the drugs named in the prescription, so he puts in substitutes. If the patient gets well, then the drug clerk compounds more of the mixture and tells the world what a wonderful "cure-all" he has found. The next prescription comes, but for another disease. The prescription is written by the same good old doctor; the same story—not all the drugs on hand, another substitute is tried. That patient dies; all is quiet. The druggist feels skittish, hunts the prescription, and keeps it to show that the doctor sent the same, and tells that it was duly filled. He keeps the world wisely ignorant of substitutes. Thus the young doctor is led off by symptomatology to the idea that he must find something to give and take.

CHEMISTRY.

As chemical compounds are not used by the osteopath as remedies, then chemistry as a study for the student is only to teach him that elements in Nature combine and form other substances, and without such changes and union no teeth, bone, hair, or muscle could appear in the body. Chemistry is of great use as a part of a thorough osteopathic education. It gives us the reasons why food is changed in the body into bone, muscle, and so on. Unless we know chemistry reasonably well, we will have considerable mental worry to solve the problem of what becomes of food after eating. By chemistry the truths of physiology are firmly established in the mind of the student of Nature. He finds that in man wonderful chemical changes do all the work, and that in the laboratory of Nature's chemistry there is much to learn. By chemistry we are led to see the beauties of physiology. Chemistry is one thing and physiology is the witness that it is a law in man as it is in all Nature. By chemistry we learn to comprehend some of the laws of union in Nature which we can use with confidence. In chemistry we become acquainted with the law of cause and change in union, which is a standard law sought by the student of osteopathy.

Osteopathy believes that all parts of the human body act on chemical compounds, and from the general supply manufacture the substances for local wants. Thus the liver builds for itself the material that is prepared in its own division laboratory. The same of heart and brain. No disturbing or hindering causes will be tolerated if an osteopath can find and remove them. We must reason that on withholding the supply from a limb it would wither away. We suffer from two causes—want of supply and the burdens of dead deposits.

PRINCIPLES OF OSTEOPATHY.

This branch of study, Principles of Osteopathy, gives us an understanding of the perfect plans and specifications followed in man's construction. To comprehend this engine of life, it is necessary to constantly keep the plans and specifications before the mind, and in the mind, to such a degree that there is no lack of knowledge of the locations and uses of any and all parts. A complete knowledge of all parts, with their forms, sizes, and places of attachment, is gained, and should be so thoroughly grounded in the memory that there can be no doubt of the use or purpose of the great or small parts, and what duty they have to perform in the working of the engine. When the specifications are thoroughly learned from anatomy or the engineer's guide-book, we will then take up the chapter on the division of forces, by which this engine moves and performs the duties for which it was created. In this chapter the mind will be referred to the brain to obtain a knowledge of that organ, where the force starts, and how it is conducted to any belt, pulley, journal, or division of the whole building. After learning where the force is obtained, and how conveyed from place to place throughout the whole body, one becomes interested and wisely instructed. He sees the various parts of this great system of life when preparing fluids commonly known as blood, passing through a set of tubes both great and small, some so very small as to require the aid of powerful microscopes to see their infinitely minute forms, through which the blood and other fluids are conducted. By this acquaintance with the normal body which has been won by a study of anatomy and in the dissecting-rooms, he is well prepared to be invited into the inspection-room, to make comparison between the normal and the abnormal engines. He is called into this room for the purpose of comparing engines that have been thrown off the track or injured in collisions, bending journals, pipes, or bolts, or which have been otherwise deranged. To repair this machine signifies an adjustment from the abnormal condition in which the machinist finds it to the condition of the normal engine. Our work would commence with first lining up the wheels with straight journals. Then we would naturally be conducted to the boiler, steam chest, shafts, and every part that belongs to a complete engine. When convinced that they are straight and in place as designated in the plans and described in the specifications, we have done all that is required of a master mechanic. Then the engine goes into the hands of the engineer, who waters, fires, and conducts this artificial being on its journey. As osteopathic machinists we go no further than to adjust the abnormal conditions back to the normal. Nature will do the rest.

SYMPTOMATOLOGY.

With anatomy in the normal properly understood, we are enabled to detect conditions that are abnormal. It may be that by measurement we can discover a variation one-hundredth of an inch from the normal, which, though infinitely small, is nevertheless abnormal. If we follow the effects of abnormal straining of ligaments, we will easily come to the conclusion that derangements of one-hundredth part of an inch are often probable of those parts of the body over which blood-vessels and nerves are distributed, whose duties, are to construct, vitalize, and keep a territory, though small in width, fully up to the normal standard of health. The blood-vessels carrying the fluids for the construction and sustenance of the infinitely fine fibres, vessels, glands, fascia, and cellular conducting channels to nerves and lymphatics, must be absolutely normal in location before a normal physiological action can be executed in perfect harmony with the health-sustaining machinery of the body. If a nerve or vessel should be disturbed, we would expect delay and a subsequent derangement in the workings of the laboratory of Nature. Thus we recognize the importance of a thorough acquaintance with the large and small fibres, ligaments, muscles, blood- and nerve-supply to all the organs, glands and lymphatics of the fascia, and the blood-circuit in general. We wish you to make yourself so thoroughly acquainted with the human antomy that your hand, eye, and reason will be unfailing guides to all causes and effects. We wish to impress upon your minds that this is a living and trustworthy symptomatology, and not speculative, having its commencement in words and winding up with unreliable rehashings of antiquated theories that have neither a father nor a mother whose counsel and milk have ever led their children beyond the yellow chalk-mark of stale custom, born and sustained to this day by the nightmare of stupidity, ignorance, and superstition. This is the book of symptomatology that I wish you to purchase. Use it in place of all others. Its price is eternal vigilance.

SURGERY.

Surgery, as taught in the American School of Osteopathy, is to be used as often or as much as wisdom finds it necessary in order to give relief and save life or limb when all evidence with facts shows that blood cannot repair the injuries. It is then and then only that we use surgery to save life, limb, and organs of the body from worse conditions, by allowing dead fluids to destroy them by poisoning absorptions. Surgeons of the Army or Government are the commissioned officers of health, with powers and instructions to use drugs or anything else for the relief of the wounded or sick soldier while in the service. Their duties extend to the use of both knife and spatula. Surgery has its place in the scientific uses, and I think it has grown to be a very great science. In the hands of a judicious person, it can be of untold benefit; but in the hands of a bigot, I think it is a deadly curse. Osteopathy is surgery from a physiological standpoint. The osteopathic surgeon uses "the knife of blood" to keep out "the knife of steel," and saves life by saving the injured or diseased limbs and organs of the body by reduction, in place of removing them.

We want to avoid the use of the knife and saw as much as possible. We must be patient, and use freely a skillful knowledge of physiology, remembering all the time that cures come only as a result of physiological action after the most skilled surgeons of this and past ages have done their best work. We do not expect or even hope to improve on the skilled arts of surgery in amputations and other legitimate uses of the knife and saw; but we do hope to understand the forms and functions of the parts of the human body to a saving degree of knowledge, and apply that knowledge in such a skillful manner that abnormal conditions demanding the use of the knife will not occur, such as tumors on and in the body, or stones in the bladder and gall-sac, which form when some function fails to keep lime and chalk and other substances in solution as Nature intended they should be while in the circulation. If we can come to the rescue by producing better drainage through the veins and excretory channels, we prove our ability as surgeons by using Nature's knife in place of the surgical knife of steel. Growths in the abdomen, such as tumors, only form when some channel of drainage is shut off. If we wish to stop or remove a growth of any organ in the abdomen, we must line up the body in good form for the appropriation of the arterial blood by the organ to which it was sent out by the heart; then fix all the vessels of drainage, turn the nerves loose, and the work will be done. Too much use has been made of the knife, and too little trust placed in Nature. The knife can be seen. Nature is known only by the power of the gift of reason well applied. The knife, particularly for the last few years, gets larger rolls of cash for its work than the pills; also the grave and heaven get more men and women—that is, if they have plenty of money to pay for their ride. Poor people seldom have tumors or appendicitis, because the doctor finds he can attend them without the knife. I tell you that it is the wealthy who generally get the deadly knife.

CHAPTER II.

Some Substances of the Body.

Two Hundred Bones.

In the human body the osteopathic machinist finds about two hundred and six bones. No two fit the same joint or move in the same place. Each one is made in a different form or shape. Each shape indicates a different place and use. He finds one skull, two jaw-bones, seven neck-bones, twelve back-bones, five lumbar bones, one sacrum, two innominates, two thigh-bones, two feet with twenty-six bones in each foot, two arms with three bones in each, two hands with twenty-seven bones in each hand, then two collar-bones and two shoulder-blades, and so on. In all no two alike. You know from your knowledge of anatomy that I am telling you the truth as to the numbers and differences in forms and uses of the bones of the human body. Your reason tells you their natural places and how to place them in their proper places for the discharge of their functions in life's machinery. When you have been trained in schools of anatomy to know just how to place all the bones of a skeleton in their proper positions, in harmony with the one or ones with which they articulate, to meet the needs of the body, I say and believe that by the time you have learned all their natural unions and articulations, that you have learned enough to know when any bone is missing or put in the wrong place. I feel then that you will have received a criticising knowledge of what is right or wrong in the spine, ribs, and limbs, and all the bones of any part of the limbs, spine, or chest.

Armed with the proof that you do know, let us begin and reason that the two hundred bones, all different in forms and uses, are all firmly fastened together with strong straps, and they must each have a differently shaped binding, strap, or ligament, and that strap must be long or short, thick, wide, or narrow, to suit the long, the short, or the flat bones of power and motion, of the head, face, neck, etc. Every bone of the back and chest, every bone of the limbs, and every other bone has muscles attached to it to hold it in its socket or place in which it moves or articulates.

Bones Considered First.

My object in this talk on the bones is to encourage your minds in plowing deeper in the fertile soil of reason. I want you to see that all force, either stimulating, quieting, motor, nutrient, sensory, or any kind or quality of nerve-supply, comes to the muscles and glands and the organs of the whole system from some depository, and has got to get to its destined muscle, nerve, vein, or flesh through gates and openings in or between the bones. When these gates are shut or closed and the nerves lose control of the blood to a single muscle or a whole system of muscles, with all supplies of the fascia and cellular system cut off, then starvation and spasms of muscles appear and they become very contracted or hard. Right here is the red rag of the masseur or the osteopath who dwells so much on the inhibiting nerves and muscles. His lack of knowledge in the field of philosophy leaves him in the field of a masseur only. He gets some good results, and thinks his rubs are the best rubs in the world. He tells you: "Have the patient lie on his breast, face down, hands hanging down to the sides of the table; then have the operator stand at the side of the table or leather-covered, upholstered bench, and look all over the spine and sacrum. If a high bone is here, a low or sunken place at the center or sides near the transverse processes where ribs are held in attachment to the spine by ligaments, you must treat here and there by pressing fingers heavily between ribs and spine and rub the back up and down with the hands on either side of the vertebral column." He has you work on the back, using a heavy pressure with a washerwoman's motion when she has a shirt on the washboard. The patient gets well or dies, and the masseur thinks his hands have a good washboard when he is pushing a lean woman's skin, fascia, and rhomboid muscles over her ribs. He thinks he has a good job in a health laundry, and rubs hard, fast, and long. He thinks her ribs, twelve on each side, make as good a washboard as "Mam" ever washed a sock on. He never stops to think that ribs are tied to muscles, that they are tied to other ribs, and from them to points on the spine, and that better results than with great pressure of a man's hands on the back with up-and-down passes could be obtained. He should remember that slipped or twisted vertebræ and ribs must be sought out and adjusted, giving intercostal nerves thorough freedom to act and soften muscles and let blood loose to feed and nourish the whole spine. I contend that the curing comes direct from the liberation of the interspinous and costal nerves, freed from bone-pressure on the nerves of motion, sensation, and nutrition.

How are we to proceed with the process of setting bones to their natural places, and what are bones supposed to do by way of hindering functional action when much or little at variance from their exact normal place on the bony framework? All nerve-power issues from the heart and brain, and both are storage batteries full of nerve-force all the time and ready to supply any set of nerves. Why should we think other than that all these two storehouses require of the nervous system is to have open channels to receive such force as they require to do all functioning incumbent upon them? Open doors and continued wires of life are all that are required by them as conditions before the brain and heart send out their active forces. Osteopathy believes that the brain and heart are fully supplied with all the living forces, and will send power to any place with which they have nerve-connections without any rubbing or manipulation further than to insure unobstructive flow of the nerve-forces. That power gets abnormally slow or fast only when the full supply is cut off or limited before it leaves the bones surrounding the brain and spinal cord. Our work is done when we leave open the nerve-channels to the perfect eye of Nature's inspection. Blood- and nerve-force return to the normal when freedom is given the nerves to act. There is no need for an operator to unnecessarily tire himself and his patient when no good is to be derived from the effort. He is dealing with cause and effect. He must not fall back to the low plane of reason on which a masseur dwells. The latter's force is applied with no lamp of reason burning in his camp. The masseur works hard and gets some good results, but does not know how nor why they came, more than that he has given the patient a good "all-over rooting." We pay for a lamp of reason to guide us. We feel that we are only tinkling cymbals or sounding brass as osteopaths until we can have reason at the beginning and the end of all our methods or efforts to cure the afflicted.

The Brain.

Of all parts of the body of man, the brain should be the most attractive. It is the place where all force centers, where all nerves are connected with one common battery. By its orders the laboratories of life begin to act on crude material and work until blood is formed and transformed into food for the nerves first, then the arteries and veins. The brain furnishes nerve-action and forces to suit each class of work to be done by that set of nerves which is to construct forms and to keep blood constantly in motion in the arteries and from all parts back to the heart through the veins, that it may be purified, renewed, and re-enter the circulation. Arterial motion is normal during all ages, from the quick pulse of the babe's arm to the slow pulse of the aged. At advanced age the pulse is so slow that heat is not sufficiently generated by the nerves, whose force is not great enough to bring electricity to the stage of heat. All temperature, high and low, surely is the effect of active electricity--*plus* to fever, *minus* to coldness. When an irritant enters the body by the lungs, skin, or in any other way, a change appears in the heart's action from its effect on the brain to a high electric action. That burning heat is called fever. If *plus*, we may have a violent type, as in yellow fever; if *minus*, we may have low grades, as in typhus and typhoid fevers, and so on through the list.

Thought Implies Action.

To think implies action of the brain. We can grade thought, although we cannot measure its speed. Suppose a person in one line of business thinks fast enough to suit that kind of work. We will take a farmer who is devoting his time and energies to hog-raising. Now the question is, How fast does he think? How many revolutions do the wheels of his head make per minute to do all the necessary thinking connected with his business? Say his mental wheels revolve one hundred times per minute. Then he adds sheep-raising to his business, and if that should require one hundred more revolutions, and he takes charge of raising draft-horses, with one hundred and seventv-five more revolutions added, you can see the wheels of his head are whizzing off three hundred and seventy-five vibrations per minute. And at this time he adds the duties of a carpenter, with three hundred more revolutions. Add them together, and you see six hundred and seventy-five. To this number he adds the duties and thoughts of a sheriff, which are numerous enough to buzz his wheels at fifteen hundred revolutions more, and you find twenty-one hundred and seventy-five to be the count of his mental revolutions so far. Now you have the great physical demands added to the mental motion which his brain has to support, yet he can do all, so far, fairly well.

He now adds to his labors the manufacturing of leather from all kinds of hides, with the chemistry of fine tanning, and this adds a strain equal to the sum of all previous mental motions. Add and you find forty-two hundred and fifty revolutions all drawing on his brain each minute of the day. Add to this mental strain the increased action of his body which has to perform the duties, and you have the beginning of a worry of both mind and body, to which we will add manufacturing of engines, iron-smelting, rolling, etc.; send him as a delegate to a national convention, give him thoughts of the death of a near relative, and add to this a security debt to meet during a money panic. By this time the mind begins to fag below the power of resistance.

A continuance of these great mental vibrations for a long time finally stops nutrition of all or one-half of the brain, and we have a case of "hemiplegia," or the wheels of one-half of the brain run so fast as to overcome some fountain of nerve-force and explode some cerebral artery in the brain and deposit a clot of blood at some motor supply center or plexus. Thus we find men from over mental action fall in our national councils, courts, manufactories, churches, and in almost all places of great mental activity. Slaves and savages seldom fall victims to paralysis of any kind, but escape, for they know nothing of the strain of mind and hurried nutrition. They eat and rest, live long, and are happy. The idea of riches never bothers their slumbers. Physical injuries may and often do wound motor, sensory, and nutrient centers of the brain; but the effect is just the same—partial or complete suspension of the motor and sensory systems. If you burst a boiler by high pressure or otherwise, your engine ceases to move. And just the same of an overworked brain or body. Hemiplegia means, when divided, "half" and "I strike," or paralysis of one-half of the body. Hemiplegia is usually the result of a cerebral hemorrhage or embolism. It sometimes occurs suddenly without other marked symptoms; but commonly it is ushered in by an apoplectic attack, and on return of consciousness it is observed that one side of the body is paralyzed, the paralysis being often profound in the beginning, and disappearing to a greater or less extent at a later period. Hemiplegia is much more rarely produced by a tumor. It then generally comes on slowly, the paralysis gradually increasing as the neoplasm encroaches more and more upon the motor tracts, though the tumor may be complicated by the occurrence of a hemorrhage and a sudden hemiplegia. A gradual hemiplegia may also be produced by an abscess or chronic softening of the brain-substance. Other conditions or symptoms presented will in such a case assist us to diagnose the nature of the lesion.

Cerebro-Spinal Fluid.

To satisfy the mind of a philosopher who is capable of knowing truth, you must come at him outside of the limits of conjecture, and address him only with self-evident facts. When he takes up the philosophy of the great subject of life, no substitute can satisfy his mental demands. The one who would deal in conjectures or "supposed sos" should be placed in the proper category to which he belongs, which is the driftwood that floats down the dark river overshadowed by the nightmare of doubt and superstition. The seeker for truth is a man of few words, and they are used by him only to show the truths or facts he has discovered. He has no patience with the unmeaning records only offered to please the credulous and which are of little or no value, being nothing but long recitations of ungrounded statements. We will take man when formed. When we use the word "formed," we mean the whole building complete, with all organs, nerves, vessels, and every minutiæ in form and material found or used in life.

We look at the body in health as meaning perfection and harmony, not in one part, but as the whole. So far we are only filled with love, wonder, and admiration. Another period of observation appears to the philosopher. We find partial or universal discord from the lowest to the highest in action and death. Then the book of "whys" is opened and displays its leaves, calling for mental labor even to the degree of agony, to seek the cause or causes that produce failure of a limb in sensation, motion, nutrition, voluntary and involuntary functional activities. Our mind will explore the bone, the ligament, the muscle, the fascia, the channels through which the blood travels from the heart to local destination, with lymphatics and their contents, the nerves, the blood-vessels and every channel through or over which all substances are transmitted all over the body, particularly the disabled limb in question. It obtains blood abundantly from the heart. We continue our investigation, but the results obtained are not satisfactory, and another leaf is opened and the question appears, Why and where is the mystery, what quality and element of force and vitality has been withheld? A thought strikes him that the cerebro-spinal fluid is one of the highest known elements that are contained in the body, and unless the brain furnishes this fluid in abundance, a disabled condition of the body will remain. He who is able to reason will see that this great river of life must be tapped and the withering field irrigated at once, or the harvest of health be forever lost.

THE SPINAL CORD.

I want to offer you facts—not advice only, but pure and well-sustained facts, the only witnesses that ever enter the courts of truth. A spinal cord is a fact; you see it—thus a fact. That which you can see, hear, feel, smell, or taste is a fact, and the knowledge of the ability of any one fact to accomplish any one thing, how it accomplishes it, and for what purpose, is a truth sought for in philosophy. The spinal cord is the present fact for consideration. You see it, you feel it, and thus you have two facts with which you can start to obtain a knowledge of the use of this cord. In it you have one common, straight cylinder, which is filled with an unknown substance. and by an unknown power wisely directed. It is wisely formed, located, and protected. It throws off branches which are wisely arranged. They have bundles, many and few. They are connected to their support, which is the brain, by a continuous cord. After it has concluded throwing off branches at local places for special purposes, then like a flashlight it throws off a bundle of branches, called the "horse-tail plexus," *caudæ equinæ*, that conveys fluids and influences to the extremities to execute the vital work for which they are formed. While the laws of life and the procedure of nerves in executing and accomplishing the work designed by Nature for them to do is mysterious, and to the finite mind incomprehensible, you can only see what they do or perform after the work is done and ready for inspection.

As we are dealing with the omnipresent nerve-principle of animal life, I will tell you this one serious truth, and support it by the fact of observation. To treat the spine more than once or twice a week, and thereby irritate the spinal cord, will cause the vital assimilation to be perverted and become the death-producing executor by effecting an abortion of the living molecules of life before they are fully matured and while they are in the cellular system, lying immediately under the lymphatics. If you will allow yourself to think for a moment, or think at all of the possible irritation of the spinal cord, and what effect it will have on the uterus, for example, you will realize that I have told you a truth, and that I have produced an array of facts to stand by that truth. Many of your patients are well six months before they are discharged. They continue treatments, because they are weak, and they are weak because you keep them so by irritating the spinal cord. Throw off your goggles and receive the rays of sunlight which forever stand in the bosom of Reason.

This is one of the most important chapters of this book, because at this point we turn over the engine of life to you as an engineer, and you are expected to wisely conduct it on its journey. Your responsibility here is doubled. Your first position is that of a master draftsman who is capable of drawing plans and specifications whereby the engineer may know what the well-constructed machine is in every particular. He knows the parts and their relations as conductor and operator, and you are supposed to be the foreman in the shop of repairs. The living person is now the engine, Nature the engineer, and you the master mechanic. This being your position, it is expected that you will carefully inspect all parts of the engines brought to your repair shop, note all variations from the normal, and adjust them as nearly as possible to the conditions of the perfect model that stands in your mental shop.

At this point it will be well to suppose a case by way of illustration. Suppose by some accident the bones of the neck should be thrown at variance from the normal by a bend or twist.

We may then expect inharmony in the circulation of the blood to the head and face, and to all the organs and glands above the neck. We will find imperfect supply of blood and other fluids to the head. We may also expect swelling of the head and face, with local or general misery. You would have a cause for headache, dizziness, blindness, enlarged tonsils, sore tongue, loss of sight, hearing, and memory, and on through the list of head diseases, all on account of the perverted circulation of the fluids. It is equally important to have perfect drainage from the parts, for without it the good results cannot be expected to follow your efforts to relieve diseases above the neck.

What Are Nerves?

Nerves are the children and associates of one mother—the heart. She, the heart, is the wise form-giving power of life. She is life centralized for the use of each and all animals. All beings are simply constructed through the wisdom in the vital energy contained in this mother's power. She plans and builds according to the forms necessary to execute the orders of her dictators. She is the mother, nerve, and soul of all nerves pertaining to this body. She orders, constructs, and repairs, and continues in constructing her work to absolute completeness. She is a graduate from the school of the Infinite, and her works are expected to show perfection in forethought, and are to be inspected, passed upon, received, or rejected by the scrutinizing mind of the Infinite, whose orders are very positive, always holding before her mind the penalty of torture and death for failing to do all her work to the fullest degree of physical perfection. The first command of the Infinite is for her to be at her post, to keep the picture of the plans forever before her eye. Before she makes a motion to construct a fiber of flesh to cover her nakedness, she must open both eyes, and scrutinize and inspect carefully every fiber that enters into the material house known as the physical heart. First is formed the material heart, in which the spiritual establishes an office in which to dwell and oversee and enforce the requirements of the specifications for constructing the human body or that of any animal, fish, reptile, or bird. Having established the office of life in which the plans and specifications stand in bold relief, she receives from her superior officer an order to prepare a laboratory in which the necessary material is prepared to enter into the construction of this divinely formed being. She runs or constructs a branch road of transportation to and from that manufactory, which is located at the proper distance from her office to give it plenty of room to carry on the business of manufacturing. She calls this, when done, the abdominal workshop. In order not to be disturbed, she sends out her foreman with instructions to build a fence or wall around herself, and calls that wall the pericardium. Outside of that are other separating walls, with attachments. At this important moment she reads in the specifications that she is expected to run out the necessary tracks for the construction of a storage battery, the brain, with the grand trunk line, the spinal cord, and connect that battery with her office, the grand central, with wires, the nerves. As she advances with the plans and specifications, she makes other connections and constructs lungs, liver, spleen, pancreas, kidneys, bladder, genital organs, limbs of locomotion, the framework and the finished house, the thorax and abdomen. She patiently continues the performance of making all conveniences necessary for the comfort of the indweller, the spiritual being. Thus we find the heart to be the mother of all the nerves of the human body, of all its parts and principles known in vital action. From her vital chamber she delivers vitality to all forms, fibers, and functioning substances of life and motion. All parts of the body are wholly dependent on this vital center, and it can move and act without the assistance of any machine or part of the machine to which she has given form and life. She charges one set of fibers with vitality, and we call them nerves of sensation; she charges another set we call nerves of nutrition, and another set of wires we call nerves of motion. They have no motion, no sensation, no nutriment; they are simply roads for the convenience of executing the orders as found in the plans and specifications of life.

My object in the foregoing description of the heart is to draw the attention of the reader to another thought that I will present as well as I can. We can all comprehend that the heart is the engine of blood-force and supply. With this statement I will ask the question, Would the severing of a nerve produce paralysis of a limb or any division of the body, or would it be the tearing up of the road between the limb and the heart? It is true enough that the brachial nerve reaches the brain from the arm. If that nerve has been severed and motion destroyed, has it not separated the limb from the storage battery, the brain, from whence it was supplied? To illustrate this thought more forcibly, I will compare the heart to a tree whose fruit is good to eat, nice to behold, fine in flavor, and surely a child of the mother tree. The wood, the leaf, and the coloring matter of the leaf, limb, and fruit are simply physical expressions of the power of the mother tree to create variations in the several divisions of the tree. What evidence have we, that is absolute and undebatable, that all physical forces of the body are not conceived, developed, and issued from the heart? We speak of sensory nerves, nutrient nerves, motor nerves, voluntary and involuntary nerves, and to some degree we have described their special locations. By the knife and microscope we have found that all systems of nerves have one universal connection. We have found nothing that would warrant us in saying that the brain has any power to create nerve-fluid or force. We can talk about the brain of the head, the abdominal brain, the brain of the liver, and go on with such speculative divisions and find a new brain in every ganglion of the body, but we have only found storage batteries from the heart that are new to our observation. We find one cluster in the lungs, one in the brain, one in the stomach and bowels, one at the kidneys, uterus, bladder, spine, and limbs, but all sing "Sweet Home" to Mother Heart when peace and harmony prevail, and cry with anguish when she fails to communicate the glad tidings of health, peace, plenty, and harmony. Thus joy is perpetual when the watchman cries, "All is well."

NERVE-POWERS.

If we make a classification of nerve-forces, we will count five nerve-powers. They must all be present to build a part, and must answer promptly at roll-call, and work all the time. The names of these master workmen are Sensation, Motion, Nutrition, Voluntary, and Involuntary. All must answer at every roll-call during life; none can be granted a leave of absence for a moment. Suppose Sensation should leave a limb for a time, have we not a giving away there of all cells and glands? A filling up follows quickly, because Sensation limits and tells when the supply is too great for the use of the builder's purpose. Suppose the nerve-power known as Motion should fail for a time; starvation would soon begin its deadly work for want of food.

Suppose, again, the nerves of nutrition should fail to apply the nourishing showers; we would surely die in sight of food. With the voluntary nerves we move or stay at will. At this time I will stop defining the several and varied uses of the five kinds of nerves, and begin to account for growths and other variations, from the healthy to the unhealthy conditions of man. The above-named nerve-forces are the five known powers of animal life, and to direct them wisely is the work of the doctor of osteopathy.

The osteopath has five witnesses to examine in all cases he has under his care. He must give close attention to the source and supply of healthy blood. If blood is too scant, he must look to the motor systems of blood-making. That would surely invite his most careful attention and study to the abdomen. He cannot expect blood to quietly pass through the diaphragm if it is impeded by muscular constrictions around the aorta, vena cava, or thoracic duct The diaphragm is often pulled down on both the vena cava and thoracic duct, obstructing blood and chyle from returning to the heart, so that it reduces the amount of the chyle below the requirement of healthy blood, or even suppresses the nerve-action of lymphatics to a degree causing dropsy of the abdomen, or a stoppage of venous blood by pressure on the vena cava so long that venous blood is in stages of ferment when it enters the heart for renovation, and when purified and returned, the supply is too small to sustain life to a normal standard.

Careful attention to the normal position of all the ribs to which the diaphragm is attached is essential. The eleventh and twelfth ribs are often pushed so far from their normal bearings that they are found turned in a line with the spine, with cartilaginous ends down near the ilio-lumbar articulation. When in such a position, they draw the diaphragm down heavily on to the vena cava at about the fourth lumbar. Then you have a cause for an intermittent pulse, as the heart finds poor passage for blood through the prolapsed diaphragm, which is also stopping the vena cava and producing universal stagnation of blood and other fluids in all the organs and glands below the diaphragm.

Three Conditions of the Blood-Corpuscles.

In this school of philosophy we are led to consider the fascia and three conditions of the blood-corpuscles By the perfectly healthy corpuscle all constructed perfection of the body is produced. Perfect health is the natural result of pure blood. By it no deformities are constructed. On the other hand, we may have diseased or wounded corpuscles, which, when deposited in the mucous membrane by the conductors from the fascia, congregate and produce abnormal growths, such as fibroid tumors, cancers, and all abnormal conditions of flesh growths. Having had the perfection of the first stage or healthy corpuscle, a biogenic life still exists in the wounded corpuscles. When these semi-normal corpuscles appear on the mucous membrane, they produce forms that are known by the name of microbes. They are natural to the body and come from the fascia, and in the condition of diminished health or vitality they are mistaken for foreign bodies, but they have not been added to the system from the outside. Thus we say membraneous croup microbes, diphtheria microbes, and so on. They are carried to the mucous membrane in this semi-vital condition of biogenic life, and, with their affinity for one another, congregate upon the mucous membrane of the trachea, mouth, or throat generally.

Now we will consider the third and last corpuscle, or the dead corpuscle. When it leaves the fascia from any part of the system and arrives in the mucous membrane of the lungs, it is simply dropped out into the lung-cells as dead matter, and we have consumption and all other wasting diseases of the lungs. We wish it to be understood that thus far we have been speaking of the lymphatics of the fascia. We can account by this philosophy for the cause of cancer and other growths, which will be mentioned as we proceed with the subject of disease and cause. We will be more elaborate as we take up and describe the diseases that come from the blood confounded in the fascia, artery, muscle, vein, or the nervous systems Through the three conditions of the blood while in the fascia we can reasonably account for effects, such as good health, or abnormal growths and physical wastes. At this time we wish to call your attention to the electrical disturbance of nerve-fibers as they cross one another and produce another manifestation known as fever heat, or lower temperature.

FLUIDS OF THE BODY.

If a thousand kinds of fluids exist in our bodies, a thousand uses require them, or they would not appear. To know how and why they exist in the economy of life is the study of the man who acts only when he knows at what places each must appear and fill the part and use for which it is designed. If the demand for a substance is absolute, its chance to act and answer that call and obey the command must not be hindered while in preparation, nor on its journey to its destination, for upon its power all action may depend. Blood, albumen, gall, acids, alkalies, oils, brain-fluid, and other substances, formed by associations while in physiological processes of formation, must be on time, in place, and measured abundantly, that the biogenic laws of Nature can have full power and time to act. Thus all things else may be in place and in ample quantities and yet fail, because the power is withheld and there is no action for want of brain-fluids with their power to vivify all animated nature. We can do no more than to feed and trust the laws of life as Nature gives them to man. We must arrange our bodies in such true lines that ample Nature can select and associate, by its definite measures and weights and its keen power of choice of kinds, that which can make all the fluids needed for our bodily uses, from the crude blood to the active flames of life, as they are seen when marshalled for duty, obeying the edicts of the mind of the Infinite.

BLOOD.

Blood is an unknown red or black fluid, found inside of the human body, in tubes, channels, or tunnels. What it is, how it is made, and what it does in the arteries after it leaves the heart, before it returns to the heart through the veins, is one of the mysteries of animal life. We have tried to analyze it, to discover of what it is composed, and when done we know but little more of what it really is than we know of what sulphur is made. We know it is a colored fluid, and it is in all parts of flesh and bone. We know it builds up flesh, but "How?" is the question that leads us to honor the unknowable law of life, by which the work of mysterious construction of all forms found in the parts of man is done. In all our efforts to learn what it is, what it is made of, and what enters it as life and gives it the building powers with the intelligence it displays in building that we see in daily observation, is to us such an incomprehensible wonder that with the "sacred writers" we are constrained to say, "Great is the mystery of Godliness." I dislike to say that we know very little about the blood—in fact, nothing at all; but such is the truth. We cannot make one drop of blood, because of our ignorance of the laws of its production. If we knew what its component parts were and their combination, we would soon have large machinery manufacturing blood, and have it for sale in quantities to suit the purchaser. But alas! with all the combined intelligence of man, we cannot make one drop of blood, because we do not know what it is. Then, as its production is by the skill of a foreigner whose education has grown to suit the work, we must silently sit by and willingly receive the work when handed out to us for use by the producer. At this point I will say that an intelligent osteopath is willing to be governed by the immutable laws of Nature, and feels that he is justified to pass the fluid on from place to place and trust results.

When Harvey solved by his powers of reason a knowledge of the circulation of the blood, he only reached the banks of the river of life. He saw that the heads and mouths of the rivers of blood begin and end in the heart to do the mysterious works of constructing man. Then he went into camp and left this compound for other minds to speculate on—how it was made, of what composed, and how it became a medium of life which sustains all beings. He saw the genius of Nature had written its wisdom and will of life, by the red ink of all truth.

Blood is systematically furnished from the heart to all divisions of our bodies. When we go any course from the heart, we will find one or more arteries leaving the heart. If we go toward the head, we find carotid, cervical, and vertebral arteries in pairs, large enough to supply blood abundantly for bone, brain, and muscle. That blood builds the brain, the bone, nerves, muscles, glands, membranes, fascia, and skin. Then we see wisdom just as much in the venous system as in the arterial. The arteries supply all demands, and the veins carry away all waste material. We find building and healthy renovation are united in a perpetual effort to construct and sustain purity. In these two are the facts and truths of life and health. If we go to any other part or organ of the body, we find just the same law of supply, arteries first, then renovation, beginning with the veins. The rule of artery and vein is universal in all living beings, and the osteopath must know that and abide by its rulings, or he will not succeed as a healer. Place him in open combat with fevers of winter or summer and he saves or loses his patients just in proportion to his ability to sustain the arteries to feed and the veins to purify by taking away the dead substances before they ferment in the lymphatics and cellular system. He shows stupidity and ignorance of support from arteries and the purifying powers as carried along through the veins when he fails to cure erysipelas, flux, pneumonia, croup, scarlet fever, diphtheria, measles, mumps, rheumatism, and on to all diseases of climate and seasons

It is ignorance of and inattention to the arteries to supply and the veins to carry away deposits that lead to the formation of tumors in lungs, abdomen, or any part of the system. Man's ignorance of how and why the blood renovates and why tumors are formed has allowed the knife to be found in the belts of so many doctors to-day. On this law osteopathy has successfully stood and cured more than any school of cures, and has sustained all its diplomates, financially and otherwise. I write this article on blood for the student of osteopathy. I want him to put Nature to a test of its merit, and know if it is a law equal to all demands. If not, he is very much and seriously limited when he goes into war with diseases.

Disease Defined.

When we use the word "disease," we mean anything that makes an unnatural showing in the body—overgrowth of muscle, gland, organ, physical pain, numbness, heat, cold, or anything that we find not necessary to life and comfort. I have no wish to rob surgery of its useful claims, and its scientific merits to suffering man and beast. My object is to place the osteopath's eye of reason on the hunt of the great "whys" that the knife is useful at all. It comes in often to remove growths and diseased flesh and bone that have formed owing to man's ignorance of a few great truths. If blood is allowed to be taken to a gland or organ, and not taken away in due time, the accumulation will become bulky enough to stop the excretory nerves and cause local paralysis. Then the nutrient nerves proceed to construct tumors, and on and on until there is no relief but the knife or death. Had this blood not been conveyed there, it would not be there at all, either in bulk or less quantities. Had it simply done its work and passed on, we would have had no material to develop such abnormal beings. If a tumefaction appears in one side and not in the other, why is it on one side and not on the other? It takes no great effort of mind to see that the veins did not receive and carry off the blood, and a growth was natural, as the conditions would not permit anything else and be true to Nature. Thus man's ignorance has made a condition for the knife. Had he taken the hint and let the blood pass on when its work was done, he would not have had to witness the guillotine taking his patients, whose early pains told him a renal vein or some vessel below the diaphragm was ligated by an impacted colon, or that a few ribs were pulling and bringing the diaphragm down across the vena cava and thoracic duct, causing excitement or paralysis of the solar plexus, or any other nerves that pass through the diaphragm, through which also passes blood to and from the heart and lungs.

How to find causes of diseases or where a hindrance is located that stops blood is a great mental worry to the osteopath when he is called to treat a patient. The patient tells a doctor "where he hurts," how much "he hurts," how long "he has hurt," how hot or cold he is. The medical practitioner then puts this symptom and that symptom in a column, adds them up according to the latest books on symptomatology, and finally he is able to guess at a name by which to call the disease. Then he proceeds and treats as his pap's father heard his granny say their old family doctor treated "them sort of diseases in North Carolina." An osteopath, in his search for the cause of diseases, starts out to find the mechanical cause. He feels that the people expect more than guessing of an osteopath. He feels that he must put his hand on the cause and prove what he says by what he does; that he will not get off by the feeble-minded trash of stale habits that go with doctors of medicine. By his knowledge he must show his ability to go beyond the musty bread of symptomatology.

An osteopath should be a clear-headed, sober, conscientious, truth-loving man, and never speak until he knows he has found and can demonstrate the truth he claims to know. I partially understand anatomy and physiology after fifty years of close attention to the subject. The last twenty years have been spent in giving close attention to what has been said by all the best writers, many of whom are considered standard guides for the student and practitioner. I have dissected and witnessed the work of the very best anatomists in the world. I have followed the knife through the whole distribution of the blood of arterial systems to the great and small vessels, until the lenses of the most powerful microscopes seemed to exhaust their ability to perceive the termination of the artery. With the same care I have followed the knife and microscope from the nerve-center to terminals of the large to the infinitely small fibers around which those fine nerve-vines entwine, first, like the bean, entwining by way of the right, and then, turning my microscope, finding the entwining of another set of nerves to the left, like the hop. Those nerves are solid, cylindrical, and stratified in form, with many leading from the lymphatics to the artery, and to the red and white muscles, fascia, cellular membrane, striated and unstriated organs, all connecting to and traveling with the artery, and continuing with it through its whole circuit from start to terminals.

Like a thirsty herd of camels, the whole nervous system, sensory, motor, nutrient, voluntary, and involuntary, seems to be in sufficient quantities and numbers to consume all the blood and cause the philosopher to ask the question, "Is not the labor of the artery complete when it has fed the hungry nerves?" Is he not justified in the conclusion that the nerves gestate and send forth all substances that are applied by Nature in the construction of man? If this philosophy be true, then he who arms himself for the battles of osteopathy when combating diseases has a guide and a light whereby he can land safely in port from every voyage.

Turn the eye of reason to the heart and observe the blood start on its journey. It leaves in great haste and never stops, even in the smaller arteries. It is always in motion, and very quick and powerful at all places. Its motion indicates no evidence of construction during such time, but we can find in the lymphatics cells or pockets in which motion is slow enough to suppose that in those cells living beings can be formed and carried to their places by the lymphatics for the purposes for which they are intended, as bone or muscle. Let us reason that blood has a great and universal duty to perform, if it constructs, nourishes, and keeps the whole nervous system normal in form and function.

As blood and other fluids of life are ponderable bodies of different consistencies, and are moved through the system to construct, purify, vitalize, and furnish power necessary to keep the machinery in action, we must reason on the different powers necessary to move those bodies through arteries, veins, ducts, over nerves, spongy membranes, fascia, muscles, ligaments, glands, and skin, and judge from their unequal density, and adjust the force to meet the demand according to kinds.

Suppose venous blood is suspended by cold or other causes in the lungs to the amount of œdema of the fascia; another mental look would see the nerves of the fascia of the lungs in a high state of excitement, cramping fascia onto veins, which would be bound to cause an interference with the flow of blood to the heart. No blood can pass through a vein that is closed by such resistance, nor can it ever do it until the resistance is suspended. Thus the cause of nerve-irritation must be found and removed before the channels can relax and open sufficiently to admit the passage of the obstructed fluids. In order to remove this obstructing cause, we must go to the nerve-supply of the lungs, or other parts of the body, and direct our attention to the cause of the nerve-excitement, and that only, and prosecute the investigation to a finish. If the breathing be too fast and hurried, address your attention to the motor nerves and then to the sensory, for through them you regulate and reduce the excitement of the motor nerves of the arteries. As soon as sensation is reduced, the motor and sensory circuit is completed and the labor of the artery is less, because venous resistance has been removed. The circuit of electricity is complete, as proven by the completed arterial and venous circuit for the reduction of motor irritation. The high temperature disappears because distress gives place to the normal, and recovery is the result.

THE FASCIA.

I know of no part of the body that equals the fascia as a hunting-ground. I believe that more rich golden thoughts will appear to the mind's eye as the study of the fascia is pursued than of any other division of the body. Still one part is just as great and useful as anv other in its place. No part can be dispensed with.

In every view we take of the fascia a wonder appears. The part the fascia takes in life and death gives us one of the greatest problems to solve. It surrounds each muscle, vein, nerve, and all organs of the body. It has a network of nerves, cells, and tubes running to and from it; it is crossed and no doubt filled with millions of nerve-centers and fibers which carry on the work of secreting and excreting fluids vital and destructive. By its action we live and by its failure we die. Each muscle plays its part in active life. Each fiber of all muscle owes its pliability to that yielding septum-washer that allows all muscles to glide over and around all adjacent muscles and ligaments without friction or jar. It not only lubricates the fibers, but gives nourishment to all parts of the body. Its nerves are so abundant that no atom of flesh fails to get nerve- and blood-supply therefrom.

This life is surely too short to solve the uses of the fascia in animal forms. It penetrates even its own finest fibers to supply and assist their gliding elasticity. Turn the visions of your mind to follow those infinitely fine nerves. You see the fascia, and in your wonder and surprise you exclaim, "Omnipresent in man and all other living beings of the land and sea."

Other great facts come to the mind with joy and admiration as we see all the beauties of life on exhibition in the wonders found in the fascia. The soul of man, with all the streams of pure living water, seems to dwell in the fascia of his body. Does it not throw hot shot and shells of thought into man's famishing chamber of reason to feel that he has seen in the fascia the framework of life, the dwelling-place in which life sojourns? He feels that he there can find all disturbing causes of life, the places in which diseases germinate and develop the seeds of sickness and death.

As the student of anatomy explores the subject with his knife and microscope he easily finds this fascia going with and covering all muscles, tendons, and fibers, and separating them even to the least fiber. All organs have coverings of this substance, though they may have special names by which they are designated. I write at length of the universality of the fascia to impress the reader with the idea that this connecting substance must be free at all parts to receive and discharge all fluids, and to appropriate and use them in sustaining animal life, and eject all impurities, that health may not be impaired by dead and poisonous fluids. A knowledge of the universal extent of the fascia is imperative, and is one of the greatest aids to the person who seeks the causes of disease. The fascia and its nerves demand his attention, and on his knowledge of them much of his success depends.

Will the student of osteopathy stop just a moment and see his medical cotemporary plow the skin with the needle of his hypodermic syringe? He drives it in and unloads his morphine and other poisonous drugs under the skin into the very center of the nerves of the superficial fascia. He produces paralysis of all the nerves of the body by this method, just as certainly as if he had put his poison into the cerebellum, but in a manner not so certain to produce instantaneous death as it would had it been unloaded in the brain. But if he is faithfully ignorant, he will cause death just as surely at one place as the other, because the poisonous effects are carried along to every fiber of the whole body by the nerves and fibers of the fascia.

When you deal with the fascia you are doing business with the branch offices of the brain, under a general corporation law, and why not treat these branch offices with the same degree of respect? The doctor of medicine does effectual work through the medium of the fascia. Why should not you relax, contract, stimulate, and clean the whole system of all diseases by that willing and sufficient power you possess to renovate all parts of the system from deadly compounds that are generated on account of delay and stagnation of fluids while in the fascia?

Our science is young, but the laws that govern life are as old as the hours of all ages. You may find much that has never been written nor practiced before, but all such discoveries are truths born with the birth of eternity, old as God and as true as life.

We must remember, as we study the fascia, that it occupies the whole body, and should we find a local region that is disordered, we can relieve that part through the local plexus of nerves which controls that division. Your attention should be directed to all the nerves of that part. Blood must not be allowed to flow to the part by wild motion. Its flow must be gentle to suit the demands of nutrition, otherwise weakness takes the place of strength, and we lose the benefits of the nutritive nerves. Suppose the nerves that supply the lungs with motion should stop acting; the lungs would also stop. Suppose they should come to a half stop; the lungs would surely follow suit. Now we must reason, if we succeed in relieving lungs, that all kinds of nerves are found in them. The lungs move, thus you find motor nerves; they have feeling, thus the sensory nerves; they grow by nutrition, thus the nutrient nerves. They move by will, or without it; they have a voluntary and involuntary system.

The blood-supply comes under the motor system of nerves, and is delivered at proper places for the convenience of the nerves of nutrition. The sensory nerves limit the supply of arterial blood to the quantity necessary, as construction is going on at each successive stroke of the heart. They limit the action of the lungs, receive and expel air in quantities sufficient to keep up the purity of the blood, etc. With this foundation, we observe that if there is too great action of the motor nerves, as shown by an abnormal increase in breathing, we are admonished to reduce breathing by addressing attention to the sensory nerves of the lungs, in order that the blood may pass through the veins, whose irritability has refused to receive the blood, further than capillary terminals. As soon as sensation is reduced, relaxation of nerve-fibers of veins tolerates the passage of venous blood, which is deposited in the spongy portions of the lungs in such quantities as to overcome the activity of the nerves of renovation, an activity that accompanies the fascia in its process of ejection of all fluids that have been detained an abnormal time, first in the region of the fascia, then in the arterial and venous circulation. Thus you see what must be done. The veins as channels must carry away all the blood as soon as it has deposited its nutrient supplies to the places for which they were intended; otherwise, by delay, vitality by asphyxia is lost to the blood, which calls for a greater force from the arterial pumps to drive the blood through the parts, rupturing capillaries and depositing the blood in the mucous membrane, until finally nerves of the fascia become powerless by surrounding pressure, and, through the sensory nerves, an irritability sets in at the heart, which is driven to still greater efforts.

As life finds its general nutrient law in the fascia and its nerves, we must connect them to the great source of supply by a cord running the length of the spine, by which all nerves are connected with the brain. The cord throws out millions of nerves to all organs and parts which are supplied with the elements of motion and sensation. All these nerves go to and terminate in that great system, the fascia.

As we dip our cups deeper and deeper into the ocean of thought we begin to feel that the solution of life and health is close to the field of the telescope of our mental searchlights, and soon we will find the road to health so plainly written that the wayfaring man cannot err though he be a fool.

Disease is evidently sown as atoms of gas, fluids, or solids. A suitable place is first necessary for the active principle of the disease, be that what it may. Then a responsive kind of nourishment must be obtained by the being to be developed. Thus we must find in animals that part of the body which assists by action and by food in developing the being in fœtal life. Reason calls the mind to the rule of man's gestative life first, and as a basis of thought we look at the quickening atom, the coming being, when only by the aid of a powerful microscope can we sêe the vital germ. It looks like an atom of white fibrin or detached particle of fascia. It leaves one parent as an atom of fascia, and, in order to live and grow, must dwell in friendly surroundings, and be fed by such food as is found in blood and lymph. The nerve-generating power must also be considered. As the fascia is the best equipped with nerves, blood, and white corpuscles, it is only reasonable to expect the germ to dwell there for support and growth.

AN ILLUSTRATION OF CONCEPTION.

When you follow the germ from the father after it has left his system of fascia, we find it flourishing in the womb, an organ which is almost a complete being of itself, the center, origin, and mother of all fascias. It there dwells and grows to birth, and appears as a completed being, a product of the life-giving powers of the fascia.

The fascia is universal in man, and stands before the world to-day a great problem. It carries to the mind of the philosopher the evidence absolute, that it is the "material man." It is the fort which the enemy of life takes by conquest through disease, and, completing the combat, unfurls the black flag of "no quarter." That enemy is sure to capture all the forts known as human beings at some time, although the engagement may last for many years. A delay in the surrender can only be obtained by giving timely support to the supply of nourishment, that powerful life force that is bequeathed to man and all other beings, and acts through the fascia of man and beast.

THE LYMPHATICS.

A student of life must take in each part of the body and study its uses and relations to other parts and systems. We lay much stress on the uses of blood and the powers of the nerves, but have we any evidence that they are of more vital importance than the lymphatics? If not, let us halt at this universal system of irrigation, and study its great uses in sustaining animal life. Where are the lymphatics situated in the body? Where are they not found? No space is so small that it is out of connection with the lymphatics, with their nerves, secretory and excretory ducts. The system of lymphatics is complete and universal in the whole body. After beholding the lymphatics distributed along all the nerves, blood-channels, muscles, glands, and all the organs of the body, from the brain to the soles of the feet, all loaded to fullness with watery liquids, we certainly can make but one conclusion as to their use, which would be to mingle with and carry out all impurities of the body, by first mixing with the substances and reducing them to that degree of fineness that will allow them to pass through the smallest tubes of the excretory system, and by that method free the body from all deposits of either solids or fluids, and leave nourishment.

Possibly less is known of the lymphatics than any other division of the life-sustaining machinery of man. Ignorance of that division is often equal to a total blank with the operator. Finer nerves dwell with the lymphatics than even with the eye. The eye is an organized effect, the lymphatics the cause, and in them the principle of life more abundantly dwells. No atom can leave the lymphatics in an imperfect state and get a union with any part of the body. There the atom obtains form and knowledge of how and what to do. The fluids of the brain are of a finer order than any fluids supplying the whole viscera. By nature, coarser substances are necessary to construct the organs that run the blast and rough-forging divisions. The lymphatics prepare, furnish, and send the atoms to the builder that he may construct by adjusting all according to Nature's plans and specifications. Nature makes machinery that can produce just what is necessary, and, when united, produces what the wisest minds would exact.

The lymphatics are closely and universally connected with the spinal cord and all other nerves, and all drink from the waters of the brain. By the action of the nerves of the lymphatics, a union of qualities necessary to produce gall, sugar, acids, alkalies, bone, muscle, and softer parts, is brought about so that elements can be changed, suspended, collected, and associated and produce any chemical compound necessary to sustain animal life, wash out, salt, sweeten, and preserve the being from decay and death by chemical, electric, atmospheric, or climatic conditions. By this we are admonished in all our treatment not to wound the lymphatics, as they are undoubtedly the life-giving centers and organs, and it behooves us to handle them with wisdom and tenderness, for by and from them a withered limb, organ, or any division of the body receives what we call a "reconstruction," or is builded anew. Without this cautious procedure, your patient had better save his life and money by passing you by as a failure, until you are by this knowledge qualified to deal with the lymphatics.

Why not reason on the broad plain of known facts, and give the cause of a person having complete prostration. When all systems are cut off from a chance to perform and execute such duties as Nature has allotted to them, we have prostration. Motor nerves must drive all substances to and sensation must judge the supply and demand. Nutrition must be in action on time, and keep all parts well supplied with power, or a failure is sure to appear. We must ever remember the demands of Nature on the lymphatics, liver, and kidneys. They must work all the time or a confusion will result, and a deficiency in the performance of their duties will mean a crippling of some function of life over which they preside.

UNIVERSALLY DISTRIBUTED.

Dunglison's definition of the lymphatics is very extensive, comprehensive, and right to the point for our use as doctors of osteopathy. He describes the lymphatic glands as countless in number, universally distributed all through the human body, containing vitalized water and other fluids necessary to the support of animal life, running parallel with the venous system, and more abundantly there than in other locations of the body, at the same time discharging their contents into the veins while conveying the blood back to the heart from the whole system. Is it not reasonable to suppose that, besides being nutrient centers, they accumulate and pass water through the whole secretory and excretory systems of the body, in order to reduce nourishment from a thick to a thin constituency, that it may easily pass through the tubes, ducts, and vessels interested in the distribution of materials as nourishment first, and renovation second, through the excretory ducts. The question arises, Whence cometh this water? This leads us back to the lungs. With a fountain of life-saving water provided by Nature to wash away impurities as they accumulate in our bodies, would it not be great stupidity in us to see a human being burn to death by the fires of fever, or die from asphyxia by allowing bad or dead lymph, albumen, or any substance to load down the powers of Nature and keep the blood from being washed to normal purity. If so, let us go deeper into the study of the life-saving powers of the lymphatics. Do we not find in death that the lymphatics are dark, and in life they are healthy and red?

What we meet with in all diseases is dead blood, stagnant lymph, and albumen in a semi-vital or dead and decomposing condition all through the lymphatics and other parts of the body, brain, lungs, kidneys, liver, and fascia. The whole system is loaded with a confused mass of blood that is mixed with unhealthy substances that should have been kept washed out by lymph. Stop and view the frog's superficial lymphatic glands. You see all parts move just as regularly as the heart does. They are all in motion during life. For what purpose do they move if not to carry the fluids to sustain the building-up processes, while the excretory channels receive and pass out all that is of no farther use to the body? Now we see this great system of lymphatics is the source of construction and purity. If this be true, we must keep the lymphatics normal all the time or see confused Nature in the form of disease. We strike at the source of life and death when we go to the lymphatics.

No part is so small or remote that it is not in direct connection with some part or chain of the lymphatics. The doctor of osteopathy has much to think about when he consults natural remedies, and how they are supplied and administered, and as disease is the effect of tardy deposits in some or all parts of the body, reason would bring us to a search for a solvent of such deposits, which hinder the natural motion of blood and other fluids in functional works, and with that solvent we are to keep the body pure from any substance that would check vital action. When we have searched and found that the lymphatics are requisite for the body, we then must admit that their use is equal to the abundant and universal supply of all the glands. If we think and use a homely phrase, and say that disease is only too much dirt in the wheels of life, then we will see that Nature takes this method to wash out the dirt. As an application, pneumonia is too much dirt in the wheels of the lungs. If so, we must wash it out. Nowhere can we go for a better place for water than to the lymphatics. Are they not like a fire company with nozzles in all windows ready to flush the burning house?

Definition of the Word "Treat."

Here I want to emphasize that the word "treat" has but one meaning—that is, to know you are right, and do your work accordingly. I will only hint, and would feel embarrassed to go any further than to hint to you the importance of an undisturbed condition of the five known kinds of nerves; namely, sensation, motion, nutrition, voluntary, and involuntary, all of which you must endeavor to keep in perpetual harmony while treating any disease. If you allow yourself to reason at all, you must know that sensation must be normal and always on guard to give notice by local or general misery of unnatural accumulation of the circulating fluids. Every nerve must be free to act and do its part. Your duty as a master mechanic is to know that the engine is kept in a perfect condition, so that there will be no functional disturbance to any nerve, or vein, or artery that supplies and governs the skin, the fascia, the muscle, the blood, or any fluid that should be in free circulation to sustain life and renovate the system from deposits that would cause what we call disease.

Your osteopathic knowledge has surely taught you that, with an intimate acquaintance with the nerve- and blood-supply, you can arrive at a knowledge of the hidden cause of disease, and conduct your treatment to a successful termination. This is not by your knowledge of chemistry, but by the knowledge of the anatomy of man, and of what is normal and what abnormal, what is effect and what is the cause. Do you ever suspect renal or bladder trouble without first receiving knowledge from your patient that there is soreness and tenderness in the region of the kidneys at some point along the spine? By this knowledge you are invited to explore the spine for the purpose of ascertaining whether it is normal or not. If, by your intimate acquaintance with a normal spine, you should detect an abnormal form, although it be small, you are then admonished to look out for disease of the kidneys, or bladder, or both, from the discovered cause for disturbance of the renal nerves by such displacement, or some slight variation from the normal in the articulation of the spine. If this is not worthy of your attention, your mind is surely too crude to observe those fine beginnings that lead to death. Your skill would be of little use in incipient cases of Bright's disease of the kidneys. Has not your acquaintance with the human body opened your mind's eye to observe that in the laboratory of the human body the most wonderful chemical results are being accomplished every day, minute, and hour of your life? Can that laboratory be running in good order and tolerate the formation of a gall- or bladder-stone? Does not the body generate acids, alkalies, and all substances and fluids necessary to wash out all impurities? If you think an unerring God has made all those necessary preparations, why not so assert yourself, and stand upon that ground?

You cannot do otherwise, and not betray your ignorance to the thinking world. If in the human body you can find the most wonderful chemical laboratory mind can conceive, why not give more of your time to that subject, in order that you may obtain a better understanding of its workings? Can you afford to treat your patients without such qualification? Is it not ignorance of the workings of this divine law that has given birth to the foundationless nightmare now prevailing to such an alarming extent all over civilization, that a deadly drug will prove its efficacy in warding off disease in a better way than has been prescribed by the intelligent God who has formulated and combined life, mind, and matter in such a manner that it becomes the connecting link between a world of mind and that element known as matter? Can a deep philosopher do otherwise than conclude that Nature has placed in man all the qualities for his comfort and longevity? Or will he drink that which is deadly, and cast his vote for the crucifixion of knowledge?

CHAPTER III.

Divisions of the Body.

Mission of the Doctor.

To find health should be the object of the doctor. Anyone can find disease. He should make the grand round among the sentinels and ascertain if they are asleep, dead, or have deserted their posts, and have allowed the enemy to get into the camp. He should visit all posts. Before he goes out to make the rounds, he should know where all the posts are, and the value of the supply he has charge of, whether it be shot, shell, food, clothing, arms, or anything of value to the company or division.

Five Divisions.

So great a subject as the study of man, not to be superficial, must be divided into two or more parts. While the head and neck are related to and connected with the whole body, their importance to that body of which they are parts cannot be comprehended without a thorough and special acquaintance with all forms and substances passing through in transit and return. Without knowing the function of the brain, we cannot know its uses. Therefore an acquaintance to a general understanding is absolutely necessary, that we may regulate our treatment, which is only an inspection and adjustment of the head to its true position with the neck. As the neck is compound in its attachments, first to the head and then to the body, the importance of knowledge has doubled itself, because the neck receives and transmits fluids from the body to the brain, through its organized machinery, and to the body or chest with all its machinery, which receives at the heart nutrient elements from below and delivers the same to the lungs for such preparation as is incumbent upon that division of life's sustaining machinery. We need a good knowledge of the head and neck and the relation they bear to the lungs, the great renovators and vitalizers of fluids previous to their return to the heart for general uses.

It is of the greatest importance to thoroughly know the parts and uses of both the heart and lungs, where and how both have received their forms, forces, and materials that enter into those forms, and the power sustaining divisions, how they are supported in their duties. We see, in order to keep the chest and lungs normally healthy, we must know how, where, and why they act, and we can only know this by an intimate acquaintance with the forms and functions of the head and all therein belonging, with the neck, in which all of the thoroughfares are found and through which forces are transmitted.

When we shall have mastered a reasonable comprehension of these divisions, we are only feebly prepared to enter a new and more extended field, with its connected oneness in receiving blood and other substances and appropriating them to the duties of constructing machinery to receive gases, blood, and other substances and associating them in such a manner that they become the living corpuscles of construction, not only with the ability to build up muscles, but the ability from a germ to begin the addition of atom to atom through all steps of fœtal life to a perfectly formed human being, with all organs, glands, and substances. We must see the great importance of the highest known intelligence that can be accumulated by the study of the human body from head to abdomen, because here we are in a city of living wonders pertaining to life. At this point, beginning with the first lumbar, we have an unexplored field of great truth presented to our minds, which should imply how much injury can be admitted and not go beyond the power of repair. In the fourth and fifth divisions, better understood as the region of the abdomen and pelvis, if wounds, falls, punctures, or other injury would cause impingement upon any nerve, vein, or artery, how far can Nature tolerate any such encroachment and still be able to keep up something of a normal appearance? How far can such injuries proceed without causing failure to a degree that would produce piles, leucorrhea, monthly convulsions, fibroid and other forms of tumefaction, ulcers, Bright's disease of the kidneys, gall-stones, bladder-stones, enlarged liver, diseased spleen, jaundice, dropsy, varicose veins, and many other diseases that we have not space to enumerate here? Has not man's inability to comprehend this important question given birth and place to a resort to try to solve such questions by the rules of hit or miss, better known as symptomatology? Does not Nature, with a knowledge of the machinery, offer a more reliable system of locating cause by adjusting that machinery so that it can remove the cause and change effect?

These five points of observation for the osteopath to remember in his examination will easily cover the whole body. We cannot overlook any one of them and successfully examine any disease of the system. Local injuries are, however, an exception to this rule, but even a local hurt often causes general effect. Suppose a fall should jar the lumbar vertebræ and push some of the articulations to the front or back or to the side. Say we have the lumbar vertebræ disturbed and one or two short ribs turned down against the lumbar nerves, with a prolapsed and loosened diaphragm and pressure on the abdominal aorta, vena cava, and thoracic duct. Have we not cause there for the stoppage or derangement of the circulation in the arteries, veins, lymphatics, and all the organs below the diaphragm? Heart trouble would then naturally result. Fibroid tumors, painful monthlies, constipation, diabetes, dyspepsia, or any trouble of the system that could be caused by bad blood would also naturally follow. If blood, lymph, or chyle are kept too long below the diaphragm, they become diseased before they reach the lungs, and after renovation but little good blood is left. Then the dead matter is separated from the blood and blown out while in a vaporous state at the lungs. Thus there is not enough nutriment to keep up the normal supply. In this state the patient loses flesh and is in an enfeebled condition generally, because of the trouble the blood and lymph have in passing through the diaphragm. The failure of the free action of blood produces general debility, congestion, low types of fever, dropsy, constipation, tumefaction, and on to the whole list of visceral diseases.

We are then called to the pelvis. If the innominate bones are twisted on the sacrum or are driven too high or too low, an injury to the sacral system of nerves would be cause for congestion, inflammation of the womb, or bladder diseases, with a crippled condition of all the spinal nerves. This would cause hysteria, and on to the whole list of diseases due to spinal injuries. The osteopath has great demand for his powers of reason when he considers the relation of diseases generally to the pelvis, and this knowledge he must have before his work can be done successfully.

As I said, five points comprise the fields in which an osteopath must search. I have given you quite pointedly, although not at length, a few hints on the spine and sacrum, which cover the territory below the diaphragm. I will simply refer you to the chest, neck, and brain, and say, "Let your searchlight always shine brightly on the brain." On it we must depend for power. Most of the nerves run through the neck and branch off to the heart and brain, the two most important parts of man. Search faithfully for causes of diseases in the head, neck, chest, spine, and pelvis, for all the organs, limbs, and parts are directly related to and depend on these five localities to which I have just called your attention. With your knowledge of anatomy, I am sure you can practice and be successful, and you should be successful in all cases over which osteopathy is supposed to preside.

CHAPTER IV.

Head, Face, and Scalp.

Causes of Effects.

It is useless to enumerate all the diseases peculiar to the head, face, and scalp. If a shortage of blood-supply should be apparent in any organ or division of the head, reason would say, "Turn on a greater supply of blood; see that there is no obstruction to the nerve-forces." On the other hand, if the scalp and face should be puffed out of shape by blood and water, address your attention to the venous and lymphatic drainage, and keep that up until completed. Your knowledge of nerve-supply for blood, lymphatics, and all organs of the head should guide you correctly here, and it will if you have given due attention to instructions in anatomy and physiology. This work is not written to teach a lazy student where to punch and pull, who has neglected to receive the benefits of the instructions provided for him in school. The same rule holds equally good with diseases of the neck, breast, and abdomen. You have all details freely given in clinic instruction.

We often find a lesion which may appear as a growth or withering away of a limb, affecting all its muscles, nerves, and blood-supply. In cases of tumors on the scalp, loss of hair, eruptions of the face, growth of tonsils, ulcers on one or both ears, growths on the outside and inside of the eyes, a cause must precede the effect in all these cases. A pain in the head is an effect. Cause is older than the effect, and is absolute in all variations from normal conditions. A tumor on the head and under the skin is an effect only. It took matter to give it size, it took power to deliver that substance. The fact that a tumor was formed shows that the power to build was present and did the work of construction. Another power should have been there to complete the work at that location. That power is the carrying off of the dead matter after the work of construction was complete.

ERYSIPELAS.

This philosophy knows no life nor death except through the motion of the blood and the inaction of that fluid, which contains life while in motion and death as the effect of motion ceasing. Without giving in detail the divisions and bones of the head, I will say, in considering the subject of diseases of the head, that the head is composed of hard bones covered with soft flesh and filled with brain, blood, nerves, and membranes. It has divisions to suit the functions of the inner chamber of the cranium or skull. On the under side or surface of the skull there are many holes, foramina, or openings, to accommodate the blood-vessels and other structures that supply and drain the brain. On the outside of the skull the head is covered with soft substances, skin, fascia, muscles, nerves, veins, secretives, and excretives. This human head shows many effects, diseases, whose cause can be traced to lack of nourishing blood-supply, to poor drainage and exhausted fluids, which should be returned through the venous or thrown out through the excretory system. With this known fact and your knowledge of anatomy, I think you are very well qualified to answer the question, What is the cause of erysipelas, with its fiery swelling which spreads over the skin of the face and scalp of the head, to the complete occupation of both? Here is a detention of blood, detained long enough to cause what is commonly known as erysipelas of the head and scalp. That visible effect is a result of an action known as fermentation of the fluids that should have passed from the veins and membranes of the scalp, the fascia, lymphatics, and cellular system of the head and face. When I ask you where and how the blood is conveyed from the face back to the heart, you will describe the blood-vessels that empty into the jugular veins, internal and external, giving a short enumeration of the external veins of the face, the facial, the temporal, the angular, the transverse nasal, the frontal, post-auricular, and occipital, which empty into the external and internal jugular. The failure or stoppage of blood that has caused this facial erysipelas can easily be traced to the large veins that should keep the face thoroughly drained. You see where the trouble is, and by that knowledge know that you must assist the obstructed drainage to the normal. Then your labor is done; the arterial and venous energies will take care of the necessary drainage and repair. When erysipelas attacks the nose only, your work is directed to the facial and nasal veins. Should the erysipelas localize itself between the ear and occipital region, your work would be to encourage the discharge of venous blood through the auricular and occipital veins. Should the tongue be swollen, your treatment would extend to the lingual, superior thyroid, and anterior jugular veins. By this method we obtain reduction of bulky deposits and swellings of the face, and know that normal action will follow judicious renovation. The student will ever remember that no action can be suspended in the arterial supply and venous drainage of the face and scalp and not leave visible marks by such failure.

Baldness.

At this time it would be well enough to point the student to baldness or hair-failure, due to a lack of nourishment on the part of the artery and lack of drainage by the vein. To this we will add dandruff, scald-head, pimples, spots, and discolorations of the face. All have absolute causes for their appearance, and it is for us to detect the cause and apply the remedy. The importance of a good knowledge of the blood-supply of the face and scalp is patent.

As we have dwelt somewhat on the venous drainage, we will now give, by way of refreshing the student's memory, a short description of the superficial arteries of the head. We will begin with the external carotid, branch off toward the nose and mouth with the facial, the coronary, the nasal, transverse facial, orbital, supraorbital, temporal, frontal branch, parietal branch, occipital, and posterior auricular. With the image of the superficial arteries of the head in your mind's eye, you are prepared to reason that the drainage of the head through the veins must be normal, or diseases of the head and face will be the result, and will show their effects upon the outer surface and all through the skin, extending down to the fascia, the lymphatics, the parotid glands, and other important structures of the head and face. We must have good and unobstructed action of the nerves of the head and face, because much depends upon their combined action. These nerves are the posterior auricular, auriculo-temporal, supraorbital, buccal, malar, nasal, supratrochlear, infratrochlear, infraorbital, and supramandibular. I think by this time I have given enough of the important nerves so that, without any other assistance, you can safely proceed with the management of erysipelas in all parts of the head and face. You will see, if you reason at all, that by constriction of the muscles and membranes around the blood-vessels we have a stoppage or almost a complete inhibition of the blood while in transit from the head to the heart. You will remember that the system of constriction is very extensive in the region of the upper part of the neck, at its junction with the head. Irritation from the constricture causes extensive congestion of the internal systems of arterial and venous circulation as well as of the external. Let me point your attention to the lungs, with their increased motion in breathing. Has not this constricture extended to the lungs by the irritation of the pneumogastric nerves in the region of the neck as they pass from the brain to the lungs? Surely, with constricture of ascending arteries, there is a demand for greater arterial force, and we find the effect we call "a hard and quick pulse," which is known to accompany erysipelas of the head and face.

Treatment of Erysipelas.

We will now take up the treatment of erysipelas; but just before entering into the discussion of the best method of treating this disease and other diseases of the head, I will say that this is an effort on my part to teach the student how to concentrate his mind on the subject of diseases presented for his skill, deliberation, and practice. I will define erysipelas by giving Gould's definition: "*Erysipelas.* An acute infectious disease, due to the streptococcus erysipelatosus (which is probably identical with the streptococcus pyogenes), and characterized by an inflammation of the skin and subcutaneous tissues. *E., Facial,* erysipelas of the face, the most common form. After an initial chill, the temperature rises very high. There may be vomiting and delirium, and the disease may rapidly spread over a great part of the body. The affected area is swollen, has a deep red color, an elevated margin, and itches. *E., Wandering,* a form in which the erysipelatous process successively disappears from one part of the body to appear subsequently at another part."

Before the student begins to treat erysipelas or any disease of the head, I wish to tell just what I mean by "treatment." If I say to treat the cervical and facial nerves, I do not mean that you must ..h the neck and hold down the muscles. I want you to adjust the bones of the neck and let blood flow to and feed the nerves and muscles of the neck and stop the constrict-ures that have been holding the blood in check until it has died for want of air. We know that in any case of erysipelas we have sour fluids, the effect of delay of blood while in the veins located in the affected area. This venous blood must be sent to heart and lungs for purification and renewal. The operator is supposed to come into this important battle, where local life is to be saved by increasing the vital force and supplying pure and healthy blood. He should halt and establish himself for observation as a seeker of the cause of this local delay in circulation, venous or arterial, and in the nerve-action, because in these three are the powers to supply the vital fluids and remove the exhausted. Vital forces must have access to the veins and arteries going to and from this irritating overplus of blood, fluids, and gases that are occupying the spaces in the skin, membranes, lymphatics, fascia, superficial and deep, in the region of the face, mouth, tongue, tonsils, Eustachian tubes, nasal air-passages, and the glands of the upper part of the neck close to the skull, the scalp included. On the wisdom of his conclusions previous to action depends the good or bad results that he will produce in diminishing the deadly supply through wisdom, or increasing the same through ignorance or inability to reach the positive cause of the constricture that has shut down the windows, doors, or openings through which nerve-force comes from the spinal cord and other branches from the brain to the face, for the purpose of giving energy to the blood in either venous or arterial action. He must know that if a hardness of the fleshy substances in the locality is found, that a stricture is caused by the nerves of constriction, and that this constricture proves itself to be strong enough to restrain the passage of blood to and from the locality of the face in which this destructive fermentation is doing its deadly work. The philosopher will seek the plexus of nerves which controls the blood- and nerve-supply and the drainage through the venous and excretory systems. He must remember that he is dealing with a spasmodic constricture of the muscles of the neck and face, and that this constricture forces bones together with such power as to draw muscles and fibers strong enough to force the upper bones of the neck so far to the right, left, front, or rear as to produce a damaging pressure on the nerves as they issue from the brain and medulla, whose duty it is to keep the fluids of the face in harmonious action for all purposes. The student will find bones varying from the normal in position in every case of facial erysipelas, nasal erysipelas, or any part of the head. I say, and know it to be true, that he will find bony variations from the skull and atlas to the first dorsal, and often to the fourth dorsal in facial erysipelas and other diseases of the head. Your patient has fever and is very hot. The educated touch will teach you this without the use of a thermometer. At this point you need reason much more than thermal instruments. My question to you is not to know whether the temperature is a 100, 106, or 160. I want to drag both of your feet out of the ruts of allopathy, and place your hands upon the handle of the pump and get some water from the lymphatics, the cellular system of the lungs, or any other place in the human body, set the excretories all to work and put the fire out, like any sensible fireman would do if a city block were on fire. Erysipelas is reasonably easily handled if seen and treated before the gangrenous period or condition sets in, or inflammation has done its deadly work. The inquirer for information would naturally ask the question, "Why do the osteopaths want the excretory system to throw water on the consuming fire?" Let me call your attention to the fact that you should know, as physiological reasoners, that phosphorus with oxygen and surface air, assisted by nerve- and blood-motion, aided by electricity, produces a union between the oxygen and phosphorus, and the addition of nitrogen, which occupies much cellular space in the body, produces the combustion known as fever heat, and that phosphorus ceases to unite with anything whilst submerged in water from secretory and excretory ducts of the system.

We think erysipelas is simply an effect of fermentation of the blood and other fluids of the surface veins, fascia, and glands, large and small, of the face and neck. We can see by a very superficial examination the internal jugular, superior thyroid, and anterior jugular, assisted by the external jugular, and furthermore assisted by the posterior auricular, occipital, temporal, facial, angular, and lingual veins. To continue with the description of the head, face, and neck, we will draw your attention to the vena cava superior, the grand outlet, the brachiocephalic, and external jugular, with all the blood-vessels draining the face and neck and emptying into the vena cava superior, the process of the fluids in which must be undisturbed by any constriction of the muscles, fascia, or membrane, that would impede and suspend the return of venous blood before asphyxia and fermentation could possibly set up their destructive action. In presenting this short description of the rivers through which venous blood is conveyed to the heart, I think it not amiss to refresh your memory by drawing your attention to the system and situation of the arteries which are universally distributed over the face, embracing the whole head, beginning with the external carotid, facial, transverse facial, coronary, nasal, orbital, temporal, parietal, occipital, posterior auricular, and inferior carotid. We present the arterial system of the supply, then the venous system of drainage, in order that by reasoning you may arrive at a conclusion that there can be no such thing as a healthy venous stagnation. We find a system of maltage in which the alcohol of decomposition does its work in erysipelas from start to finish. This process goes on and on poisoning the blood with its deadly yeast until the whole lump is in fermentation. A simple question seems to be in place at this time.

If a man will die by means of poisonous medicines administered by way of his mouth, will he not also die from poisons generated in his own system by the law of fermentation and decomposition? It is thus that we reason of the death of a part or of the whole body. This poison has come through the self-generated fluids, which are poisonous and are absorbed in quantities sufficient to produce death to the part affected. It may embrace the whole system. Is it not reasonable to suppose that all the nerve-forces of Nature found in man will come forward in great haste and combine all their forces to discharge this deadly enemy? The heart labors with great force and rapidity. The lungs increase the process of breathing to many times the normal. The constrictor nerves naturally come in to do their work as much as possible by a convulsive process of relieving the lymphatics of the face, head, and neck of unwholesome contents. If successful in this effort to disgorge, we have as a result a natural tendency to health and recovery. The human body will sicken and die from imperfect drainage just as certainly as the inhabitants of a great city would become extinct by collapse or any method that would block the sewerage main, the vena cava of a great city. The more we know of perfect drainage of the human body, the more satisfactory will be results obtained by keeping up the natural drainage, which should be perfect at all times. As we have referred to the heart and lungs and to the importance of keeping them free from all obstructions, that they may do their work to the degree required of them by Nature, we must also by our reason embrace the importance of keeping the brain free from impingement by any stagnation in the face or neck that would diminish freedom of action to and from the brain, the known local center of nerve-action. Our success as osteopaths in treating erysipelas depends altogether upon good nerve-action, blood-supply, and normal drainage.

CHAPTER V.

The Neck.

ORGANIZED SUBSTANCES OF THE BODY.

The organized substances in the human body, to the student of osteopathy, should be in divisions when he begins to philosophize as an operator. The organized substances of the body are the skin, fascia, membrane, muscle, ligament, bone, etc. All parts of the body when in form consist of the substances above named. The student having passed through descriptive and demonstrative anatomy, histological; chemical, and physiological studies, will find all parts of the body, without an exception, to consist of bone, skin, fascia, membrane, cells, glands, brain, nerves, blood-vessels, etc. If health is perfect, it only proves perfect harmony in the physiological action of the body in all its parts and functions. Any variation from perfect health marks a degree of functional derangement in the physiological department of man. Efforts at restoration from the diseased to the healthy condition should present but one object to the mind, and that is to explore minutely and seek the variation from the normal. The first search for this knowledge would confine us to the bony system, in order to see if any lesion presents itself by any abnormally large place or places. First examine the neck, because of its position and connection with the brain, which is the physiological source through which nerve-force is supplied and suited to the convenience of the heart, to assist in delivering such burdens as it may send forth to nourish and sustain the body. Every articulation of the neck should report itself to the skilled operator as absolutely normal. He should remember that there are hundreds of ligaments in the neck, and that any strain or twist may produce an irritating tangle of nerves that should be wholly free to keep up the functional action of the glands that are so numerously distributed in the region of the neck, throat, and jaw. A scalenus, a sterno-mastoid, an omohyoid muscle may be irritated to contraction sufficient to disturb the nerves of the constrictor muscles, which, when tightened down upon the blood-channels and nerve-supply, would cause a dangerous constriction and stop blood and other fluids from passing to and from adjacent parts, to a degree of congestion followed by fermentation, which universally attacks all stagnant fluids of the body. He who has educated his eye and hand to carefully explore the neck and detect and adjust variations is the man who is armed and equipped to bring relief to the child or person suffering with throat or glandular diseases of the neck. Your knowledge of anatomy has taught you that the hard and soft parts of the neck were put there for a purpose, and must come up at all times and in every place to the plans and specifications of this great and important division of human health and happiness. It is your eye of reason and your finger of touch that I exhort to be instant in season and out of season. You must know what a neck is, with all its parts and responsibilities, or you will fail in proportion to your lack of knowledge, not theoretical, but practical, which you can only obtain by experience.

Treatment of the Neck.

One writer says that you must stimulate or inhibit the nerves here for lost voice and there for weak eyes, here for sore throat, and this set of nerves for coughs, that set for caked breasts, and so on. I wish to emphasize that when I say you must treat the neck for fits, sore throat, headache, dripping eyes, and so on through the whole list of troubles whose causes can be found in slips of bones of the neck between the skull and the first dorsal vertebra, I mean, if you know what a neck is, to treat that neck by putting each bone of the neck in place, from the atlas to the first dorsal, and go away. You have done the work and all the good you can do. Reaction and ease will follow just as sure as you have done your work right. Begin at the head and start at the first bone of the neck, and don't guess, but know that it fits to the skull properly above. Then see and know that it sets squarely on the second bone. Then go on to the third, fourth, fifth, sixth, and seventh bone. Now go up that neck with your finger and push all the muscles of the neck into their places. Blood and nerves will do the rest of the work. Follow this course once or twice a week, and don't fool away any time fumbling to "stimulate and inhibit"

The Arm.

When he is brought face to face with the stern realities of the sick-room, the osteopath begins his inquiries and follows with his questions just far enough to know what division of the body is in trouble. If he finds that an arm has lost motion, he goes to the arm to explore for the cause. He can begin his hunt for the cause at the hand and explore it carefully for wounds, strains, or any lesion that could injure the nerves of the arm. If he finds no probable cause there, he should explore the bones for dislocations or strains of ligaments at the elbow or wrist. If he finds no defect in these articulations sufficient to locate the cause, he has only two more places to inspect—the shoulder and the neck, with their articulations of bones and muscles. If you find all things normal at the shoulder, then go to the neck, from which all the nerves of the arm are derived. If you find no lesion or cause equal to the trouble so far, then you have been careless in your search, and should go over the work again. Carefully look, think, feel, and know that the head of the humerus is true in the glenoid cavity; that the clavicle is perfect at both ends of its articulation with the sternum and acromion process. See that the biceps is in its groove; that the ribs are true at the sternum and the spine; that the neck is true on the first dorsal. Everything must be true in all joints of the neck, as the nerves of the arm come from the neck. There can be no variation from the normal, or trouble will appear. As the neck has much to do with the arm, we should keep with us a living picture of the forms of each vertebra, how and where it articulates with others, how it is joined by ligaments, and what blood-vessels, nerves, and muscles cross or range with it lengthwise, because from overlooking a small nerve or blood-vessel you may fail in removing a goitre or in curing many of the diseases of the head, face, and neck.

Structure of the Neck.

Previous to entering upon the discussion of croup, diphtheria, tonsillitis, pneumonia, spasms, inflammation of the brain, and other diseases peculiar to children of a few months or years of age, I would think it wholly useless without impressing again upon your minds the importance of a thorough knowledge of anatomy. When a child dies by disease, he dies all over. The limit of the ravages of the disease can only be described by the anatomy of the whole human body, with its physiological and anatomical systems of blood, both to and from the heart, as directed by such vessels and delivered by the forces of the nerves. To-day our most eminent authors who have written on such subjects have sent us into the field of action wholly incompetent to combat the enemy successfully. At this point of the discussion allow me to call your attention to the fact that the cause of disease has been for all ages a silent mystery, lying in ambush and shooting its smokeless powder, and with its deadly bullets slaying its countless millions. No author whom I have ever consulted has intimated that the cause of such diseases had planted its battery and skirmishers to do their destructive work in the nerves of the pelvis. Let us reason from our knowledge of anatomy, giving special attention to the spinal cord from the occiput to the coccyx, with the many nerves that branch off from the cord to all divisions of the body, to construct, nourish, and move the whole machinery of life, as found in the human body by anatomical and physiological research. Like the sensitive plant, these nerves cause the machinery of life to dilate when it receives its nourishment, and contract just as surely when assailed by enemies that would inflict injury. Carefully follow me to about the tenth dorsal vertebra, at which point you will see the beginning of the cauda equina, with its legions of nerves, which I am satisfied have secrets in their bosoms not yet unfolded. As they approach the lumbar, the pelvis, and the coccyx, and line themselves up for roll-call, we find them to be that innumerable host that no man has ever been able to number. Let me ask a few questions: Is it not plainly probable that this is the great quartermaster on whom every soldier of human life depends? Does not the mother give life and form by the constructive labors of this uncounted host? If this division of the body be as valuable to the human life as indicated by its system of telephoning that is hinted at by Nature when she has unfolded her great bunch of wires that are to converse with all parts of the body, we are led not only to think, but to know, that the language is positive, that this is the system of telegraphy, and that those wires conducted from the main branch, off at a few local stations until they get to that great city of life that is situated below the tenth dorsal. This system of wires or nerves is liable to be torn down, as are the telegraph and telephone wires of St. Louis, New York, or any other city, by sleet, wind, and storm. We see how completely all parts of the body are supplied with nerves for all purposes. Would it not be folly to try to treat local effects when the wisest author's eye has never seen any farther than the effects of which he tells you? Diphtheria affects the upper systems of glands even to death. The disease also destroys nerves of motion and sensation, of voice and swallowing, and even causes partial and total paralysis and death. Many kinds and quantities of drugs have been used, only to be baffled by the disease, of whose mysterious cause nothing is known. Authors tell us that while diphtheria does its deadly work in the glandular system, croup does its deadly work in the surface membranes of the trachea and lungs, but is just as fatal. They leave the cause, and prescribe calomel, whisky, opium, emetics, and chloroform, and prepare for tracheotomy and the death of the babe or child of three or five summers.

Croup, Diphtheria, Tonsillitis.

If we reason on any subject, we can offer only one cause for such mental effort; *i. e.*, conviction in the mind of the person who thinks and speaks has grown to the conclusion that the truth pertaining to the subject has not been unfolded with that degree of wisdom that it should be. As a child, I was taught that the difference between a doctor of law and a doctor of medicine existed in the fact that the doctor of law reasoned from cause to effect, while the doctor of medicine reasoned from effect to cause. The lawyer seeks evidence or testimony of truths with the expectation of a favorable verdict, and on this foundation he proceeds in all cases. If he has presented the whole truth and nothing but the truth before a just and competent jury, he has no fear of the result. Still he knows that both ignorance and dishonesty may exist with bench or with jury. Thus ends the story of the doctor of common law. Having presented the condition of the lawyer as we understand it, we will try just as honestly to present the condition of the doctor of medicine, or, in other words, the lawyer who deals with physiological laws. From the day he enters this great field of usefulness to the end of his career as a physician, he finds himself confronted with the effects of hidden causes, which are far back in the dark fogs of mystery. He knows that much depends on his diagnosis, which, being translated, means to guess from the effect to the cause that has produced the effect. His experience is very short before he discovers that nothing pleasant or unpleasant can exist without a cause. He reasons that darkness is an effect, caused by the absence of light; that when the earth becomes wet, it is an effect of falling water; therefore, a pain in any part of the body has a cause, notwithstading its mysterious workings. He has reason to believe that the cause exists in brain, blood, nerve, electric, or magnetic confusion in the physiological action of the machinery which sustains animal life.

At this point we will take up croup for discussion. We will commence our method of reasoning by setting out with an apple that falls to the ground from its mother tree, and receives a bruise which destroys the healthy condition of a small spot on the surface by that concussion, which soon proceeds to a destructive condition known as fermentation, or rot, and continues to the destruction of the whole apple, which dies undoubtedly from the diffusion of its own dead blood. It is evident to any observer that in the fall the apple received a deadly wound, that an inflammatory action followed and the fever or fermentation became general, and the apple died because of diffusion of deadly fluids to all parts of the body of the apple, even to death. You see that from the first small bruise it was natural with the apple and its qualities, when this chemical laboratory was put in motion by the active laws of fermentation, to go on and on to the destruction of the last vital drop of fluid.

I think you fully understand by this time that something else is expected to be illustrated by the apple. We will bring in the child of a few summers from the mother's breast and set it down with the pelvic, gluteal, and lower spinal nerves on the cold ground, which is electro-magnetic without a doubt, but just as reliable in its effects and as mysterious in its methods of procedure in producing a deadly shock upon the pudic and lower spinal nerves and starting it on its deadly work as the law that governs the apple. Thus we bruise or chill the nerves of the rectum, because it is the nature of cold to contract tissues. We will proceed from the plexuses there and journey upward, to observe the powerful action these nerves exercise over membranes, ligaments, and fibers. A powerful shock surely is received by the fascia, with its cellular and lymphatic systems, which extend to every muscle. It is the fascia that I am speaking of now, and I want you to hold it in your memory because of its universality through the whole human body. The fascia has much to do in feeding its own and other nerves, even on to the spinal cord, which is the one great conductor from the brain. The nerves which the spinal cord throws off, be they sensory, motor, or nutrient, their harmony must not be tampered with any more than that of the apple. By an irritation of those nerves you are warned to look for danger. The constrictor nerves, that have already produced constriction at the buttock, are as sure to reach the lungs, with their overpowering quantities of albumin, fibrin, and asphyxiated blood from the lymphatics and the whole cellular system, as the shock or bruise is certain to extend to and cause constriction of the kidneys and leave them in a spasmodic condition, during which time they cease to receive and excrete all substances not healthy in the territory they should drain. So far we find constriction of bowels, bladder, and all membranes and muscles of the abdomen and all its organs. In croup we find both kidneys drawn convulsively together, forming a pyramid over the aorta, vena cava, and thoracic duct. We find the buttock of the child extremely cold, with no arterial action below the crus. On examination, we find the diaphragm constricted, rigid, and tight. We find the diaphragm almost inactive during spasmodic croup. Here I think I am warranted in saying that the spasmodic action beginning at the buttock and extending to the diaphragm has been presented plainly enough so that you can fully comprehend what I think is the initial cause of croup. A shock to the nerves of the cellular system and their contents when unloaded and carried to the lungs becomes deadly from the fact of the resistance the blood receives at the diaphragm. The deposits called membranous deposits are exuded matter from the cellular system to the mucous membrane of the trachea and lungs, with their appendages.

Diphtheria.

"Our doctor said the child died from the effects of diphtheria, which ran into malignant sore throat and tonsillitis of gangrenous nature. Our doctor is a mighty good man. He did all he could for sister. He said he wanted to save sister, and, in consultation with two doctors that he had summoned from Boston and New York, he did all he could to save her life. They used all remedies, new and old. They swabbed her throat with caustics and used the most powerful throat-washes known in Europe and America. They exhausted all the simple family remedies, and even put a tube in sister's windpipe to let the air into the lungs, but she died in spite of all that could be done."

The girl is dead. The disease was called diphtheria, a very dangerous and contagious disease. It was reported to the board of health, who ordered out flags as a warning for others to keep out. This has been the practice and treatment in these cases for lo these many years. Who has ever questioned our sages and our systems of reason and treatment in colds and diseases of the throat, tonsils, and glands of the neck and their passages? Did we ever halt and reason that the white patches found in the mouth and throat were put there to guard the parts against coming injuries that hurried breathing, cold air, food, and drink might produce? Did we ever ask why God put such a covering over these exposed surfaces? When we remove these natural guards to life, have we not flatly disputed the wisdom of Nature? If we remove them and say we do no harm, would we not, under such a rule of reasoning, be just as wise in removing the bark from our fruit-trees, expecting the trees to do better without the bark than to let it stay where Nature put it until the tree grew its wood and fruit and dropped its old bark, when it had made new and was prepared to part with the old that was of no further use to the life of the tree? Would it not be wisdom for a few times in our practice among sore throats to let the bark stay where Nature had placed it until it had done the work for which it had been formed?

A word from long experience in diseases of the mouth, throat, and neck of the young. We have given much more faith to local symptoms and local treatments than we should. The best we can say of such is that it leads us into a system of routine work, which is followed by the school the doctor of medicine hails from. Forty years ago I began to let throats alone, by keeping all kinds of washes out of sore throats. For sore spots I gave the baby, boy or girl, starch gruel, the white of an egg, gum Arabic, or some pasty drink to cover the sore spots. Give such often until soreness leaves the throat.

I am proud to report that I have lost no case of croup, sore throat, tonsillitis, or diphtheria since I quit the unphilosophical practice of washing and swabbing children's throats, which I think kills 75 per cent of the cases that have died from infantile throat troubles. Give your patients sensible osteopathic treatment, and keep washes out; give them plenty of gruel to eat and cover the sore spots, and you will have but few dead babies, if any, out of your list of throat diseases among children.

In talking on diphtheria and other throat diseases to the students of my school, I do so with the knowledge that I am before men and women of intelligence, who are well read in the very best of American literature, which is equal to the very best of the most advanced nations of the earth. I know, too, that you did not come here for any foolishness or child's play, at a heavy loss of time and money. You came to this military school for drill, that you could be better prepared to combat with the great army of diseases that is dealing death by the millions annually to the human race all over the earth. I know you mean business, and I propose to talk business to you during your sojourn with us.

Our medical doctors are men of our race, and they have bravely fought for the lives of our children. They have used the best weapons they could plan and build. They have failed to batter down and take the forts of the enemy. The enemy has guns and ammunition of better strength and longer range. The enemy has made the most skilled generals of medicine run up the white flag of surrender and the blue flags of danger, which warn others to keep out of range of diphtheria, smallpox, and so on to the full list of contagions and infections.

Who has ever run up a white flag except the man who realized that he had no power to resist longer, nor hope of victory? What has the doctor done but multiply his drugs and chronicle defeat? He knows and says that drugs are strong compounds, of which he is just as ignorant as a bootjack. Like a rhinoceros, he sees and fights only the smoke of the gun that throws the deadly bullets that tear asunder his frame and let the life out. The medical man ends with his little book on symptomatology, and doses and kills babies just as fast now as at any time for a thousand years. He knows his practice is not trustworthy. He cuts and tries, and does not know whether the tree will do better or worse if he skins the bark off the babies' throats. He swabs, and daubs, and tries to keep up with the last antitoxin fad, and then turns the dead baby over to the deacon who levels all babies for heaven, and tells us, "The Lord giveth, and the Lord taketh." Then the hunter sets out on a hunt for more quail He shoots on the wing only, but he gets a heap of quail, and asks all legislatures to give him a good quail law and keep out all hunters but him and his kind.

Croup, diphtheria, tonsillitis, and kindred diseases of the neck, throat, and lungs that appear with the quick changes of weather in fall and winter, should be well reasoned upon by the osteopath before he begins his treatment. He finds, when called to treat a sore and swelled tonsil, in some a croupy cough, fever on face, head, and breast; but he will find the baby's hips, and in fact the whole body, with the usual flatness lost, and round from the base of the skull to the pelvic bottom. We run to our little book of symptomatology, and find we have what is called croup, diphtheria, tonsillitis, and so on. Here we ask no more questions, but begin to dose, drop, cut the throat, and send for more doctors and the latest antitoxin or the last fad that we have read in some journal. The babe dies. A next comes, to run the same gauntlet that many have tried, failed, and died in.

Treatment of Diphtheria.

With a knowledge of the beginning of these diseases, the operator has but few points to observe, and they are physiological facts of functioning and mechanical skill. Thus armed, we will find diphtheria to be the effect of cold acting on constrictor muscles of the neck by irritation of constricted nerves, by atmospheric changes from hot to cold. Such changes appear at all times of the year, but are more common in the fall and winter.

Much ignorance prevails as to its contagious nature. No known cause for its appearance has been found that is not in doubt. I think that troubles that appear to be contagious in times of their prevalence are called so on opinions formed on quantity more than on any known facts as to their infectious nature. The children of one family may take diphtheria and die, and all their school- and play-mates visit at all times during the worst stages to the hour of death, and not a single one takes the disease, or sore throat, or anything like it. It appears as a cold and does its work as a cold. It confounds the harmony of the nervous system. It acts as a wound or a shock to the vaso-dilators, causing them to give way to the constrictor nerves and stop the motion of the lymph in the lymphatic vessels long enough to ferment, heat up and dry the lymph of the epithelial and adipose tissues and cellular membrane of the tonsils, trachea, and all air-passages, tubes, and cells of the lungs, till by inflammation the mucous membrane is sloughed off, with such deposits as accumulate in the mouth, throat, and trachea. If there is any truth in the theory that bacteria of the same kind and form are found in all places of diphtheria, I would suggest inquiring into the health of the cow's udder from which the milk is taken that the children have been drinking. Perhaps that cow has but three teats that give "sound" milk, and the other gives lumpy or bloody milk from an ulcer, cancer, or tubercular bag. I fear that the bacteria are swallowed in diseased milk.

Whooping-Cough.

I have perused all the authorities obtainable, and have advised and counseled with them for information in reference to the cause of whooping-cough until I am constrained to think, whether I say so or not, that I have had many additions of words during the conversation, and, to use a homely phrase, less sense than I started out with. My tongue is tired, my brain exhausted, my hopes disappointed, and my mind disgusted, that after all this effort to obtain some positive knowledge of whooping-cough, I have received nothing that would give me any light whatever, pertaining to the subject. The writers wind up thus: that it may be due to a germ that irritates the pneumogastric nerve. I go off as blank and empty as the fish lakes on the moon. I supposed that the writers would say something in reference to the irritating influence of this disease on the nerves that would contract or convulsively shorten the muscles that attach at the one end to the os hyoid, and at the other end at various points along the neck, and force the hyoid back against the pneumogastric nerve, hypoglossal, cervical, or some other nerve that would be irritated by the pressure.

The above picture will give the reader some idea why I became so thoroughly disgusted with the heaps of compiled trash. I say "trash," because there was not a single truth, great or small, to guide me in search of the desired knowledge. And at this point I will say, on my first independent exploration I found all of the nerves and muscles that are attached to the os hyoid contracted, shortened, and pulling the hyoid back, bringing pressure against the pneumogastric nerve and all the nerves in that vicinity. Every muscle was in a hard and contracted condition in the region of this portion of the trachea, and extending up and into the back part of the tongue. Then I satisfied myself that this irritable condition of the muscles was possibly the cause of the spasms of the trachea during the convulsive cough. I proceeded at once with my hand, guided by my judgment, to suspend or stop for awhile the action of the nerves of sensation that go with and control the muscles of the machinery which conducts air to and from the lungs. My first effort, while acting upon this philosophy, was a complete relaxation of all muscles and fibers of that part of the neck, and when they relaxed their hold upon the respiratory machinery, the breathing became normal. I have been asked, "What bone would you pull when treating whooping-cough?" My answer would be: "The bones that hold by attachment the muscles of the hyoid system in such irritable condition, beginning with the atlas and terminating with the sacrum." To him who has been a faithful student in the American School of Osteopathy, the successful management of whooping-cough should be reliable and successful in all cases, when the case is received for treatment in anything like a reasonable time.

Before we leave that wisely constructed neck, I want to press and imprint on your minds in the strongest terms that the wisest anatomist and physiologist, the oldest and most successful osteopath, knows only enough of the neck and its wondrous system of nerves, blood, and muscles, and its relation to all above and below it, to say, "From everlasting to everlasting, Thou art great, O Lord God Almighty! Thy wisdom is surely boundless." For we see that man must be wise to know all about the neck, for by a twist of that neck we may become blind, deaf, spasmodic, lose speech and memory, and many other ills befall us. Think for a moment of the thousands and tens of thousands of large and small vessels that pass through the neck, to and from the heart and brain, to every organ, bone, fiber, muscle, and gland in the body.

CHAPTER VI.

The Thorax.

Inhibition and Stimulation.

When we use the terms "inhibition" and "stimulation," we mean to cut off or to excite to greater activity blood or any fluids, magnetic, electric, or life forces. One has said, "Life is that calm force sent forth by Deity to vivify all nature." Let us accept and act on it as true, that life is that force sent forth by the Mind of the universe to move all nature, and apply all our energies to keep that living force at peace, by retaining the house of life in good form from foundation to dome. Let us read a few lines in the book of Nature. If we stop blood in transit and note a few changes that Nature's chemistry takes on to remove dead blood, that has died because of delay in veins and arteries, we will note that if blood fails to pass a point owing to an obstructing cause, the lungs begin to labor, taking in much more than the usual amount of air. This fills the chest so full that the blood is forced into the arterial system for a short time by the force of all five lobes of the lung. At this time but little blood is left in the chest, because the air in the lungs is so great in bulk that to make room for that bulk the blood had to be pushed from the chest to other places. Now you see blood forced from chest to arteries by atmospheric pressure, which fills all space in the chest; but as soon as the air is taken out of the chest, a vacuum is made, large enough to hold three quarts of blood which has been detained by stop-valves in the veins and kept back and out of the chest until the air is forced out by exhalation; then the blood rushes in from the whole venous system, by force of contraction of the flesh of the whole body, which drives the venous blood back to the heart. Thus we see atmospheric pressure acting on arteries. The air is in the lungs, and forces blood from the heart by inside pressure of the atmosphere; then we see venous blood forced back to the heart through the veins by outside atmospheric pressure, fourteen pounds to the square inch of skin surface. The body during animal life has internal and external atmospheric pressure to assist arterial and venous circulation.

Lungs—Place, Power, and Use.

We see, when we open the chest, that the lungs are centrally situated in the chest and directly behind the heart. We find them located at a place where they change form by inhaling air, which change calls for over two hundred cubic inches of space, which can only be prepared for by removals. If we look and reason, we will conclude that as the ribs are moved outwardly from the heart, the diaphragm downward and the abdomen filling out and down, there is some power making this pressure. This is evident to him who reasons at all. Then he is ready to hunt and locate the cause. He has only to consult his own power of reason, aided by his observation, to learn that the inner side of the chest is the location and the lung is the organ that wedges out ribs, blood, and flesh while in distention. One thought of the power of atmospheric pressure will start reason in motion, and we will see that atmospheric pressure is one of the most important powers that any philosopher can conceive of, for pressing the blood forward from the heart through the arterial distribution; then again, as the air leaves the chest a vacuum is made and venous blood naturally comes to the lungs to be purified, and when purified, the next breath filling up the chest, it is naturally forced to the heart, to have this newly prepared blood conveyed to its destiny.

Here I will insert all I have to say of lung diseases. By some force the lungs open and fill to the full capacity of the chest. How the lungs are filled is not of so much importance to an osteopath as to know that they do fill the chest so full that it pushes blood, ribs, and flesh off to make room for themselves. That is one of Nature's methods for keeping blood in motion, both by pressure while filling the lungs and by forming a vacuum when letting air escape from the lungs. We find a great power and use in the pressure of the lungs when filling,on arterial blood to drive it through the system, and a vacuum to receive venous blood when air escapes, that has been held in the veins by valves which keep blood from being pushed back while the artery is being aided by pressure to supply all parts of the system.

The lungs open and shut; they swell and shrink. They open to take in air and also hold the air for a short period. They run by involuntary action. When they fill with air, they take up from one hundred to two hundred and forty cubic inches of space in the chest, and to get that space blood must be removed, ribs must be pushed out, diaphragm down; that coming bulk has to be hauled into the chest by the ability of the cups or cells to drink, swallow,or suck in the air. So far the "how" is but little understood. Still, it goes in and out of the lungs. Authors try to tell of muscle, bone, and other aids and "hows." We read much, but know little when we read from twenty to a hundred pages on lung-action by this and that author, for they give no real and positive light on their use and power. What I want to say is in reference to the power of the lungs when filling or full. There is pressure, power, and force that does, can, and will wedge, push, or force blood and other substances out of the way as the lungs expand to the full size of all the space allotted them in the pleural cavity. We soon see, if we observe at all, that pressure will assist in driving the blood through the arterial system as it leaves the heart. We find the veins, both great and small, provided with two-stop valves, which prevent the blood from falling back when on its course to the heart. No amount of pressure, short of rupture, can cause the blood to return from whence it came. But as soon as the pressure is taken off the veins of the lungs, the blood naturally flows or pours into the heart. We look upon this as the provision by which the arterial flow is assisted by lung-pressure and the venous flow checked until the arterial system has supplied all demands upon the surface. Then the pressure eases up and the blood naturally flows to the heart for the next process of distribution to the lungs, to receive such chemical substances as are necessary to purify and qualify the blood to be returned to the heart for universal distribution. Thus we see not only the chemical use of the lungs, but by them the blood receives assisting pressure and acts by that pressure to keep the blood and other substances in perpetual motion.

A question like this would be quite natural to the student: If blood is driven by lung-force, how does it move in fœtal life before the lung is formed? A good answer to that would be, that in fœtal life the mother's lungs give purity to the child's blood, and her arterial force takes the place of after-birth action and force demanded previous to birth. Thus we see Nature has filled all demands in animal life.

Following this lengthy description of the form and location of the lungs, we have your mind in a prepared condition to take up lung diseases, to lead you to the causes of the effects better known as diseases of the lungs.

Pneumonia.

Under this familiar name or title we will say to the inexperienced student that in changes of atmospheric conditions the lungs receive shocks which wound or disturb the natural harmony of lung-action by irritating the nerve-terminals as they appear in the mucous membrane of the lungs. This irritation after a time produces constriction of fibers, tissues, and muscles of the lungs, so as to prohibit freedom in the passage of the blood while in the venous system to such a degree as to suspend atmospheric assimilation long enough to produce asphyxia and death of blood-corpuscles and other substances that may be or should be in action in a healthy condition of the lungs. We find stagnation, stoppage, accumulation, and congestion to the degree of irritability of a part or whole of the lungs. Now we have a condition of inactive fluids deposited in some part of one or all five divisions of the lungs, which take on themselves the first step of fermentation. This is followed by another action caused and known as inflammation, which brings in the higher and more active forces, which produce an increase in temperature to the degree known as fever, which may be many degrees hotter than the normal temperature of the body. We may have what is well known as pneumonia or lung fever, which passes on in quick succession to other stages, such as coughing up blood for a day or a longer period, until this increased temperature and augmented action have changed the dead blood into gaseous fluids and thrown them off from and out of the lungs. With the change from coughing up of blood we have healthy and healing pus.

We see in pneumonia a disease beginning in an irritation of the sensory nerves, and progressing from that condition of irritation to congestion, inflammation, recovery, or death.

CONSUMPTION.

I have not written much on "Consumption," because I wanted to test my conclusions by long and careful observations on cases that I have taken and successfully treated without drugs. I kept the results from public print until I could obtain positive proof that consumption can be cured. So far the discovered causes give me little doubt, and the cures are a certainty in very many cases. An early beginning is one of the great considerations in incipient consumption.

I believe so many deaths by consumption will soon be with the things of the past, if the cases are taken early and handled by a skilled mind, one trained for that responsible place. That mind must be taught this as a special branch. It is too deep for superficial knowledge or imperfect work. Life is in danger, and can be saved by skill, not by force and ignorance. He who sees only the dollar in the lung is not the man to trust with your case.

It is such men as have the ability to think, and the skill to comprehend and execute the application of Nature's unerring laws, that obtain the results required. We believe the day has come, and long before noon the fear of consumption will greatly pass from the minds of people. We have long since known and proven that a cough is only an effect. If an effect, then a wise man will set his mental energy on the track to hunt the cause. He has all the evidence in the cough, location of pain, tenderness of spine and chest, and quality of the substances coughed up, to locate the cause, and to know, when he has found it, how to remove it and give relief. It will grow more simple as he reasons and notes effect. We do not think that this result will be obtained every time by even an average mind, unless it has a special training for that purpose. The physician must not only know that the lungs are in the upper part of the chest, close to the heart, liver, and stomach, but he must know the relations all sustain to each other, and that the blood must be abundantly supplied to support and nourish the five sets of nerves—sensory, motor, nutrient, voluntary, and involunatary. If the supply should be diminished on the nutrient nerves, weakness would follow; reduce the supply from the motor and it will have the same effect. Motion becomes too feeble to carry blood to and from the lungs normally, and the blood becomes diseased and congested, because it is not passed on to other parts with the force necessary for the health of the lungs.

At this time the nerves of sensation become irritated by pressure and lack of nutriment, and we cough, which is an effort of Nature to unload the burden of oppression that congestion causes with the sensory nerves. If this be effect, then we must suffer and die, or remove the cause, put out the fire, and stop waste of life. Nature will do its work of repairing in due time. Let us reason by comparison. If we dislocate a shoulder, fever and heat will follow. The same is true of all limbs and joints of the body. If any obstructing blood or other fluid should be deposited in quantities great enough to stop other fluids from passing on their way, Nature will fire up its engine to remove such deposits by converting fluids into gas. As heat and motion are important as remedies, we may expect fever and pain until Nature's furnace produces heat, forms and converts its fluids into gas and other deposits, and passes them through the excretories to space, and allows the body to work normally again.

We believe consumption causes the death of thousands annually who might be saved. We must not let stupidity veil our reason, and we are to blame if we let so many run into "consumption" from a simple hard cough. The remedy is natural, and, we believe, from results already obtained, 75 per cent can be cured if taken in time. What we generally call "consumption" begins with a cough, chilly sensations, and lasts a day or two. Sometimes fever follows with a cough, either high or low. The cold generally relaxes in a few days, the lungs get "loose," and much sputa is raised for a period, but the cough appears again and again with all changes of weather, and lasts longer each time, until it becomes permanent. It is called "consumption," because of this continuance. Medicines are administered freely and frequently, but the lungs grow worse, cough more continued and much harder, till finally blood begins to come from the lungs and there is a wasting of strength. A change of climate is suggested and taken, but with no change for the better. Another and another travels to death on the same line. Then the doctor in council reports "hereditary consumption," and with his decision all are satisfied, and each member of the family feels that a cold and cough means a coffin, because the doctor says the family has "hereditary consumption." This shade-tree has given comfort and contentment to the doctors of the past.

If you have a tiresome and weakening cough at the close of the winter, and wish to be cured, we would advise you to begin osteopathic treatment at once, to enable the lungs to heal and harden against the next winter's attack.

A Description of Consumption.

For fear you do not understand what I mean by "consumption," I will write on a descriptive line quite pointedly. I will give the start and the progress to fully developed consumption. We often meet with cases of a permanent cough, with expectorations of long duration, dating back two, five, ten, even thirty years, to the time the patient had measles. The severity of the cough and strain had congested even the lung-substances, and a chronic inflammation was the result. If we analyze the sputa, we find fibrin and even lung-muscle. Does all this array of dangerous symptoms cause an osteopath to give up in despair? It should not, on the other hand, he should go deeper on the hunt for the cause. He may find trouble in the fibers of the pneumogastric nerve. The atlas or hyoid, vertebra, rib, or clavicle may be pressing on some nerve that supplies the mucous membrane of air-cells or passages. If a cut foot will often produce lockjaw, why will not a pressure on some center, branch, or nerve-fiber cause some division of the nerves of the lungs that govern venous circulation, to contract and hold blood indefinitely as an irritant, and cause perpetual coughing?

This is not the time for the osteopath to run up the white flag of defeat and surrender. Open the doors of your purest reason, put on the belt of energy, and unload the sinking vessel of life. Throw overboard all dead weights from the fascia, and wake up the forces of the excretories. Let the nerves all show their powers to throw out every weight that would sink or reduce the vital energies of Nature. Give them a chance to work, give them full nourishment, and the victory will be on the side of the intelligent engineer. Never surrender, but die in the last ditch. Let us enter the field of active exploration, and note the causes that would lead us to conclude we have the cause that produces "consumption," as it has ever been called.

Begin at the brain, go down the ladder of observation, stop and whet your knives of sharp mental steel, get your nerves quiet by the opium of patience. Begin with the atlas, follow it with the searchlight of quickened reason, comb back your hair of mental strength, and never leave that bone until you have learned how many nerves pass through and around that wisely formed first part of the neck. Remember it was planned and builded by the mind and hand of the Infinite. See what nerve-fibers pass through and on to the base and center, and each minute cell, fascia, gland, and blood-vessel of the lungs. Do you not know that each nerve-fiber for its place is king and lord of all?

The Effects of Consumption.

I think consumption begins by closing the channels in the neck for the lymph, which stands as one of, if not the most highly refined elements in animal bodies. Its fineness would indicate that it is a substance that must be delivered in full supply continually to keep health normal. If so, we will, for experimental reasons, look at the neck ligated, as found in measles, croup, colds, and eruptive fevers. Supply is stopped from passing below the atlas for three days. During such diseases fever runs high at this time and dries up the albumen, giving cause for tubercles, as fever has dried out the water and left the albumen in small deposits in the lungs, liver, kidneys, and bowels. If this view of the great uses of lymph is true as a cause of glandular growths and other dead deposits, have we not a cause for miliary tuberculosis? Have we not encouragement to prosecute with interest, in the hope of an answer to the question, "What is tuberculosis?" Our writers are just as much at sea to-day as they were a thousand years ago. I will give the reader some of the reasons why I think the mischief was started while fluids were cut off by congestion of the neck. By the crudest method of reasoning, we would conclude that from the form of the neck many objects are indicated, and the material of which it is composed would give reason to turn all its powers of thought, to ask why it is so formed as to twist, bend, straighten, stiffen, and relax at will, to suit so many purposes? A very tough skin, a sheath, surrounds the neck with blood-vessels, nerves, muscles, bones, ligaments, fascia, glands, great and small, throat and trachea. In bones we find a great canal for the spinal cord. It is well and powerfully protected by a strong wall of bone, so no outer pressure can obstruct the flow of passing fluids, to keep the vitality supplied by brain-forces, but with all the protection given to the cord, we find that it can be overcome by impacted fluids to such a degree as to stop blood and other fluids from supplying the lungs and everything below.

The Cause of Consumption.

Consumption to an osteopath should be known as the graveyard in which the dead have been sent from the hospitals of the physical forms of the body, and directly from the fascia of all. We reason, when the lungs throw off dead matter, that the blood-corpuscles have died in the hospitals of the fascia, omentum, and mesentery, and in proportion to the death of the corpuscles so is the supply of sputa deposited and coughed up, until the putrid bodies exceed both the able-bodied and the wounded; then the vital powers yield in death to universal putrescence, a total collapse, or to the death of the man, and he is listed "died of pulmonary consumption." I hope that this method of reasoning to the student of osteopathy will enable him to reach further back into the cause that has produced the effect that has been so little understood, so deadly in its ravages and so extended in its field of destruction to the human family. At this time in our investigation we will ask the student to refresh his mind by reviewing his anatomy, looking very carefully to the nerve- and blood-supply, both superficial, deep-seated, and universal.

Miliary Tuberculosis.

"A tubercle is a separate body being enveloped." All descriptions of a tubercle amount to about this, that the tubercle is a quantity of fleshy substance, which may be albumen, fibrin, or any other substance collected and deposited at one place in the human body, and covered with a film composed generally of fibrinous substances, and deposited in a spherical form and separated from all similarly formed spheres by fascia. They may be very numerous, for many hundreds may occupy one cubic inch, and yet each one is distinct. They seem to develop only where fascia is abundant, in the lungs, liver, bowels, and skin. After formation, they may exist and show nothing but roughened surfaces, and when the period of dissolution and the solvent powers of the chemical laboratory take possession to banish them from the system, the work of banishment generally begins when some catarrhal disease is preying upon the human system. Nature seems to make its first effort at the catarrhal period for the purpose of disposing of such substances as have accumulated. At that time it brings forward all the solvent qualities and applies them, with the assistance of the motor force, to driving out all irritating substances through the bowels, the lungs, and the porous and excretory system. Electricity is called in as the motor force to be used in expelling all unkindly substances. By this effort of Nature, which is an increased action of the motor nerves, electricity is brought to the degree of heat called fever, which, if better understood, we would possibly find to be the necessary heat of the furnace of the body to convert dead substances into gas, which can travel through the excretory system and be thrown from the body much easier than water, lymph, albumen, or fibrin.

During this process of gas-burning, a very high temperature is obtained by the increased action of the arterial system through the motor nerves, permeating the tubercles and causing an inflammation by the gaseous disturbance so produced; another effort of Nature to convert those tubercles into gas and relieve the body of their presence and irritable occupancy.

As an illustration, we will ask the reader if he could reasonably expect to pass a common towel through a pipestem? Nevertheless Nature can easily do it. Confine the towel in a cylinder and apply fire, which in time will convert the towel into gas or smoke, and enable it to pass through the stem. Is it not just as reasonable to suppose those high temperatures of the body are Nature's furnaces, making fires to burn out of those dead bodies, while passing them through the skin in order to get rid of these substances that are packed all through the human fascia, and can only be passed from the body in a gaseous form.

The blackened eye of the pugilist soon fires up its furnaces and proceeds to generate gas from the dead blood that surrounds the eye. Though it may be in considerable quantities under the skin, the blood soon disappears, leaving the face and eye normal to all appearances. No pus has formed, nor deposit left; fever disappears; the eye is well. What better effort could Nature offer than through its gas-generating furnace? I will leave any other method for you to discover. I know of none that my reason can grasp.

When reason sees a white corpuscle in the fascia not taken up as a nutrient, it attaches itself to the fascia with all its uterine powers during the time of measles or other eruptive diseases, and soon takes form and is a vital and durable being whose name is "tubercle." All tubercles are unappropriated substances whom Mother Fascia has clothed and ordered in camp for treatment and repairs, and has placed on the list of enrolled pensioners, to draw on the treasury of the fascia until death shall discharge them.

The mothers of the human race give birth to children from the time of their puberty to sterility. They may give birth a dozen times, but Nature finally calls a halt, and the whole system of life-sustaining nerves of the womb which are in the fascia, with blood in great abundance to supply fœtal life, ceases to go farther with the processes of building beings. Vitality for that purpose stops, never to return. Nature has no longer a demand for her system to act as a constructing cause for other beings of her kind, and she is free the remainder of her days.

Variety of Births.

A question arises, Are children the only beings she can develop in her system and give birth to? No; she can go through other processes of breeding. In her fascia there is one seed which, if vitalized, will develop a being called "measles." She never has but one confinement. That set of nerves that gave support and growth to measles died in the delivery of the child, and never can conceive and produce any more measles. Another seed lives in her fascia waiting to be vitalized by the male principle of smallpox, and when it is born it always kills the nerves that gave it life and form. And the person never can have but one such child or being during life. Still another seed awaits the coming of the commissary to nourish while it consumes that vitality in the fascia of the glands to develop the portly child we call "mumps." Both male and female conceive and give birth to these beings, and then tear up the tracks and roads behind them, by killing the demand for such kinds.

I want to draw the mind of the reader to the fact that no being can be formed without material, a place in which to be developed, and with all forces necessary for the work. And as all excrescences and abnormal growths, diseases, and conditions must have the friendly assistance of the fascia before development, the fascia is the place to look for the cause of disease and the place to begin the action of remedies in all diseases.

"We can arrive at truth only by the powerful rules of reason," the philosopher has shouted from the housetops during all these ages. He adjusts his many supposable causes, and adds to and subtracts from until he arrives at a conclusion based upon the facts of his observations. We must know the principles that exist in substances and seeds by which, when associated with proper conditions, that powerful engine known as "animal life" gives truth, with fact and motion as its voucher. We reason, if corn be planted in moist and warm earth, that action and growth will present the form of a living stalk of corn, which has existed *in embryo*, and still continues its vital actions as long as the proper conditions prevail, until the growth and development are completed. If you take a seed in your fingers, push it in the ground and cover it up, incubation, growth, and development is expected in obedience to the law under which it serves. Thus we see, in order to succeed, we must deposit and cover up the seed, that the laws of gestation may have an opportunity to get the results desired. As Nature always presents itself to our minds as seeds deposited in proper soil and season, and it is loyal to its own laws only, we are constrained by this method of reasoning to conclude that disease must have a soil in which to plant its seeds before gestation and development. It must have seasonable conditions, the rains of nourishment, also the necessary time required for such processes. All these laws must be fulfilled to the letter; otherwise a failure is certain. As the great laboratory of Nature is always at work in the human body, the chilling winds and poisonous breaths, with extremes of heat and cold at different seasons of the year by day and night, and the lungs and skin are continually secreting and excreting every minute, hour, and day of our lives, is it not resonable to suppose that we inhale many elements that are floating in the common winds that contain the seeds of some destructive element, to the harmony of fluids that are necessary to sustain the healthy animal forms? Suppose it should start the yeast, or kind of substance that lives mainly upon lime. If this yeast, in its action and thirst for food to suit its life and appetite, should call in from the earth, water, and atmosphere for its daily food lime substances only, and by its power destroy all other principles taken as nourishment, is it not reasonable to suppose it would deposit such elements in overpowering quantities in the fascia of the mucous membrane of the lungs, so as to overcome the renovating powers of the lungs and excretory system? This deposit acts as an irritant to the sensory nerves to such an extent that the electricity of the motor nerves is forced to take charge of and run the machinery of the human body, with a velocity sufficient to raise the temperature of the body, by putting the electricity above the normal action of animal life, and thereby generate that temperature known as fever.

The two extremes, heat and cold, may be the causes of retention and detention. One is detained by the contraction of cold until the blood and other fluids die by asphyxia. The warm temperature produces relaxation of the nerves, blood, and all other vessels of the fascia, during which time the arteries are injecting too great quantities of fluids to be renovated by the excretory system. Then you have a cause for decomposition of the blood and other substances. You have a logical foundation and a cause for all diseases, catarrhal and climatic, contagions, infections, and epidemics. The fascia proves itself to be the probable matrix of life and death. When harmonious in normal action, health is good; when perverted, disease results.

Lung Diseases.

In America man has dreaded diseases of the lungs more than any other one disease. If we compare pulmonary diseases with other maladies, we find that more persons die of consumption, pneumonia, bronchitis, and nervous coughs than from smallpox, typhus and bilious fever, and all other fevers combined. Many diseases of contagious nature stay in the city or country or in an army but a short time; they kill a few and disappear, and may not return for many years. This is the history of yellow fever, cholera, and other epidemics. They slay their hundreds, and cease as unceremoniously as they began. But when we think of diseases that begin to show their effects in tonsils, trachea, and lining membranes of the air-passages, we find we are in a boundless ocean.

It takes no great mind to know from past observation that a common cold often holds on and settles down to chronic inflammation of the lungs, and the patient dies of consumption, croup, diphtheria, or tonsillitis. Catarrhal troubles stay and waste vitality by causing a failure in oxidation while in the lungs. Diphtheria paves the way for the young and old to die of consumption. Vitiated air in dance-halls, opera-houses, churches, and school-houses never fails to inspect and deposit the seeds of consumption in weak lungs.

As one delves deeper and deeper into the machinery and exacting laws of life, he beholds works and workings of contented laborers of all parts of one common whole, the great shafts and pillars of an engine working to the fullness of the meaning of perfection. He sees that great quartermaster, the heart, pouring in and loading train after train, and giving orders to the wagonmaster to line his teams and march on quick time to all divisions, supply all companies, squads, and sections with rations, clothing, ammunition, surgeons, splints, and bandages, and put all the dead and wounded into the ambulances to be repaired or buried with military honors by Captain Vein, who fearlessly penetrates the densest bones, muscles, and glands with the living waters to quench the thirst of the blue corpuscles that are worn out by doing fatigue duty in the great combat between life and death. He often has to run his trains on forced marches to get supplies to sustain his men when they have had to contend with long sieges of heat and cold. Of all officers of life, none has greater duties to perform than the quartermaster of the blood-supply, who borrows from the brain, which gives motion to all parts of active life, the force with which he runs his deliveries.

Found Effects.

In all ages the mind and pen of man have been content to dwell and rest or agree that the lungs generate tubercles and other destructive substances; that a lung is an insane suicide; that it takes its own life. The doctor analyzes by his chemistry the substances coughed up from the lungs. He takes the diseased lung to his microscope for physical examinations.

He finds knots, lumps, and much variation from the normal lungs in cells, muscles, tissues, blood-vessels, and nerves, the sensory, motor, and nutrient. He finds great abnormalities in the form and fluids of the lungs, and drops further search. He has found the effects, and only charges all this bad work to the lungs. He knows he has found the guilty party, and proceeds to punish. He never asks why. He asks no question about the cause of the lungs giving way and failing to perform their function, nor does the thought occur to him that they must be helped by being nourished from the lymph prepared in the omentum, pleura, diaphragm, and the peritoneum generally. He has failed to ask why the lungs fail to be normal when the omentum is diseased. He seems to have totally failed to see that in all cases of diseased lungs no perfectly normal omentum can be found, or at least no treatise on lung diseases has even mentioned that the remote cause of consumption might be traced to the omentum, or failure in its functioning before disease of the lung appeared. It seems to be due to osteopathy that the discovery has been made. In all post-mortems of people who have died from lung diseases and been examined at the American School of Osteopathy, the omentum has been found to be diseased, torn, wounded, cancerous, or disabled in such a manner that it was not possible to perform its functions. We have reason to believe that the lung dies or fails to do its part normally when the omentum is diseased.

Digestion.

In our physiologies we read much about digestion. We will start in where they stop. They bring us to the lungs with chyle fresh as made and placed in the thoracic duct, previous to flowing into the heart to be transferred to the lungs to be purified, charged with oxygen, and otherwise qualified, and sent off for duty, through the arteries, great and small, to the various parts of the system. But there is nothing said of the time when all blood is gas, before it is taken up by the secretions, after refinement, and driven to the lungs to be mixed with the old blood from the venous system. A few questions about the blood seem to hang around my mental crib for food. Reason says we cannot use blood before it has all passed through the gaseous stage of refinement, which reduces all material to the lowest forms of atoms, before constructing any material body. I think it safe to assume that all muscles and bones of our body have been in the gas state while in the process of preparing substances for blood. A world of questions arise at this point.

The first is, Where and how is food made into gas while in the body? If you will listen to a dyspeptic after eating, you will wonder where he gets all the wind that he rifts from his stomach, and continues for one or two hours after each meal. That gas is generated in the stomach and intestines, and we are led to believe so because we know of no other place in which it can be made and thrown into the stomach by any tubes or other methods of entry. Thus, by the evidence so far, the stomach and bowels are the one place in which this gas is generated. I have spoken of the stomach that generates and ejects great quantities of gas for a longer or shorter time after meals. This class of people have been called dyspeptics. Another class of the same race of beings stand side by side with him without this gas generating. They, too, eat and drink of the same kind of food, without any of the manifestations that have been described in the first class. Why does one stomach blow off gas continually while the other does not? As No. 2 throws off no gas from the stomach after eating, is this conclusive evidence that his stomach generates no gas? Or do his stomach and bowels form gas just as fast as No. 1, and the secretions of the stomach and bowels take up and retain the nutritious matter and pass the remainder of the gas by way of the excretory ducts through the skin? If the excretory ducts take up and carry this gas out of the body by way of the skin, and he is a healthy man, why not account for the other one's stomach ejecting this gas by way of the mouth, because of the fact that the secretions of the stomach are either clogged up or inactive, for want of vital motion of the nerve-terminals of the stomach.

Another question in connection with this subject, Why is the man whose stomach belches forth gas in such abundance also suffering with cold feet, hands, and all over the body, while No. 2 is quite warm and comfortable, with a glow of warmth passing from his body all the time?

With these hints I will ask the question, What is digestion?

THE PHILOSOPHY OF DIGESTION.

All digestion is the result of electric shocks, sent forth from the brain by way of the motor system of nerves. Such shocks are in perpetual motion from the center of the earth to the soul of the surface. Not only do these shocks tear asunder all substances found in the alimentary channel, but they impart, inject, and associate a moving principle, called vitality. Yet it is only vital to the work of decomposition, selection, and association for the purpose of forming flesh, muscle, sinew, hair, teeth, and bone. The different qualities found in the fluids of the different localities, such as brain, liver, and kidneys, are effects of those living shocks. The same law is just as applicable in reason and as true in effect in creating and imparting odors to the various glands in the whole system. The heart, being the center electro-motor engine, at every vibration is regulated by the velocity demanded to modify and keep the electric battery or the brain supplied with electricity to the normal capacity to supply the electro-motor, without which some degree of failing weakness is perceptible by beholding sluggish action and abnormal quantities of deposits in some or all parts of the cellular system of the lungs, heart, stomach, bowels, uterus, lymphatics of the fascia, and system generally.

The Heart.

Diseases of the chest are generally confined to the lungs, heart, pleura, the pericardium, mediastia, with their blood-vessels, nerves, and lymphatics. As we open the breast we behold the heart conveniently situated to throw blood to all parts of the body. From it we see vessels or pipes that go to all muscles and organs, the stomach, bowels, liver, spleen, kidneys, bladder, womb, etc., and all bones, fibers, ligaments, membranes, lungs, and brain. When we follow the blood through its whole journey in feeding the different parts, be they organ or muscle, we find just enough unloaded at each station to supply the demand as fast as it is consumed. Thus life is supplied at each stroke of the heart with blood to keep digestion in full motion while other supplies of blood are being made and put in channels to carry to the heart. This blood is freely given to keep the channels strong, clean, and active. Much depends on the heart, and great care should be given to its study, because a healthy system depends almost wholly on a normal heart and lung. The study of the framework of the chest should be done with the greatest care. Every joint of the neck and spine has much to do with a healthy heart and lung, because all vital fluids pass through the heart and lungs, and any slip of bone or strain or bruise of muscle or nerve will affect to some degree the usefulness of that fluid in its vitality, when it is appropriated in the place or organ it should sustain in a good healthy state. The osteopath's first and last duty is to look well to a healthy blood- and nerve-supply. He should let his eye rest day and night on the spinal column, to know if the bones articulate truly in all facets and other bearings, and never rest day or night until he knows the spine is true and in line from atlas to sacrum, with all the ribs in perfect union with the processes of the spine.

DEVELOPMENT

The heart, from the first visible drop of blood to the termination of all its work in the human body, seems to follow specifications that were wisely written and adapted to all purposes necessary to sustain animal life. If we follow the blood from the heart and observe its first work after giving form to itself, we will see two arteries passing off to a distance After watching the action and work of construction at that place, we find as a result the formation of the brain, which is universally recognized as the seat of the machinery that produces the forces necessary to supply the nerves that have their beginning in the brain and extend to every fiber, muscle, organ, and ligament necessary to be used in propelling the machinery of animal life. Not only does it provide for the machinery of force that is stationed at a considerable distance from the heart, but it throws out another great river of nourishment, known as the abdominal aorta, out of which many rivers branch off to supply and sustain another great manufactory, which is located from the first lumbar to the end of the sacrum. This manufactory has carried on its labors for countless ages, busily pounding away at its work of preparing the material that supplies every fiber and part of the human body. No author has been kind enough, if wise enough, to give us any information on this great and important question. I wish to emphasize it very positively and draw your attention, with your minds separated from all else, while thinking, to answer this question: What would be the deleterious effects on the nerves of the kidneys if a sudden fall, the feet slipping out directly in front, the body still erect, dislocated the sacrum by the velocity of the force against the frozen ground, ice, floor, stones, or any other unyielding surface? The wedge-formed sacrum between the two innominate bones would be driven downward toward the ischii one-fourth, one-half, or one whole inch. What effect would it have on the shape of the coccyx, the coccygeal ligaments being fastened to the innominate? Would it not leave the coccyx bent in and upward? What effect would it have on the sacral nerves? the whole glandular system? the circulation of the blood to and from all parts below the crura? At this point I want to call your attention to the location and function of the cauda equina, the crura, the solar plexus, the sympathetic nerves generally of the abdomen, the nerves of sensation, motion, and nutrition, the nerves of the pancreas, the spleen, liver, and bladder, the lymphatics, the cellular system, the receptaculum chyli, the pudic nerves, the nerves of the uterus, and all nerves of the generative system of either male or female. Does not your compass of reason conduct you to a cause of Bright's disease of the kidneys, monthly disturbances, enlargement of the ovaries by stagnated blood to the degree of hardened deposits, to growths of enormous size of the various organs of the abdomen, such as the liver, kidneys, spleen, and so on? Have you ever observed that the woman with monthly convulsions has a sacrum twisted or driven from its normal position by blows, falls, or otherwise?

I can refer you to no author on this subject whose pen has ever described this arrangement as being the parent cause of hundreds of diseases and malformations, from the ponderous fibroid tumor to the rose cancer of the bladder or uterus. Here I wish to draw your attention to the duty of the various nerves found situated and distributed from one extremity of the abdomen to the other.

Heart Disease.

In speaking of diseases of the heart and remedies therefor, I think it best to give the student a knowledge of what is received and practiced by the medical profession as found in text-books of practitioners of the drug system. For this purpose I will quote in full from the "American Text-Book on Therapeutics," by Wilson, on diseases of the heart: "In all acute affections of the heart, therapy can be looked upon, first, as casual; secondly, as symptomatic. Nearly all inflammatory conditions of the pericardium are secondary, and, as the cause of such conditions has already become operative, the field of treatment is limited to the prevention of further damage from the primary cause (and is in so far then casual), the relief of suffering and other symptoms, and finally the prevention of death, which may result either from the operation of the original cause or from ensuing complications."

In the Dark.

I do this to show the osteopath that one of the most learned authors speaks about all that is offered for the student of medicine to guide him in his practice. He begins in conjectures of cause, such as rheumatism, which you know is an effect, coming from the failure of the heart to deliver blood in living quantity to the joints and vicinity. At this point he raises his club and bangs away in the dark for want of knowledge of the cause. He begins by advising the shoveling in of mercury, digitalis, opium, calomel, acids, alkalies, stimulants, and sedatives, and so on to the ice-bag, hot pack, blood-letting, or venesection. Has he said anything that he can swear by? Has he said anything that you can go by? He leaves you a blank, because his diagnosis and treatment are blanks also. After having read his "able" definition, and knowing that you do know something of anatomy and physiology, I will say that you know too much anatomy and physiology and the results gained by osteopathy to be satisfied to go into the treatment of the diseases of the heart with no knowledge of diseases or the drugs you are about to administer. On that line you travel without hope. Right here, as osteopaths, we will take up the heart and see if we know the responsible duties it has to perform as headquarters of the blood-supply. I do not wish to consume your time unnecessarily in a lengthy description of the heart and the millions of rivers it supplies, with all of which you have been made acquainted by descriptive and demonstrative anatomy, histology, and physiology. We feel the importance of asking you to refresh your memories once more by a vivid mental painting of the whole arterial system, both great and small, that you may be the better able to think with me as I present the subject.

Causes.

At this time we will introduce the subject of "heart diseases" and the mechanico-physiological causes. We will try to arrive at some reasonable conclusion as to the cause of intermittent heart, heart of great commotion or palpitation, heart of feeble force, and all those conditions which would produce effects known as "heart disease." They are described by ancient and modern writers under many names, such as angina pectoris, valvular disturbances, and many other names. But all previous writings end with "ifs," "buts," and a few "howevers" and "possiblies," without a single rock for the doctor to stand on. The student of medicine goes forth with his diploma under his arm and begins a new life of guessing at cause and cures, with both eyes goggled by ignorance of the diseases he meets. He blindly begins to experiment with the drugs of which he has no knowledge, so far as their effects are known in heart disease. He is ordered and instructed by his preceptor to use calomel freely and frequently, morphine and digitalis with caution, venesection with caution, and so on, and to be patient with his patients; they may get well anyhow.

Suppose we stop and camp at this place, light our pipes

and take a good social smoke, and ask our venerable old "medicine-man" what object he had in prescribing the deadly mercury, digitalis, or morphine in case of heart disease. At this time we will saddle up our horses and go on. The old doctor has told us very kindly that he made use of these remedies because they have long been used by the doctors, who did not know anything about cause and effect.

Now I have given you the sum total of the procedure of the medical practitioners of the past up to the present date, with their acknowledgment that they do not know the cause of the disease nor the effect of the drug they have been free to administer, with all the dignity and wise looks that could be painted to represent an angelic philosopher.

A Few Facts.

With the limited knowledge that I have of anatomy and physiology, I feel some degree of boldness and pleasure in presenting my views of mechanico-physiological cause of heart diseases, which I think I can present to you in a simple and philosophical manner, clear enough that with your knowledge of anatomy you will concede that I have given you the only true foundation on which heart-disturbances can be clearly traced to the causes of commotions called palpitation, angina pectoris, and the whole column of heart diseases. We will begin by supposition. Suppose in a person in perfect health, anatomically and physiologically perfect in all parts and functions, we find the heart infinitely correct in receiving and discharging blood in quantities just enough, with force exactly equal to all demands. In this picture of life we see the engine in motion, count the strokes, and record them at seventy per minute. At this time we begin in a small way to experiment with the body, which this engine supplies, by tying a cord around one of the little toes, the body lying in exactly the same position as when the heart-beat was timed and recorded at seventy. Would we expect to find or would we have reason to expect the heart to make seventy strokes, no more, no less, in motion or energy? If we find seventy-one beats to be the number per minute with a small artery stopped by ligation of one little toe, what would be the number of beats with two toes tied? Suppose we take the strings off the toes and the heart falls back to seventy; then drive a shingle-nail through one toe. Would you be surprised if the heart made seventy-five beats? Then drive a nail through the other little toe. Would you be surprised to see the heart running eighty beats per minute? One was simple stoppage of blood by a cord, the other a wound which produced contracture of muscles, ligaments, and blood-vessels to a greater degree than the ligation did. I think any man with anatomical and physiological knowledge will be able to reason and come to the conclusion that if an obstruction in the least toe, and that at the greatest distance from the heart, disturbs its regularity and pulsation, that other causes of irritation and stoppage of either arterial or venous blood will also cause demands that the heart use greater energy to force blood through the involved channels, just in proportion to the resistance it has to meet. When the heart has overlabored for many days and months to force blood through compressed arteries and veins, would it not be reasonable and would it not be safe to conclude that when a heart had labored to exhaustion it would tire out, quiver, and palpitate? I will ask your indulgence and a little more patience. I began at the little toe with the view of giving you a homœopathic dose on obstructed circulation as evidence of the cause for heart disturbance. We will now commence on a larger scale. We have to deal with the allopathic "czar" of ignorance. It is not supposable that he has time to dabble with the little blood-vessels, and one at a time. We will hit him, if we can at all with reason, with the anatomical fact that numerous arteries are thrown off from the aorta for the purpose of supplying certain demands, and that by jars, twists, strains, and a world of accidents that the human body is liable to meet and pass through, he may have one, ten, or even all of his ribs pushed down, up, out, or in, so as to obstruct any or all of the intercostal arteries, veins, and nerves. In this deformity would he suspect that rheumatism was the cause of the unnatural labor and misery of the man's heart? I think if this venerable old sage will consult his anatomy, he will find that this philosophy has a foundation in truth, with Nature and all its works as a voucher, and that arterial obstruction precedes all variations from the normal action of the heart. As you have had your mind refreshed upon the mechanical causes that will produce trouble of the heart unto death, I will tell you a few things to assist you in your work when called to treat persons laboring under diseases of the heart. Carefully explore the neck, with its union to the head, and ascertain positively that every joint in the neck is perfect at all bearings with other joints, and that all the muscles are free from entanglement with other muscles and processes of the neck. A slipped bone of the neck will limit the passage of the vertebral artery on its way from the heart to the brain. If the artery is obstructed in the bones of the neck, a disturbed heart will follow as one of the effects. If all joints have been found normal in the neck and nothing found there that could obstruct an artery, we will begin with the first rib as it articulates with the first dorsal vertebra, ascertaining whether it is normal in position with the spine and transverse articulation. You may find that rib pulled forward enough to close the vertebral foramen and stop the vertebral artery at that point. If so, you will find commotion and irregularity of the heart's action. If we find nothing wrong at the first ribs, we may find a serious luxation of the second, third, or fourth ribs, which may shut off the intercostal branches. When the heart brings the blood to supply the first, second, third, and fourth ribs of either side and is met by intercostal spaces impinged upon by twists, strains, or dislocations of the ribs, another positive cause of heart-disturbance is established, and the heart will give that peculiar long and heavy stroke in its effort to supply intercostal arteries. In our process of reasoning we will surely be sustained in the conclusion that all so-called heart diseases are only so many effects, with each effect having a cause in blood being suppressed at some point, which is the cause of the effect known as valvular, nervous, and other "diseases of the heart."

I think we have said enough on the philosophy and causes of heart trouble to be easily understood by the pupils of my school, with their thorough understanding of anatomy, which I trust they will wisely apply in treating heart diseases.

Aneurisms.

Some arteries are enlarged to enormous sizes. We call them aneurisms or accommodation-chambers for deposits of blood. The artery should pass farther on; thus you must know by reason an obstruction has limited the flow of the blood, and a tumor is an effect, and obstruction is the cause of all abnormal deposits, either from vein or artery. Unobstructed blood cannot form a tumor, nor allow inharmony to dwell in any part of the system. Flux is an effect caused by a variation in blood-supply and circulation. Blood finds veins of the abdomen irritated and contracted to such a degree that it cannot enter the veins with its cargo and deposits it at terminal points in the mucous membrane of the bowels. When the membrane fails to hold the blood so delivered, then the first blood which dies of asphyxia finds an outlet into the bowels, to be carried off and out by peristaltic action. Thus you have a continuous deposit and discharge of blood until death stops the supply.

RHEUMATISM.

Before pain begins at the joints, you are sure to find that all gas or wind has left the joints. Thus, electricity burns because of bone friction. Some gas must be between all bone joints. Thus we find great use for atmospheric pressure to hold bones far enough apart to let the "joint water" pass freely over the opposing ends of bones. There is a natural demand for gas in all healthy joints of the body. Reason leads us to believe that gas is constantly being conveyed to or generated in all joints. Before rheumatism appears the separating gas has been exhausted, and there follows friction and electric heat because of there being two or more joints in one electric circuit or division, in place of the bone or bones between two or more articulating ends of a bone, or more bones thrown into the battery, in place of each division being independent while in functional action in its own division. By way of explanation I will take the thigh-bone, at the socket or knee articulation, filled with fluids and gas. Bind the bones by ligaments or membranes so as to hold the bones in place, with a chamber to hold joint fluids. Would it be complete without gas pressure to hold the bones from pressing so closely together as to cause friction and heat to cause an electric action equal to nerve-poison? We thus get what we call neuralgia, rheumatism, sciatica, and so on to the full list of aches and pains not accounted for to date by our philosophers. Let us ask, if we force the hard ends of two bones together, as we do in jumping from elevations, with nothing to modify the concussions, will the bones not be bruised or mashed enough to become irritated if not protected by fluids and gas? Then if that will be the case, how can we reason better than to conclude that by contracting the ligaments at joints and holding air in that ligamentous sheath, the air will prevent the ends of the bones from meeting with a rushing force. We must be prepared to take care of those bones so as not to receive destructive injuries. Will not such gasless joints be the beginning of the fat man? also of the lean condition?

On this plane of reason many rich harvests await the sickle of reason. On this plane you can see and know the "whys" of consumption, dropsy, tumors, fits, gray hair, baldness, and so on to a surprising number of diseases.

THE INTERNAL AND EXTERNAL MAMMARY ARTERIES.

A confused and suspended circulation, either of the arterial, venous, or lymphatic circulation, or a disturbance of the nerves of either the arterial, venous, or lymphatic circulation of the mammaryglands, would be cause sufficient to draw the attention of the osteopathic diagnostician to a very careful investigation of the causes of diseases of these glands. He should know that the mammary artery is not oppressed or disturbed by ribs that have been pushed or knocked from their articulation with the sternum or spine, before he would be justified in giving a scientific diagnosis of the cause of tumors of the breast, goitre, diseases of the tonsils, the glands and lymphatics of the neck or breast, the eyes, or the giving way of important functions of any organ, internal or external, of the whole chest. We must remember that the internal mammary is a very long artery, beginning at the first rib and extending to the pelvis. Much good health depends upon its good work, and much bad health and disturbance can reasonably be expected to follow imperfect supply by arterial action or imperfect drainage through the venous and lymphatic vessels. Therefore we have a natural admonition to give the subject a deep and thorough investigation for mechanical variations from the true and normal. The length and width of the territory through which this river of life travels for the purpose of supplying organs, glands, membranes, and muscles is a standing evidence to its importance to life.

CHAPTER VII.

The Diaphragm.

NEW DISCOVERIES.

Previous to all discoveries there exists the demand for the discovery. Any discovery is an open question for a time and free to all, because in some new fact all are interested. The lack of something may be felt and spoken of by agriculturists, and inquiry directed to a better plow, a better sickle or mowing-machine with which to reap standing grain. The thinker reduces his thoughts to practice, and cuts the grain, leaving it in a condition that a raker is needed to bunch it previous to binding. His victory is heralded to the world as the king of the harvest, and so accepted. The discoverer says, "I wish I could bunch that grain." He begins to reason from the great principle of cause and effect, and sleeps not until he has added to his discovery an addition so ingeniously constructed that it will drop the grain in bunches ready for the binder. The discoverer stands by and sees in the form of a human being, hands, arms, and a band. He watches the motion; then starts in to rustle with cause and effect again. He thinks day and night, and by the genius of thought produces a machine to bind the grain. By this time another suggestion arises, how to separate the wheat as the machine journeys in its cutting process. To his convictions nothing will solve this problem but mental action. He thinks and dreams of cause and effect. His mind seems to forget all the words of his mother tongue except "cause" and "effect." He talks and preaches cause and effect in so many places that his associates begin to think he is failing mentally and will soon be a subject for the asylum. He becomes disgusted with their lack of appreciation, seeks seclusion, and formulates the desired addition and threshes the grain ready for the bag. He has solved the question and proved to his neighbors that the asylum was built for them and not for him. With cause and effect, which are ever before the philosopher's eye, he plows the ocean regardless of the furious waves, and he dreads not the storm on the seas, because he has constructed his vessel with a resistance superior to the force of the lashing waves of the ocean, and the world scores him another victory. He opens his mouth and says, "By the law of cause and effect, I will talk to my mother, who is hundreds of miles away." He disturbs her rest by the rattling of a little bell in her room. Tremblingly, the aged mother approaches the telephone and asks, "Who is there?" The answer comes, "It is I, Jimmie." Then he asks, "To whom am I talking?" She says, "Mrs. Mary Murphy." The reply comes, "God bless you, mother; I am at Galveston, Texas, and you are in Boston, Massachusetts." She laughs and cries with joy; he hears every emotion of her trembling voice as she says to him: "You have succeeded at last I have never doubted your final success, notwithstanding the neighbors have annoyed me almost to death, telling me you would land in the asylum, because no man could talk so as to be heard a thousand miles away; his lungs were too weak and his tongue too short."

"EUREKA!"

I have given you a long introduction previous to giving you the cause of disease, with the philosophy of cause and effect. I think it absolutely clear and the effect so unerring in its results that with Pythagoras I can say, "Eureka!"

To find a general cause for disease, one that will stand the most rigid and vigorous direct and cross-examination of the high courts of cool-headed reason, has been the mental effort of all doctors and healers since time began its record. Doctors have had to treat disease as best they could, by methods that custom had established as the best, notwithstanding the failures and great mortality under their system of treatment. They have not felt justified to go beyond the rules of symptomatology as adopted by their schools, with diagnosis, prognosis, and treatment. Should they digress from the rules of the "ethics of the profession," they would lose the brotherly love and support of the medical associations, under the belief that "a bad name is as bad as death to a dog."

Medical Doctor.

The medical practitioner says that in union there is safety, and resolves to stick to this, and live and do as his school has disciplined all its pupils, with this command: "The day thou eatest anything else, thou shalt surely die. Stick to the brotherhood."

The explorer for truth must first declare his independence of all obligations and brotherhoods of any kind whatsoever. He must be free to reason and think. He must establish his observatory upon hills of his own; he must establish them above the imaginary high planes of rulers, kings, professors, and schools of all kinds and denominations. He must be the czar of his own mental empire, unincumbered with anything that will annoy him while he makes his observations. I believe the reasons are so plain, so easily comprehended, the facts in their support so brilliant, that I will offer them, though I be slaughtered on the altar of bigotry and intolerance. This philosophy is not intended for minds not thoroughly well posted by dissection and otherwise on the whole human anatomy. You must know its physiological laboratories and workings, with the brain as the battery, the lungs as the machine that renovates the blood, and the heart as the living engine or quartermaster, whose duty is to supply the commissaries with blood and other fluids to all divisions and subdivisions of the body, which is engaged in producing material suited to the production of bone and muscle and all other substances necessary to keep the machinery of life in full force and action.

Without this knowledge on the part of the reader, the words of this philosophy will come out as blanks before reaching his magazine of reason. This is addressed to the independent man or woman that can, does, and will reason.

The Importance of the Splanchnics.

Let us halt at the origin of the splanchnics and take a look. At this point we see the lower branches, sensation, motion, and nutrition, all slant from above the diaphragm, pointing to the solar plexus, which sends off branches to the pudic and sacral plexuses of sensory systems of nerves, just at the position to join the life-giving ganglia of the sacrum with orders from the brain to keep the process of blood-forming in full motion all the time. A question arises: How is this motion supplied, and from where? The answer is: By the brain as the nerve-supply and the heart as the blood-supply, both of which come from above the diaphragm, to keep all the machinery in form and supplied with motion, that it may be able to generate chyle to send back to the heart, to be formed into blood and thrown back into the arteries for the construction of the parts as needed and to keep the brain fed up to its normal power-generating needs. We see above the diaphragm the heart, lungs, and brain, the three sources of blood- and nerve-supply. All three are guarded by strong walls, that they may do their part in keeping up the life supplies as far as blood- and nerve-force is required. But as they generate no blood- or nerve-material, they must take the place of manufactories and purchase material from a foreign land, to have an abundance all the time. We see that Nature has placed its manufactories above a given line in the breast, and develops the crude material below that line. Now, as growth means motion and supply, we must combine these departments in a friendly way, and conduct the force from above to the regions below the septum or diaphragm, that we may use the powers as needed. This wall must have openings to let the blood and nerves penetrate with their supply and force to do the work of manufacturing.

After all this has been done, and a twist, pressure, or obstructing fold should appear from any cause, would we not have a cut-off in the machinery returning chyle and lymph, sensation to supply vitality, and in the venous motion to carry off arterial supply that has been driven from the heart above? Have we not found a cause to stop all processes of life below the diaphragm? In short, are we not in a condition to soon be in a state of complete stagnation? As soon as the arteries have filled the venous system, which is without sensation to return the blood to the heart, then the heart can do nothing but wear out its energies trying to drive blood into a dead territory below the diaphragm known as the venous system. It is dead until sensation reaches the vein from the solar, sacral, and pudic plexuses.

The Diaphragm in Health.

At this point we will again take up the diaphragm, which separates the heart, lungs, and brain from the organs of life that are limited to the abdomen and pelvis. What has the diaphragm to do with good or bad health? We will analyze the diaphragm. We will examine its construction and its uses. We will examine its openings through which the blood passes. We will examine the opening through which food passes to the stomach. We will carefully examine the passages or openings for nerve-supply to the abdomen below, running this great system of chemistry, which is producing the various kinds of substances necessary to the hard and soft parts of the body. We must know the nerve-supply of the lymphatics, womb, liver, pancreas, kidneys, the generative organs, what they are, what they do, and what is demanded of them, before we are able to feed our own minds from the cup that contains the essence of reason as expressed by the tree of life.

The diaphragm surely gives much food for one who would search for the great "whys" of disease. It may help us to arrive at some facts if we take each organ and division and make a full acquaintance with all its parts and uses before we combine it with others.

he medical doctor has, owing to a lack of knowledge of the true causes of diseases, combated effects with his remedies. He treats pain with remedies to deaden pain; congestion by an effort to wash out overplus of blood that has been carried to parts or organs of the body by arteries of blood and channels of secretions, and not taken up and passed off and out by the excretories. He sees the abnormal sizes and leaves the hunting of the cause that has given growth to such proportions, and begins to seek rest and ease for his patient. Then he calls on medicine to carry the waste fluids to the bowels, bladder, and skin, with tonics to give strength, and stimulants to increase the action of the heart, in order to force local deposits to the general excretory system. At this time let the osteopathic doctor take a close hunt for any fold in the muscles of the system that would cut off the normal supply of blood, or suspend the action of nerves whose office is to give power and action to the excretory system sufficient to keep the dead matter carried off as fast as it accumulates. Let us stop and acquaint ourselves with the true conditions of the diaphragm. It must be normal in place, as it is so situated that it will admit of no abnormality. It must be kept stretched, just as Nature intended it should be, like a drumhead. It is attached all around to the chest, though it crosses five or six ribs on its descent from the seventh rib to the sternum at the lower point and down to the fourth lumbar vertebra. It is a continuous slanting floor above the bowels and abdominal organs and below the heart and lungs. It must, by all reason, be kept normal in tightness at all places, without a fold or wrinkle that would press the aorta, nerves, œsophagus, or anything that contributes to the supply or circulation of any vital substance. Now can there be any move in spine or ribs that would or could change the normal shape of the diphragm? If so, where and why?

Out of Position.

The diaphragm is possibly least understood as the cause of diseases, when its supports are not all in line and in normal position, than any other part of the body. It has many openings through which nerves, blood, and food pass while going from the chest to the parts below. It begins at the lower end of the breast-bone and crosses to the ribs back and down, in a slanting position, to the third or fourth lumbar vertebra. Like an apron, it holds all that is above it up, and is the fence that divides the organs of the abdomen from the chest. Below it are the stomach, bowels, liver, spleen, kidneys, pancreas, womb, bladder, the great system of lymphatics, and the nerve-supply of the organs and systems of nutrition and life-supply. All parts of the body have a direct or indirect connection with this great separating muscle. It assists in all animals, when normal; but when prolapsed by the falling down and in of any of the five or six ribs by which it is supported in place, then follow the effects of suspended normal arterial supply, and venous stagnation below the diaphragm. The aorta meets resistance as it goes down with blood to nourish, and the vein, as it goes back with impurities contained in the venous blood, also meets an obstruction at the diaphragm, as it returns to the heart through the vena cava, because of the impingement caused by a fallen diaphragm on and about the blood-vessels. Thus heart trouble, lung disease, brain, liver, and womb diseases, tumors of the abdomen, and so on through the list of effects, can be traced to the diaphragm as the cause.

LOCATION.

I am strongly impressed that the diaphragm has much to do with keeping all the machinery and organs of life in a healthy condition, and will try to give some of the reasons why, as I now understand them. First, it is found to be wisely located just below the heart and lungs, one the engine of blood and the other the engine of air. This strong wall holds all bodies or substances away from either engine while it is performing its part in the economy of life. Each engine has a sacred duty to perform, under the penal law of death to itself and all other divisions of the whole being, man. If it should neglect its work, or should we take down this wall and allow the liver, stomach, and spleen to occupy any of the places allotted to these engines of life, a confusion would surely result, and the ability of the heart to force blood to the lungs would be overcome and cause trouble.

Suppose we take a few diseases and submit them to the crucial test of reason, and see if we can find any one of the climatic fevers not having some connection with an irritated diaphragm. For example, take a case of common bilious fever. It generally begins with a tired and sore feeling of the limbs and muscles, with pain in the spine, head, and lumbar region. At this point of our inquiry we are left in an open sea of mystery and conjecture as to cause. One says, "Malaria," and goes no further; gives a name and stops. If you ask for the cause of such torturous pain in the head and back, with fever and vomiting, he will tell you that the very best authorities agree that the cause is malaria, with its peculiar diagnostic tendency to affect the brain, spine, and stomach, and he administers quinine, and leaves, thinking he has said and done all.

Reason would lead seekers for the cause of the pain to remember that all blood passes first as chyle up to the heart and lungs, directly through the diaphragm, conducted through the thoracic duct, first to the heart, thence to the lungs; at the same time rivers of blood are pouring into the heart from all the system. Much of it is very impure from diseased or stale food, coming from the lymphatics below the diaphragm. Much of the chyle is dead before it enters the thoracic duct and goes to the lungs without enough pure blood to sustain life. Then disease appears. The diaphragm, when dropped front and down, and across the aorta and vena cava, by a lowering of the ribs on both sides of the spine,would cause pressure over the cœliac axis, with a complete abdominal stoppage. Then we have obstructed and damaged blood, with no hope that it can sustain life and health of the parts for which it was designed. We know that Nature would not be true to its own laws if it would do good work with bad material.

NERVOUS PROSTRATION.

Why not reason on the broad scale of known facts, and give the "why" this or that patient has complete prostration, when all systems are wholly cut off from a chance to move and execute the duties that Nature has allotted to them? Motor nerves must drive all substances to a part and sensation must judge the supply and demand. Nutrition must be in action all the time and keep all parts well supplied, or a failure is sure to appear We must ever remember the demands of Nature on the lymphatics, liver, and kidneys, and that nerves work all the time, and that any confusion in nerves will make a cripple of some function of life over which they preside.

We see that no delay in passage of food or blood can be tolerated at the diaphragm, because any irritation is bound to cause muscular contraction and impede the natural flow of the blood through the abdominal aorta to a temporary, partial, or complete stoppage of arterial supply to the abdomen; or the vena cava may be so pressed upon as to completely stop the return of venous blood from the stomach, kidneys, bowels, the lymphatics, pancreas, fascia, cellular membranes, nerve-centers, the ganglionic and all systems of supply of the organs of life found in the abdomen. Thus, by pressure, stricture, or contraction, the passage of blood can be stopped, either above or below the diaphragm, and be the cause of blood being detained long enough to die from asphyxia, thus causing disease.

Thus you see a cause for Bright's disease of the kidneys, diseases of the womb or ovaries, for jaundice, dysentery, leucorrhœa, painful monthlies, spasms, dyspepsia, and on through the whole list of diseases now booked as "causes unknown," and treated by the rule of "cut and try." We know that all of the blood for the use of the whole system below the twelfth dorsal vertebra passes through the diaphragm, and the nerve-supply also passes through the diaphragm. This being a known fact, we have only to use our reason to know that an unhealthy condition of the diaphragm is bound to be followed by many diseases. The diaphragm is a musculo-fibrinous organ, and depends for blood- and nerve-supply above its own location, and that supply must be given freely and pure for nerve and blood, or we will have a diseased organ to start with. We may find a universal atrophy or œdema, which would, besides causing its own deformity, not be able to rise and fall, to assist the lungs to purify the venous blood, previous to returning it to the heart. It is only in keeping with reason that without a healthy diaphragm, both in its form and action, disease is bound to be the result. How can a carpenter build a good house out of rotten, twisted, or warped wood? If he can, then we can hope to be healthy with diseased blood; but if we must have good material in building, then we should form our thoughts as careful inspectors and inspect the passage of blood through the diaphragm, pleura, pericardium, and the fascia. Disease is just as liable to begin its work in the fascia and epithelium as at any other place. Thus the necessity for pure blood and healthy fascia, because all functions are equally responsible for good and bad results.

God the Judge.

At a given period of time the Lord said, "Let us make man." After He had made him, He examined him and pronounced him good, and not only good, but very good. Did He know what good was? Had He the skill to be a competent judge? If He was perfectly competent to judge skilled arts, His approval of the work when done was the fiat of mental competency backed by perfection. Since that architect and skilled mechanic has finished man and given him dominion over the fowls of the air, the beasts of the field, and the fishes of the sea, hasn't that person, being, or superstructure proven to us that God, the creator of all things, has armed him with strength, with the mind and machinery to direct and execute? This being demonstrated, and leaving us without a doubt as to its perfection, are we not admonished by all that is good and great to enter upon a minute examination of all the parts belonging to this being and acquaint ourselves with their uses and all the designs for which the whole being was created? Are we honestly interested in an acquaintance with the forms and uses of the parts in detail, of the material, its form and the object of its form; from whence this substance is obtained, how it is produced and sustained through life in kind and form; how it is moved, where it gets its power, and for what object does it move? A demand for a crucial examination of the head, the heart, the lungs, the chest, the stomach, the liver, and other organs of the abdomen, the brain, the pericardium, and the diaphragm is ever present. In this examination we must know the reasons why any organ, vessel, or any other substance is located at a given place. We must run with all the rivers of blood that travel through the system.

We must start our exploring boat with the blood of the aorta and float with this vital current, and watch the unloading of supplies for the diaphragm and all that is under it. We must follow and see what branch of this river will lead to a little or great toe, or to the terminals of the entire foot. We must pass through the waters of the Dead Sea by way of the vena cava, and observe the boats loaded with exhausted and worn-out blood, as it is poured in and channeled back to the heart. Carefully watch the emptying of the vena azygos major and minor, with the contents of the veins of the arms and head all being poured in from little or great rivers to the vena innominate, on their way to the great hospital of life and nourishment, whose quartermaster is the heart, whose finishing mechanic is the lung. Having acquainted ourselves with the forms and locations of this great personality, we are ready at this time to enter into a higher class in which we can obtain an acquaintance with the physiological workings. We become acquainted with the "hows" and "whys" of the production of blood, bone, and all elements found in them necessary to sustain sensation, motion, nutrition, voluntary and involuntary action of the nervous system, and the "hows" and "whys" of the lymphatics, the life-sustaining powers of the brain, heart, lungs, and all the abdominal system, with its parts and various actions and uses, from the lowest cellular membrane to the highest organ of the body.

When we consult the form of the cross-bar that divides the body into two conjoined divisions and reason on its use, we arrive at the fact that the heart and lungs must have ample space to suit their actions while performing their functions. What effect would follow the removal of the fence between the heart, lungs, and brain above that dividing muscle and the machinery that is situated below the cross-bar? We see at a glance that we would meet failure to the extent of the infringement on demanded room for normal work of the heart in its effort to deliver normal supplies below, the lungs to prepare blood, and interference with the brain and its duty of passing nerve-power to either engine above and all organs below the diaphragm.

The Lesson of the Tree.

The life of the living tree is in the bark and superficial fascia which lies beneath the bark. The remainder of the tree performs the duties of secreting. Its excretory system is first upward from the surface of the ground. It washes out frozen impurities in the spring, after which it secretes and conveys substances to the ground through the trunk of the tree to the roots, like unto a placenta attached to Mother Earth, qualifying all substances of fiber and leaf of the part of the tree above the ground. Each year produces new tree additions, which are seen and known by circular rings called annular growths. That growth which was completed last year is now a being of the past and has no vital action of itself. But, like all stale beings, its process is life of another order, and dependent upon the fascia for its life and cellular action which lies under the bark. It can only act as a chemical laboratory and furnish crude material which is taken up by the superficial fascia and conveyed up to the lungs, and exchange dead for living matter to return to all parts of the tree, keeping up the vital formations. Its vital process ceases through the winter season, until Mother Earth stimulates the placenta and starts the growth of the next new being, which is developed and placed in form on the old trunk.

Should this form of vitality cease in the tree, another principle, which we call "stale life," takes possession and constructs another tree, which is just the reverse of the living tree. It builds a tree after its own power of formulation from the dead matter, to which it imparts a principle of stale life, which life produces mushrooms, frogstools, and other peculiar forms of stale beings. Thus we are prepared to reason that blood, when ligated and retained in that condition of dead corpuscles, and no longer able to support animal life, can form a zoöphyte and all the forms peculiar to the great law of association: tumefactions of the lymphatics, pancreas, kidneys, liver, uterus, with all the glandular system, be they lymphatics, cellular, ganglia, or any other parts of the body susceptible of such growths. We can thus account for tubercles of the abdomen and all organs found therein. The same law is equally applicable to the heart, lungs, brain, tissues, glands, fascia, and all parts capable of receiving and lacking the ability to excrete stale substances, As œdema marks the first tardiness of fluids, we have the beginning step which will lead from miliary tuberculosis to the largest known forms of tubercles, which are the effect of the active principles of stale life or "the life of dead matter."

We will draw the attention of the reader to the fact that the diaphragm can contract and suspend the passage of blood and produce all the stagnant changes from the beginning to the completed tubercle, the cancer, the wen, glandular thickening of the neck, face, scalp, and fascia. In this stale life we have a compass that will lead us as explorers to the causes of tubercles, tumors, cancers, and ulcers. This diaphragm says, "By me you live and by me you die. I hold in my hands the powers of life and death. Acquaint now thyself with me and be at ease."

CHAPTER VIII.

The Abdomen.

INHIBITION.

Much stress has been laid on the idea of inhibition of the nerves as a remedial agency. Allow me to say that inhibition is almost universally the cause of disease. Dunglison defines "inhibit," to restrain or suppress, and defines "stimulation," to goad; that which excites the animal economy.

For the reader's benefit, I wish to refresh his mind on anatomy, that he may fully understand what I wish to present as a truth, to guide him while treating his patients, and to point him to the danger of doing more harm than good by pushing, pulling, and kneading the abdomen, with the idea that he inhibits the nerves or excites them to greater energy, thereby helping Nature do the work of restoration of the normal functional action of the organs of the abdomen.

I will say, after forty years' observation and practice, that no good can come to the patient by pulling, pushing, and gouging in the sacred territory of the abdominal organs; but much harm can and does follow bruising the solar plexus, from which a branch of nerves goes to each organ of the abdomen. Upon that center depends all the elaborate work of the functioning of the abdomen. I say, "Hands off." Go to the spine and ribs only. If you do not know the power of the spinal nerves on the liver to restore health, you must learn or quit, because you are only an owl of hoots, more work than brains. I want the man who wishes to know the work that is done by the organs or contents of the abdomen also to know the danger of ignorance, and that wild force in treating the abdomen cannot be tolerated as any part of this sacred philosophy.

Be Original.

You must reason. I say reason, or you will finally fail in all enterprises. Form your own opinions, select all facts you can obtain. Compare, decide, then act. Use no man's opinions; accept his works only.

Having passed through the head, neck, and thorax with a short description of the diseases belonging to each division, and as our work is divided for observation and discussion into five parts, we will now take up the fourth division. According to the number, the head is one, the neck two, the thorax three, the abdomen four, and the pelvis five. I have established this arbitrary classification for the purpose of observing the workings of the various divisions of the body systematically, especially the abdominal viscera, with the view of obtaining a more definite knowledge of their perfect workings in good health. It is important to know the exact place that each organ occupies while in its normal position. Not only know it on general principles, but to a greater degree of perfection than any other lesson that is before the student of disease. We should know the perfect position of each organ, the blood-, nerve-, and nutrient supply by which its work is accomplished, from whence the support comes, how applied, and how kept in its pure state by the natural functions of excreting all exhausted and diseased substances. By this knowledge only can we expect to detect the many variations, both great and small, in nutrition and renovation, which is the sum total of what is meant by good health. Each organ seems to be a creator of its own fluid substances, extracted from the channels of nutrition upon which it depends. The quantity and quality necessary for this process are absolute beyond dispute. This being the case, we must, in dealing with the abnormal, work for readjustment to normal perfection.

A Great Host.

We will look over the abdominal field, count the host, and try to be as systematic as possible. We will begin at the diaphragm, the wall that separates the thorax from the abdomen. The abdomen contains the liver, spleen, pancreas, stomach, two kidneys, the bladder, small and large intestines, the omentum, abdominal aorta and vena cava, the blood-supply for the whole system of abdominal organs, the lymphatics with all secretory and excretory organs, and all there is found on to the pelvic floor. All the organs of the territory of the abdomen must be kept before the eye, and we must feel that we are in the presence of perfection of all organs. We can then begin to compare any variation, real or imaginary, in place, form, or function of all that is before us. The perfect diaphragm means perfection at all points of its whole circular attachment, beginning with the sixth rib and ending with the third and fourth lumbar vertebræ. No spine can be varied from the sixth rib to the fourth lumbar and show perfection of the diaphragm. No rib thrown from its perfect position with the spinal articulation can leave the diaphragm perfect in its functions. Perfection of spine and ribs is imperative and absolutely required before we can hope for perfection in the flow of blood and other fluids that pass through the throat, aorta, vena cava, and thoracic duct. All must pass freely, and also their accompanying nerves, motor and sensory, that enter into the solar plexus and all its branches, or a halt will appear and begin the work of creating disease by tardy renovation of abdominal organs as the result of such shortage in the function of that part or organ that must be kept normal by perfect renovation. Suppose we select a kidney that is normally perfect, and twist the spine at the renal nerve origin enough to disturb the nutrition of the kidney; we would expect dwarfage in its functioning to set up and build tubercular deposits, congestion, fermentation, and pus. Suppose we overpower sensation and the motion of the nerve by a lap or a strain of the spine where the spinal cord throws out the nerve-branches that supply the kidneys; we would have paralysis of the kidneys, with all the diseases peculiar to that organ, the result of a deadened condition of the renal nerves.

Geography of the Abdomen.

As we are about to camp close to the abdomen for a season of explorations, to gain a more reasonable knowledge of its organs and their functions, we will search its geography first and find its location on the body or globe of life. We find a boundary line established by the general surveyor, about the middle of the body, called the diaphragm. This line has a very strong wall of striated muscle that can and does contract and dilate to suit the phenomenon of breathing, and the quantities of food that may be stored for a time in the stomach and bowels. The abdomen is much longer than it is wide. It is a house or shop builded for manufacturing purposes. In it we find the machinery that produces rough blood or chyle and gives it out to be finished to perfect living blood, to supply and sustain all the organs of this and other divisions. This diaphragm or wall has several openings through which blood and nutrient vessels pass to and from the abdomen to heart, lungs, and brain. I want to draw your special attention to the fact that this diaphragm must be truly normal. It must be anchored and held in its true position without any variation, and in order that you shall fully understand what I mean, I will ask you to go with me mentally to the ribs. Begin with the sternum, see the attachments, follow across with a downward course to the attachments of the diaphragm to the lower lumbar region, where the right crus receives a branch or strong muscle from the left side. The left crus in turn receives a muscle from the right, and the two become one common muscle, known as the left crus. You will easily comprehend the structure by examining descriptive cuts in Gray, Morris, Gerrish, or any well-illustrated work on anatomy. You see at once a chance for constriction of the aorta by the muscles under which it passes, frequently causing without doubt the disease known as palpitation of the heart, which is only a bouncing back of the blood that has been stopped at the crura. Farther away from the spine, near the center of the diaphragm, we find another opening through this wall to accommodate the vena cava. To the left, a few inches below the vena cava, we find another opening provided for the œsophagus and its nerves. Two muscles of the diaphragm cross directly between the œsophagus and aorta, in such a manner as to be able to produce powerful prohibitory constriction to normal swallowing.

The Thoracic Duct.

At this point I will draw your attention to what I consider is the cause of a whole list of hitherto unexplained diseases, which are only effects of the blood and other fluids being prohibited from doing normal service by constrictions at the various openings of the diaphragm. Thus prohibition of the free action of the thoracic duct would produce congestion of the receptaculum chyli, because it would not be able to discharge its contents as fast as received. Is it not reasonable to suppose that a ligation of the thoracic duct at the diaphragm would retain this chyle until it would be diseased by age and fermentation, and be thrown off into the substances of other organs of the abdomen, setting up new growths, such as enlargement of the uterus, ovaries, kidneys, liver, spleen, pancreas, omentum, lymphatics, cellular membranes, and all that is known as flesh and blood below the diaphragm? Have you not reason to urge you to explore and demand a deeper and more thorough anatomical knowledge of the diaphragm and its power to produce disease while in an abnormal condition from irritation, wounds, etc.? Remember that this is a question that will demand your knowledge of the mechanical formations and physiological actions and the unobstructed privileges of fluids when prepared in the laboratory of Nature, which must be sent at once to their destination before they become diseased or die from age. You must remember that you have been talked out of patience in the room of symptomatology, and all you have learned is that something ails the kidneys, and that their contents, when analyzed, have been found defective. In urinalysis you are told, "Here is fat," "Here is sugar," "Here is iron," "Here is pus," "Here is albumen," and "This is diabetes," "This is Bright's disease," but no suggestion is handed to the student's mind to make him know these numerous variations from normal urine are simply effects, and the diaphragm has caused all the trouble, by first being irritated by ribs falling, spinal strains, wounds, and so on, from the coccyx to the base of the brain. Symptomatology is very wise in putting this and that together and giving it names, but it fails to give the cause of all these lesions. Never once has it said or intimated that the diaphragm is prolapsed by misplaced ribs, to which it is attached, or that it is diseased by injury to the spine and nerves.

THE NERVES MUST ACT.

Remember there are five sets of nerves that are important factors in their divisions of life. They are the sensory, motor, nutrient, voluntary, and involuntary. With all of these you, as an engineer, must be familiar, and by proper adjustment of the body you must be able to give them unlimited power to perform their separate and united parts in sustaining life and health.

Now, as I have tried to place in your hands a compass, flag, and chain that will lead you from effect to cause of disease in any part or organ of the whole abdomen, I hope that many mysteries that have hung over your mental horizon will pass away, and give you abiding truths, placed upon the everlasting rock of cause and effect. You have as little use for old symptomatology as an Irishman has for a cork when the bottle is empty. Osteopathy is knowledge, or it is nothing.

Feast of Reason.

Let me invite you to a feast at the table of reason. This feast is to consist of materials furnished by the greatest of authors of anatomy. The material man, with all his parts, is to be spread upon the broad dishes of observation, and the divine currents of life, displaying their wonderful works in the physiological laboratory, will be spread upon this table before the hungry mind as choice bits or dainties that belong to the man who loves to reason, and to the man who wishes to enjoy some of the fruits from the trees of mental life. Our bill of fare is all before you. We will have sixteen changes of dishes at this feast. Each dish will contain the greatest amount of vital nourishment that the human tongue of reason has ever been called upon to sample and taste. Our bill of fare reads, "Brain, heart, lungs, diaphragm, pancreas, spleen, stomach, liver and gall-sac, large and small intestines, rectum, kidneys and ureters, uterus, and bladder." The length of the table is from the coccyx to the occiput, and its width the diameter of the human body. This feast will be one of but little interest or relish to the man who does not understand the combined beauties of anatomy and physiology. The sweetness of taste comes with an intimate acquaintance, by long and deep study of the composition and use of each dish of organic life set before the invited host. Without such acquaintace, no dish upon this table will be relished; therefore, the invitation is only for him who has qualified himself to partake of the interesting discourse. When every dish appears upon this table without a flaw or crack, and the dainties are as pure as Nature's God prepares and sends forth, then we will have a feast whose joys can neither be fathomed nor imagined. These dainties on which you are invited to feast are as eternal as the ages, as wisely prepared as the God of the universe has been able to furnish by His law of absolute perfection. All are invited. This table to which you are invited is durable. The choice nourishment which is to be spread before you is as inexhaustible as the days of both ends of eternity; therefore, this feast will neither end with mortality nor immortality. Come one, come all.

On our bill of fare at this abdominal feast we have enumerated by number and name all the dishes to be served. The osteopath feasts upon the dishes that are found upon the table of the abdomen, and each course will be required to be eaten systematically by the invited guests. The plates will appear in each course by threes. Of the plates of the first course, one will contain the stomach, another the small intestine, while the third and last will be the large intestine. We feast you upon this course of the alimentary canal, first, that you may know, from the entering to the expelling of all material substances, the extent of the whole road through which the alimentary substances pass. The second course will consist of three darker colored dishes, with a purple tint. One contains the liver, another the spleen, and the third the kidneys. The third course consists of the heart, arteries, and veins. The fourth course, of an equal number of dishes, contains the brain and the motor and sensory nerves. The lungs, with their physical and chemical laboratory for purifying and preparing the blood for universal distribution and use throughout the body, when presented to the heart for that purpose, constitute the fifth. The sixth course will be the diaphragm, with its vessels of secretion and nutrition, its form, locality, and its use. The seventh will contain the bladders, ureters, and the general system of collecting and excreting lifeless fluids through the excretory channels. The ovaries and nerve- and blood-supply of the generative system are the eighth course.

Lessons to Learn.

This allegoric illustration has been given in order to accustom your mind to feast and learn something of the forms of the organs of life in the human body. As you seem to be quite handy in eating through each change of courses, and seem to be familiar with the anatomical form and location of the various systems of organs, we will hand you out the ninth change, consisting of four dishes, the number required to contain the different divisions by name and locality of the one system known to us as the absorbing laboratory of nutritious substances from the alimentary canal. The first very large dish will contain the greater and lesser omenta; the second, third, and fourth will contain the different divisions of the mesentery, beginning with the meso-cæcum, meso-transversalis, meso-colon, and meso-rectum. The mesentery is shown by examination to be made of very strong and elastic substances, supplied with blood-vessels, lymphatics, and secretory and excretory systems, with nerves to suit its functioning process. We also find its attachments to the spine and bowels to be very extensive, extending many inches in length, about four to six up and down the anterior surface of the spinal column, beginning with the second lumbar. Its attachment at the other extremity from the spine is to the bowels. The small intestine attachment is very extensive. When the fan-shaped edge of attachment is measured, it equals about eighteen or twenty feet, as generally observed and reported by authors on anatomy and according to our own observations in dissections. The meso-cæcum is firmly attached both to the spine and that part of the intestines known as the ascending colon.. This membrane is quite strong and elastic. The meso-transversalis and meso-colon are also firmly attached to the spine at the one extremity and to the bowels at the other. This membranous sheet is very elastic and very liable to be stretched when the bowels are pressed down. by mechanical weights or great quantities of fæcal matter. The cæcum and the transverse and sigmoid flexure are often forced from their normal positions and piled into the pelvis, dragging the uterus and small intestine down with the cæcum and obstructing all possible chance for the fluids of the small intestine to pass through the ileo-cæcal valve and reach the colon. Thus we have a visible, philosophical cause for obstruction of fæcal matter. That is not debatable by any person who is endowed with any power to reason from cause to effect.

HARMONY MUST EXIST.

We will say to the student of the philosophy of diseases of the abdomen and their remote, active, and present causes, that he is better prepared to take up the subject of diseases of the many or few organs of the abdominal viscera if he knows what is meant by disease of the organs of the abdomen, pelvis, and chest. All these organs must work in perfect harmony to produce health. Health requires the continuous action of every organ, all nerves, all blood-vessels, all lymphatics, all the secretory system, and all the excretory system, in order that when the united products are thrown into the thoracic duct or any other duct that conveys lymph or any other fluid, they will be conveyed to the lungs. It is reasonable that this fluid, from the many thousands of cells and channels through which it is passed, will become as a unit. In order that health may be perfect, every drop of fluid must be conveyed from the lower bowels, beginning with the rectum, ascending through the sigmoid and up the left side of the abdomen, through the descending colon and transverse colon and down to the iliac fossa, which is the normal position allotted to the cæcum. Reason will teach you at once that each drop of lymph or venous blood coming from the whole system of the large bowels, and absorbed by the mesentery and conveyed through that system to the thoracic duct, must be absolutely and chemically pure, or disease will mark the amount of variation caused by the amount of impurities that are taken up by the mesenteries of any division, from the rectum to the ileo-cæcal valve.

An Obstruction.

The importance of a knowledge and a very thorough knowledge of the form and place, the function and object of the productive ability, application, and use of the fluids necessary to the production of good health is apparent. If after this preparation is completed by the lungs and we have good blood, any diseased condition of the viscera of the pelvis or thorax should appear, in the form of thickening of the membranes, congestion, thickening, or tumefaction of any organ or its appendages, then we have a positive witness that a lymphatic duct, an excretory duct, or a venous duct is stopped by the ligation of its channel by constriction, weight, or a cramp, or from pressure of bone or muscle, preventing the passage of the fluid that has been detained and has given size and form to this abnormal tumefaction found adjacent to some gland. All interferences are labeled to your understanding at once, by enlargement through stoppage of fluids which ferment, inflame, and produce erysipelas and other manifestations of inflammations. The same method of reasoning will enable the doctor of osteopathy to prove to his understanding and satisfaction that acute and chronic dysentery have origin and continuation from these obstructing causes. The same method of reasoning is just as good in typhoid dysentery. The genius of anatomy and physiology, with any ordinary amount of mechanical skill, will see by all methods of reasoning that the cæcum, the sigmoid, and the small intestine are ditched into the pelvis, pressing and compressing the nerves, veins, and arteries that should at all times be free to act normally, or congestion, inflammation, and sloughing away of the mucous membrane of the bowels, with blood, lymph, and other substances, will follow. This disturbance will produce irritation of other glands, through the nervous system, and cause those irritated organs to unload their diseased substances into the lymphatic and nervous channels and convey this confused and poisonous mass of fluid back to the lungs from the whole alimentary canal, the bladder, the uterus, the kidneys, the liver, the spleen, the pancreas, and by this physiological and chemical manifestation you can easily account for variation in temperature known as the hot and cold stages that accompany typhoid and other classes of fevers.

The Omentum.

We have spoken in another place of the importance that should be attached to the mesentery, uterus, and other organs, and how they can become diseased, and in their effort to return to the normal have generated tumors, inflammation, sloughing away, and so on. We will now take up the omentum, and try to treat this organ with consideration and due respect. We are satisfied that it has much to do, if not all, in keeping the lungs in a healthy condition. We have reason to believe, from the history of post-mortems following tuberculosis and other diseases of the lungs, that had this organ, the great omentum, been kept normally in position, form, and size, well nourished and properly renovated, we would have had but very little, if any, tuberculosis of the lungs to report. We believe that we have abundance of evidence to prove the responsibility that is upon the omentum to sustain life and health and keep the lungs forever pure. This subject will be discussed at greater length under the head of "Diseases of the Lungs."

Blood- and Nerve-Supply.

We will insist on the student giving particular attention to a knowledge of blood- and nerve-supply, and we insist on his obtaining an exact and very comprehensive knowledge of both supplies before he can expect to do acceptable work, satisfactory to himself and to his patients. The blood and nerves have much to do in producing and sustaining health. To have perfection in blood-flow and nerve-power in health, means union and action of both. Of what use would incomplete action be, when perfect health is the result of the full and free action of the nerves on blood that is to pass from the heart to all places, if either blood- or nerve-currents should be stopped by any cause? In the abdomen are many organs and functions that must act all the time, and they must have blood to act on and nerve-energy with which to act.

The Pancreas.

The pancreas opens the subject of demand and supply for its use. This organ in healthy action gives back that finest of milk, the pancreatic juice, that supplies, feeds, and nourishes the whole system of the mucous membrane, tissues, and general structures of the small intestine, while it receives and mixes the gall with the food as it passes through the small intestine, preparatory to being elaborated in the large intestine and given back as blood in its first stages to the lymphatics, to be conveyed to the heart and lungs for the final finishing to blood. This blood is sent forth by the heart by way of the arteries, great and small, to each gland for its use. A plentiful supply of blood branches off from the greater arteries after leaving the heart to supply each organ, with all its attachments, all to perfect fullness of supply. This blood system and the spinal cord, the brain, the nerves, with force equal to all, demands healthy action in each organ of the head, neck, chest, abdomen, and limbs, with no exception to the law of demand and supply, which is absolute through all nature.

Away with Quackery.

But our present work, for a time, is to fight the battles of the abdomen and free it from drug quackery and the abuses that the viscera receive from ignorance of drugs and their effects, and the continued blind faith kept up by the drug doctors in their efficacy. If Nature requires drugs, where would it go to find the laboratory that could be trusted to make drugs that would benefit the body? Would it trust its own liver to make the gall? Would it, in time of need, trust the pancreas to make good juice? Would it trust the heart and lungs to make or finish good blood and dose it out to the invalid organs of the body? Would it trust each organ for its own products as the system should need its remedial agency?

The Importance of Pure Blood.

If the abdomen provides the rough material for the blood of the system, and perfect health can only come from good blood, and perfect blood cannot be furnished by imperfect viscera nor any imperfection in form, location, or function of any organ of the abdomen, chest, or brain, why not hunt for some cause of disease in the machinery that produces blood from the start to its finish? If we find a failure in health, we would surely show wisdom by going into the machine-shop to find defects in the machine or system of organs which starts with crude material and brings forth pure blood. We would have to begin with the mouth and critically examine for imperfections in both jaws; examine the articulations, the muscles, nerves, tongue, and teeth. If found good, mark "O. K." Then take the throat. Be a careful critic, and find to a certainty that every muscle, ligament, nerve, and all blood-supply are perfectly normal from mouth to stomach, and if so, mark "O. K." Take up the stomach; if good, pass on to the duodenum and the rest of the small intestine, and follow that channel to its ending in the colon at the ileo-cæcal valve. If normal, take up the colon; begin at the cæcum and find that it is not too far down in the pelvis; see that the sigmoid colon does not force the cæcum into the pelvis and pull womb, bladder, and small intestine into the pelvic cavity and close the cæcal valve. If all is found to be in a normal condition, we will seek further for some cause for the failure in production of healthy blood. We will explore the whole extent, beginning with the ileo-cæcal valve, and up the right side to the point of curvature, where the transverse colon starts to cross the abdomen. If that division be found good after careful examination, we will then take up the subject of exploring the descending colon. Follow down the left side as far as it is firmly attached to the spine by the mesentery to that loose division generally known as the sigmoid flexure or division of the descending colon. This division is very liable to drop into the pelvis in such a manner as to make a stoppage of fæcal matter by short and obstructing kinks of the colon, through which fæcal matter cannot pass on account of obstructions just described. If no trouble is found after a careful examination of the ileo-cæcal valve, the ascending colon, transverse and descending colon, we will move on to the rectum for further observations. If that division is found to be truly normal, it would be useless to prosecute a further exploration of the alimentary canal for the cause of diseased blood. We will now take up the mesentery at its highest attachment, pass on down to the cæcum, and see that there is no undue elongation of the membranes that hold the bowels in their normal position. If the spinal attachment is found to be truly normal with the spine and the large bowel, with no abnormal kinks or twists in the folds of the mesentery, and our search has been complete, we will also have to report this part of the investigation as good. The colon, from the cæcal valve to the rectal termination, being normal, we will proceed no further with the exploration of the large bowel, but take up the small intestine for the purpose of exploration from the duodenum to the cæcum. If we find no undue proportions of the mesentery in the region of the duodenum, particularly in the vicinity of the connection of the gall-pipe with the duodenum and the pancreatic duct, we will journey from this point downward to the point where the ileum connects with the colon. If there are no kinks, folds, intussusception of the bowels, or no obstructions by hernia or fæcal matter, and no adhesions, we will be in duty bound to report the whole alimentary canal normal from mouth to anus, and seek the cause of physiological disturbance in some other system of the viscera.

Diseased Blood.

Let us reason from the known facts that we possess, when we seek for causes of diseases of the organs of the abdomen. What effect does diseased blood of the organs of any part of the body, by its progressive injury, produce on the general system by its poisonous compounds on blood, lymph, and nerve? First, we know that the aorta supplies the abdominal viscera, direct from the heart, and it is easy to find just where the blood comes from that supplies the pancreas, spleen, liver, stomach, bowels, kidneys, uterus, omentum, and the mesentery system or any part of the abdomen. Also, we can just as easily find the venous system that returns the blood to the heart. We can find and follow the lymphatic system of the abdomen, in all its functions, to the heart and lungs, with its supply of raw material to keep up the supply of blood for the whole system. We know the nerve-supply, both spinal and sympathetic, for the whole abdominal viscera, its uses and location. With this knowledge of nerve-, blood-, and lymph-supplies, we are well prepared to begin to reason and search successfully for causes of diseases that arise in the abdomen from injuries to the viscera, from mechanical or other causes, or hurts to the organs, muscles, glands, or membranes of the abdomen. In diseases of the pancreas, cause for disease would be found in a deranged nerve-, blood-, or lymph-supply, or the ducts that deliver the pancreatic juice to the duodenum. If the disease should appear in the spleen, the same system of searching for the cause would be indicated, to find the cause for blood- and nerve-failure in keeping up the normal functioning of the spleen. The same method would apply to the liver and direct the seeker to the cause that was responsible for diseases of the liver and gall-sac, and banish from the doctor's mind all doubt as to the cause of tumors, gall-stones, cancers, and on through the list of liver and gall diseases.

We all know, if we have even a little knowledge of anatomy, that the cœliac axis branches out from the aorta just below the diaphragm, and supplies the pancreas, spleen, liver, and stomach. We know how the blood returns from each one of them, and also how the nerve-supply leaves the solar plexus to give blood-action to and from each organ of the abdomen. Perfection in blood-flow to and from all organs must be perpetually normal or disease will show its work in lack of blood to supply the local or general nourishment to the organ that is diseased or starved for want of blood. If the arterial supply is good, the venous and lymphatic systems must do the work of draining, or we will have a large spleen or liver, a congested stomach or pancreas, all from the break in the blood-, lymph-, or nerve-chain of supply. This law holds good in supplies, drainage, purity, and health of all organs of the system, just as well as those I have named. The cause of uterine growths, and of diseases of the intestines, is absolute; Nature never changes. To find the obstruction of the blood- and nerve-functioning is the object of the person who reasons and cures by osteopathy.

How about Nature?

Does Nature do its work to a finish? If so, we have a lasting foundation on which to stand. Then we must work to acquaint ourselves with the process by which it proceeds to do its work in the physical man. Not only to make a well-planned and well-builded superstructure, but to care for and guard against the approach and possession of foreign elements, that either cripple or hinder perfect action in all functions of the organs to form protective compounds that will ward off the formation of fungous growths of blood and flesh before the latter can get deadly possession of the laboratory of animal life. Such fungous growths as microbes, germs, bacteria, parasites, and so on to all abnormal formations, are reported to have been found in the bodies of the sick by many authors, as results of their investigations of the compounds in the blood, sputa, and stools of the sick. We will not dispute the fact that they have been and often are found in the blood, sputa, and fæcal and other substances of the body. We will willingly admit that they are truths as reported as the results of discoveries made by many of the most learned and painstaking scientists of years of the past and of the years of our own day and generation. That the student may the better comprehend my object, I will admit and agree that such organisms as described are found in lung disease, disease of the stomach, bowels, liver, kidneys, or any organ of the system. I do not wish to disprove their existence, but wish to take such witnesses and try to prove that all such abnormal changes have a cause in suspension of arterial or venous blood, or lymph, the excretory systems, or by their nerve-supply being cut off at some important point of the physical work. A clean shop is just as necessary to good work as the skilled mechanic is to the construction of the part desired. A careful hunt for the broken link that has allowed the chain of life to fail to make the work complete throughout, and let life substances spoil in the blood or lymph before it has been used in the place or purpose for which it was designed, must be instituted. I want to impress upon you that all bad sputa, poor lymph, and defective blood are effects only, and a broken link is the cause, and bacteria are only the buzzards formed by the biogen that is in the dead blood itself.

Based on Facts.

The science of osteopathy is based on a system of reasoning that does not go beyond principles and truths that can be proven to exist in all of man's make-up, both physical and vital. A truth can always be demonstrated; otherwise, we may have only a theory that is awaiting demonstration, but which until demonstrated does not merit adoption, neither should it be taught until abundantly proven by reliable demonstration. Then, such truths are ever-living facts and will lead the possessor to good results all the time. An organ is supplied by an artery sent as a branch from some principal trunk, and that trunk is connected to others that run back to the heart from the territory in which the organ is situated. If the work has been done well and the organ is found to be normal in size and action, we have found a demonstrated truth that the blood was delivered and used normally by the forces necessary to give form and function to organized life. We prove by observation that the work necessary to that organ is true, because the organ is perfect, in place, size, and function, which could not be if there were an imperfection in the blood, its vessels, or the nerves of the organ, or those by which it was constructed and kept up to meet the normal demands of organic life. We must aim to gain a commanding knowledge of all parts of the body and the methods necessary to keep all parts in position, to insure the delivery and appropriation of the blood to its intended use, to build the organ and keep it normally pure. If we find perfection to be the condition of an organ, we are justified to pronounce that part good, until some accident befalls it that causes abnormal features, which will teach you that a failure has appeared in some part of the supply or appropriation. With your knowledge, you are warranted in seeking the cause and proceeding to readjust the parts from any imperfection discovered to the original condition of the organ and all thereunto belonging, provided there is an open approach from the heart to the organ and in return from the organ back to the heart. When you have adjusted the physical to its normal demands, Nature universally supplies the remainder. I think I have said enough of the importance of the truly normal in form and functions of the organs of the body to take up and make special application of this philosophical guide to a careful search for the true cause of any variation from the healthy condition.

Begin at the Rectum.

I will proceed to draw your attention to natural causes that would produce the beginning of diseases. We will begin our observation at the very foundation of the abdominal viscera, the rectum, the colon, back and up the left side to the point that would lead across the abdomen to the cæcum, whose normal position is the right iliac fossa. It here makes connection with the small intestine, and is also provided with a valve to admit fluids when passing in one direction and to refuse the return passage of any substance from the cæcum back and through the small intestine. We wish to travel as explorers from the rectum through the large and small intestines, stomach, and throat, with a view toward a practical knowledge of the normal position of the different divisions of the alimentary tract. Knowing that the alimentary system is an all-important part of the body mechanism, we can only expect good and healthy results from that which is normal in the whole canal, in form, size, and position, before we can ask for normal functioning, because every organ's health depends without doubt upon normality in every principle and action of the parts of the alimentary canal from the mouth to the anus. We must recognize the importance of knowledge, and much knowledge, of the alimentary system, without which the osteopath is a failure.

THE FUNCTION OF THE VISCERA.

It is my object and intention to prove by philosophy, history, and demonstration that the abdominal viscera are responsible for our good health, and that they are the sole dependence for our normal physical forms and forces. I want to admonish the student of this philosophy that if the anatomical forms are definitely correct in position, and held in that position by normal ligaments, we can expect perfectly natural work in every department of all the organs of the abdomen, the present field of exploration. It is just as reasonable to expect that variations from the normal in any organ, nerve, or blood-vessel will produce diseases in the functioning or the nerves, blood-vessels, and adjacent organs, and add to the already diseased or disturbed conditions by bulky deposits in the lymphatic cells and glands. We have in this manner a new obstruction created from the thickened membranes and flesh through which blood and other substances are conveyed from one organ to another. This would be a good cause to set up deranged conditions, fermentation, inflammation, and pus-formation. We have reasoned and demonstrated to the physiological anatomist, who is aided by his knowledge of chemistry, that diseased conditions must follow soon after stoppage and deposits of any substances. Local fermentation will set up and become extended by progressive encroachment.

That the student may understand what we mean by ligaments, or ligamentous attachments, we will begin with the ascending colon and ask your attention to its attachment to the spine, also to its composition, its elasticity, and its contractile power, because of the great importance to know how far this muscle, meso-cæcum, will allow the cæcum to descend into the pelvis with other divisions of the bowels, if at all, without tearing away from its spinal attachment. Then, we will carefully note the attachment of the anchorage of the transverse colon, and find how much stretching of the wandering muscle toward the pelvis, with the weight of the bowels and their contents, will be allowed before a tear or separation would occur. By this observation we wish to be informed how far from the spinal column the transverse colon could fall down toward the pelvis. We will now take up the descending colon, drawing your attention to its attachments by such membranes as confine it to the spine. Carefully note, with great caution, how much the descending colon will be allowed to descend by the elasticity of its mesentery. The mesentery in post-mortems has been found to have grown to great lengths from the spine, which would permit the bowels to wander from their natural position, filling the pelvis with impacted fæcal matter. We invite the attention of the patient reader particularly to the mesenteries, for the purpose of receiving and giving more light on the cause of typhoid fever, constipation, flux, dysentery, etc.

THE MESENTERY.

The bowels are attached to and held in place by a web or flat rope or elastic sheet attached to the front of the spine at one extremity and the other extremity attached to the bowels. This web is long enough to allow the bowels to change, roll, or move to different places in the abdomen. It is well for the student to know about how far that muscle will allow the bowels to move from their normal position, while diagnosing any disease. He should know if that change in the position of the bowels would or could impinge on the natural flow of the blood and other fluids for general purposes in animal life. How much variation, if any, of the bowels can be tolerated and not cause bad results? Many grave questions arise in the minds of the students when reasoning on the failure of health and the causes that have given rise to that abnormal condition in the functioning of one, many, or all of the organs of the body. As there is something of a sameness in the symptoms of many diseases, we would naturally reason that equal causes would be required to give a soreness of spine, limbs, flesh, and brain, hot or cold sensations and stupor, and other symptoms that are common to all climatic diseases. As we have spoken of the similarity of symptoms that are given by all works or authors on general practice or therapeutics, we can contrast or compare their general symptoms as proof that they do act on the same nerves in just about the same way. If they affect the nervous system similarly, then the causes of such effects belong to the same systems of lymphatic glands, cells, and systems of nutrition that belong to the deep and superficial fascia or pancreas.

The human being is one of the animals whose body stands erect or perpendicular to the earth. He stands upon two feet. Other animal bodies have four feet, on which they stand and hold the body in the horizontal position or parallel with the earth's surface. It is reasonable to suppose that the bodies of both organs are fastened to the spine by muscles and ligaments (mesentery), which are prepared in size, form, and strength to hold each organ to its normal position during motion and rest. As the organs of the four-footed animals are suspended under the spine and hang directly toward the earth's center, the ligaments would be normal only when they accommodate the organ to that horizontal spine. The erect body of the two-footed animal must have its sustaining ligaments correspond with the erect position of the body, with the strength and forms to suit the weights which they are intended to support, and at the same time be more powerfully attached to the spine than in the four-footed animal. In man we may expect much flopping, twisting, and kinking in the mesentery, producing all sorts of variation from the normal condition, health.

The Omentum.

This chapter is on diseases that follow injuries of the greater or lesser omentum, the mesentery, and fascia. All contain great amounts of blood-vessels and lymphatic vessels and glands, peculiarly arranged to supply and drain each system, with all the nerves necessary to the force required in the functioning labors of secreting and preparing material substances to be used as blood-force. Any person who has ever been in a butcher-shop, slaughter-house, or on a farm, and has seen the farmer kill hogs for fresh meat, knows that the hog has a fatty covering over the bowels, and that the farmer calls that sheet of fat the "caul fat" of the hog. He sees the farmer cut this fatty sheet loose from the stomach and the ligaments that join it to the spine, spleen, pancreas, and diaphragm. He thus gets a general idea of the size and form of the omentum or "caul fat," but he has learned nothing of its use, more than that it is spread out over the bowels. The student of anatomy soon learns that it is in man about twelve to sixteen inches wide at the upper end and rounds off to suit the abdomen as it descends from the stomach. It is about one-half of an inch thick. It has a few large arteries distributed through its body and a full supply of very fine arteries that furnish blood for the lymph-vessels and glands. The muscular and fibrinous tissue-cells are equally well supplied with blood.

What Is the Function?

But all this knowledge does not give light on the function of that organ. Let us halt and hunt for more light. It is evident as we approach the omentum and take into consideration its form, its blood-, nerve-, and lymph-supply, that we are in the presence of some kind of a manufacturer, and it is our object to become, if possible, better acquainted with the object for which Nature has constructed and placed the omentum in such an important location. If it is the office of this organ to take up the lymph and other crude materials and construct vital substances, we want to be benefited by a knowledge of that fact. We see lymph-, blood-, and nerve-systems all through the omentum and its attachments in all its parts. We see the channels through which substances enter the omentum. We know the origin of blood-, nerve-, and lymph-supplies from dissections. We know this is a laboratory, and have reason to believe it is a very fine one, and we also believe that it is responsible as an official for the performance of great duties in producing and sustaining healthy conditions of the whole system by the purity of the substances it collects, prepares, and sends forth. Without that perfection we cannot reasonably expect or hope for good health. If perfect normality in all its active principles is a guarantee of good health, is it not just as reasonable to guarantee diseased condition of the whole body when the omentum becomes diseased by wounds or injuries of any kind?

I have taken up my pen with the view of giving a few thoughts on the use of the omentum, in conjunction with the mesenteries, in keeping the body physiologically normal. I take up this subject and approach it with consideration to the cause of disease and death, in the hope that I may present the responsibility that naturally falls upon the mesentery and the omentum. We will begin with the membranous attachments, starting at the neck and following the spine clear on down to the last division of the sacrum. These membranes are attached first to the spinal column, and then to the various organs of the neck, chest, abdomen, and pelvis. We wish to go beyond the simple fact that organs are attached to and held in position by some part of this system of membranes, well known to the anatomist by the name of peritoneum. It is the physiological action and productive power found in this almost continuous system from the neck to the sacrum to which we wish to draw the student's attention. All these membranous attachments from the neck to the sacrum are abundantly supplied with nerves, blood, and lymphatic vessels. Their office as such is known to be that of secreting and sending lymph and other substances to the heart and lungs, to be prepared and returned in due time to construct and keep various organs and divisions of the body in a healthy condition, that each organ, separate and united, can keep the system in the normal condition which we recognize and call good health. In order that we may proceed correctly in considering nutrition as being prepared and sent forth to the heart and lungs for sustaining the body normally, we will halt for observation in the vicinity of the meso-rectum, meso-colon, transversalis and descending colon, and the small intestine throughout the attachment of this whole system of the mesentery. We will first take the thought of the mechanical preparation of the secretion and reception of the digested fluids as absorbed by the secretories of the mesentery. We will also seriously consider the physiological functioning during the collection of this fluid and its course in receiving the finishing touches, previous to its being sent out from the heart and handed over to the constructing machinery of animal life. We wish to ask of your reason, how much of this mesentery system would be required to produce and sustain perfect health? It appears to me that no other answer would be given that would be satisfactory to the man of reason short of, that all of the entire mesentery system must pull together all the time, or a failure of some organ to perform its duty will undoubtedly appear. At this time we wish to dwell particularly upon the omentum and its power to sustain the lungs in a healthy condition by furnishing in part or in whole the substance necessary to keep lung, muscle, and tissue supplied with muscular form and force to receive the coming substances that pass to the lungs, through the vena porta, to be prepared by the chemical action which separates the impurities, and the physiological power necessary to reject those impurities, to receive and deliver to the heart the suitable substances to be sent out and keep up the continuous repair of the body, and to retain the lungs themselves in the very best working order, that they may be able through the muscular and nerve power to do all the work incumbent upon them. Perhaps it would be best to say to the student at this time that so far as the writer can ascertain from post-mortems reported in great number by anatomists after investigations of diseases of the heart, kidneys, bowels, uterus, and the spleen, universally the omentum has been found in an abnormal condition in cases of tuberculosis of the lungs. I wish to call your attention to the fact that, so far as I can obtain any evidence, all post-mortems show that the omentums examined have been diseased or found misplaced. Foreign growths or shrinkage of the omentum have been found in all post-mortems. Since then, the attention of the writer has been called to the thought that possibly tuberculosis was more of a disease of the omentum and mesentery than of the lungs. With this view, I believe that at an early day we will be successful with lung diseases—in fact, with diseases of all organs of the body—in proportion to our acquaintance with the omentum and mesentery. Almost the whole list of diseases of climate and season will show a failure of the mesentery to sustain health through normal action, which, when properly understood, will reveal variations from the normal and physiological workings of the omentum, mesentery, or peritoneum from the neck to the sacrum. In proof of this, we will report observations on our conclusions as to the cause of diseases of the glandular and lymphatic systems. With the evidence we have, we believe such variations mark the beginning of the mesenteric failures in some function, either of the blood-, nerve-, or lymph-supplies, and physiological failures to act to their full normal capacity as required by the exacting demands of health.

Established One Cause.

When the beginning cause of disease is found and established as positively as can be reasoned out by paralytic falling of the bowels into the pelvis, when a wrench of the spinal column has been given with force enough to slip the vertebral articulations and inhibit nerves, then we have proven one cause that has let the muscles of the mesentery give up contractility and allow the colon to fall into the pelvis. Thus we see the importance of a perfectly normal spine at all points of articulation. In this case, to fall into the pelvis is just as certain to follow and will be observed by the bowels as strictly as falling bodies observe the laws of gravitation. We have a heavy pulling of the mesentery attachment at the spine by the weight applied at the point of attachment to the large bowels, giving the bowels abnormality in position and weight. That weight rests directly upon the organs that have preceded this fall of the bowels and now occupy a position in the pelvis, to be tortured by the oppressive weight of the bowels loaded with immovable fæcal matter. We have the weight lying across both ureters, descending from the kidneys to the bladder. We have irritation of the kidneys by cut-off of the flow of urine between the kidneys and the bladder. This urine, suspended or prohibited from entering the bladder, accumulates to an irritable quantity between the point of suspension or inhibition and the kidney end of the ureter. We have a qualified condition for the absorption and distribution of uremic poisons in poisonous quantities by the secretory system of the abdomen. We have a known cause, in reason, for so-called kidney diseases. We feel we have proven the frequent and even common occurrence of "wreckage" of the bowels, bladder, and womb, held down by contracture of the abdominal wall, the weight of the bowels with their contents, the womb and its congested body, and all attached membranes and fascia, with the added weight of congestion caused by detained venous blood. Further wreckage continues by interference with the arterial blood, which is stopped from reaching its natural landings. Another consequence is a great enlargement of veins, lymph-cells, cysts, and tubes of receipt and distribution. The excretory channels also become shocked and confused as effects of the first pelvic wreck. From that confused pile of wreckage, we can easily account for the formation of tumors on the uterus, bladder, rectum, and for all diseases of the abdominal viscera, such as tuberculosis of the bowels, kidneys, liver, pancreas, and spleen. All these effects are possible, all are reasonable, and all are indisputable effects that follow wreckage of the organs of the abdomen.

Appendicitis.

At the present time, more than at any other time since the birth of Christ, the men of the medical and surgical world have centralized their minds for the purpose of relieving local conditions, excruciating pain, below the kidneys, in both the male and female.

For some reason, possibly justifiable, it has been decided to open the human body and explore the region just below the right kidney in search of the cause of this trouble. The explorations were made upon the dead first. Small seeds and other substances have been found in the vermiform appendix, which is a hollow tube several inches in length. These discoveries led to explorations in the same locality in the living. In some of the cases, though very few, seeds and other substances have been found in the vermiform appendix, supposed to be the cause of inflammation of the appendix. Some have been successfully removed, and permanent relief followed the operation. These explorations and successes in finding substances in the vermiform appendix, their removal, and successful recovery in some cases, have led to what may properly be termed a hasty system of diagnosis, and it has become very prevalent, being resorted to by many physicians, under the impression that the vermiform appendix is of no use, and that the human being is just as well off without it.

Therefore it is resolved, that as nothing positive is known of the trouble in the location above described, it is guessed that it is a disease of the vermiform appendix. Therefore they etherize and dissect for the purpose of exploring, to ascertain if the guess is right or wrong. In the diagnosis, this is a well-defined case of appendicitis. The surgeon's knife is driven through the quivering flesh in great eagerness in search of the vermiform appendix. The bowels are rolled over and around in search of the appendix. Sometimes some substances are found in it, but more often, to the chagrin of the exploring physician, it is found to be in a perfectly healthy and normal condition. So seldom is it found containing seeds or any substance whatever that, as a general rule, it is a useless and dangerous experiment. The percentage of deaths caused by the knife and ether, and the permanently crippled, will justify the assertion that it would be far better for the human race if they lived and died in ignorance of appendicitis. A few genuine cases might die from that cause; but if the knife were the only known remedy, it were better that one should die occasionally than to continue this system.

Another Victory.

Osteopathy furnishes the world with a relief here which is absolutely safe, without the loss of a drop of blood, that has for its foundation and philosophy a fact based upon the longitudinal contractile ability of the appendix itself, which is able to eject by its natural forces any substances that may by an unnatural move be forced into the appendix. My first osteopathic treatment for appendicitis was in 1877, at which time I treated a Mr. Surratt and gave permanent relief. During the early eighties I treated and permanently cured Mrs. Emily Pickler, of Kirksville, mother of our former representative, S. M. Pickler, and mother of former Congressman John A. Pickler, of South Dakota. The infirmary has had bad cases of appendicitis, probably running in numbers up into hundreds, without failing to relieve and cure a single case. The ability of the appendix to receive and discharge foreign substances is taught in the American School of Osteopathy and is successfully practiced by its diplomates. In the case of Mr. Surratt, I found lateral twist of lumbar bones. I adjusted the spine, lifted the bowels, and he got well. When I was called to Mrs. Pickler, she had been put on light diet, by the surgeon, preparatory to the knife. She soon recovered under my treatment without any surgical operation, and is alive and well at this date.

Many Queries.

To many, such questions as these will arise. Has the appendix at its entrance a sphincter muscle similar in action to that of the rectum and œsophagus? Has it the power to contract and dilate, to contract and shorten in its length and eject all substances when the nerves are in a normal condition? And where is the nerve that failed to act to throw out the substance that entered the cavity of the appendix? Has God been so forgetful as to leave the appendix in such a condition as to receive foreign bodies, without preparing it by its power of contraction, or otherwise, to throw out such substances? If He has, He surely has forgotten part of His work. Reason has taught me that He has done a perfect work, and on that line I have proceeded to treat appendicitis for twenty-five years, without pain and misery to the patient, and have given permanent relief in all the cases that have come to me. With the diagnosis of doctors and surgeons that appendicitis was the malady, and the choice of relief was between the knife and death, or possibly both, many such cases have come for osteopathic treatment, and examination has revealed in every case that there has been previous injury to some set of spinal nerves, caused by jars, strains, or falls. Every case of appendicitis and renal or gall-stones can be traced to some such cause.

These principles I have proclaimed and thought for thirty years.

God's Work Complete.

We should use caution in our assertions that Nature has made its work so complete in animal forms and furnished them with such wisely prepared principles that they could produce and administer remedies to suit the occasion, and not go outside of the body to find them. Should we find by experiment that man is so arranged and wisely furnished by Deity as to ferret out disease and purify and keep the temple of life in ease and health, we should hesitate to make known the fact. The opposite opinion has had full sway for centuries, and man has, by habit, long usage, and ignorance, adjusted his mind so as to submit to customs of the great past, so that should he try, without previous training, to reason and bring his mind to the altitude of the thought of the greatness and wisdom of the Infinite, he might become insane or fall back in a stupor and exist only as a living mental blank in the great ocean of life. It would be a great calamity to have all the untrained minds shocked so seriously as to cause them to lose the might of reason they now have, and be sent back once more to dwell in Darwin's protoplasm. I tell you there is danger, and we must be careful to show the people small stars, and but one at a time, till they can begin to reason and realize that God has done all that the wisest can attribute to Him.

What Are Abdominal Tumors?

At this time the term "abdominal tumors" applies to the womb and its appendages, but really it should include the tumefaction of any organ, muscle, or membrane of the abdomen. But the tendency to attribute such growths to the womb as natural to its various productive powers seems to veil the eye of the gynæcologist to all else excepting the native ability of the womb to grow tumors by the bushel. Suppose they do grow, where and what is the parent cause that deposited the germ? as nothing can appear or exist without a cause. Either close to or remote from, we should seek with determined diligence for the cause that is behind, giving life and form to tumors on any organ, muscle, or membrane of the abdomen. Abdominal tumors are as natural as gravitation. Tumefaction is only the natural effect that follows or appears in the abdomen or pelvis when lymph is stopped in its natural channels in any organ or part of the viscera or abdominal wall. In the abdomen we find a house or chamber, all nicely prepared, lined or calcimined with tissues, membranes, and fascia, with lymphatic glands, cells, nerves, veins, and arteries. Then in the abdomen we see or find just room enough for the easy working of the organs while functioning in all divisions, and reason demands that to succeed in good and perfect work no two or more organs can work perfectly when one is crowding on another. If not, what can we expect but strangulation at points, and the appearance of growths that develop owing to the stoppage of lymph in the lymph-channels and cells? Thus it is that piles are caused by pressure on the bowels. When the cæcum falls down into the pelvis, it shuts off the returning blood in the hemorrhoidal veins and gives us a cause for tumors of the rectum. Let me draw your attention to the fact that as sure as the cæcum drops low in the pelvis, and obstruction of fæcal matter appears, then you have irritation of the bowels and constipation, with the weight of the fæcal matter of the large and small intestines to completely stop free and natural action of the nerve- and blood-supply of the contents of the pelvis. Thus we have no pelvic action, because it is wedged full to overflowing with foreign bodies and substances that ought to be held back and off by their own mesenteries. They have failed to keep the large bowels up and out of the pelvis, and we see cause for confusion, the beginning of pelvic and abdominal growths, from œdema to the great tumors of the abdomen. The student of anatomy and physiology will see at once the cause, beginning in the pelvis and proceeding from the anus to the tonsils, creating all forms and kinds of abdominal tumors and cancers of the bladder, womb, bowels, kidneys, appendix, pancreas, stomach, gall-sac, liver, spleen, heart, lungs, and brain. How would any person account for the growth of a fibroid tumor of the uterus, pelvis, or any section or organ of the abdominal viscera? To stop a river with an ice-gorge does not stop the flow of water, but sends it to surrounding territory just as fast as the gorge builds the dam up higher, and it is just as reasonable to know that a dam across a river of blood will drive the blood to other places just as long as the supply comes.

PROLAPSED VISCERA.

Prolapsed viscera create or are the cause of many disturbances of the nerve- and blood-currents. Venous blood dies in the veins to such a degree that it can only be applied to build up by the vital help given by the lymphatic veins. We reason that this is the cause of the growths in regions of venous oppression by weights or strictures. An artery has much force to propel blood through its channel, while the vein has but little if any. Thus the arteries can keep up the vitality of the venous blood or lymph and build mountains or great-sized tumors. In this way we can account for tumors appearing in many places in the body, particularly in the abdominal viscera. A venous current of blood stopped in return does not die, but is kept alive by the vitality of the arterial blood, and builds the excrescences of the abdomen. Beginning at the sphincter ani and ending at the brain, we see the effects of congestion in tumefactions and general or special abnormalities, loss of hair, sight, and hearing, diseased tonsils, nasal membranes, and air-passages. All are directly or indirectly accounted for, and it can be quite easily demonstrated that they will follow disturbances of blood- and lymph-circulation. This should be well comprehended by the student of natural philosophy, particularly the one in the study of the machinery of life. He can demonstrate this law to his own mind by adjusting that part or foundation over which the blood should travel from the aorta to the pancreas, for the purpose of giving nourishment to that organ and all its functioning apparatus. Having already adjusted the territory through which the arterial vessels pass, to the absolutely normal, with the flow of blood free and easy from the aorta to the pancreas, we will take up the consideration of the venous flow from the pancreas back to the vena cava. This returning current of blood is more liable to do mischief if suspended or stopped beyond its normal time in the veins of the pancreas, becoming a cause of disease and death by imperfect production of pancreatic fluids, which should be perfect before entering the duodenum. We then have reason to decide that imperfection of the functioning of the bowels, both large and small, would follow. We would expect fever, thirst, constipation, and chronic inflammation of the bowels from the duodenum to the ileo-cæcal valve. Also, for the want of this nourishment, we would expect to discover a weakness in the nerves of the mesenteries, which would be followed by elongation of the mesentery. This would lengthen the mesentery and allow the bowels, by their weight of fæcal matter and blood- and lymph-stagnation, to fall very low down into the abdomen and pile up in a confused mass. The cæcum would fall to the very bottom of the pelvic floor, and the ileo-cæcal valve would be obstructed under this pile of fallen bodies.

Go into Camp.

Let me refresh your minds that in dissections the spleen, kidneys, stomach, uterus, bladder, and large and small intestines have frequently been found in the pelvis. I want you to camp on the borders of the pelvis again, and stay there with your microscope, both in hand and head, until you know what this great wreckage of the viscera has produced by having been thrown into the pelvis from any cause whatsoever, either mechanical or chemical. We must remember that the pelvis is well supplied with systems of nerves, on which the health and vitality of every organ that is in the body is dependent, for health and harmonious systemic support.

With us the foundation of life must be solidly constructed of stones of the highest grades of purity, or your house will lean toward the imperfect stones in the foundation; your building will bulge, crack, decay, and fall down, and become simply a heap of ruins that will write the history of ignorance on the part of the architect and builder. The foundations of life must be absolutely good, and we must have them perfect before we proceed from the pelvis to judge and adjust other organs of the abdomen.

THE LIVER.

The liver swings in a hammock formed of five ligamentous ropes, attached to the spine and diaphragm, and with the abdominal ends firmly fastened to the liver until they have surrounded the whole organ and returned to the spine and diaphragm, making a swinging bed or hammock, or basket, to suit the form and functions of this organ. Normality of this hammock in which the liver rests must be expected, or the reverse of health predicted. This hammock is provided with the necessary openings for the passage into the liver of blood and other fluids necessary to the functioning process, that should not be disturbed by the interference of blood-, nerve-, and lymph-supplies. The spine must show mechanical correctness in all its bearings when inspected by the line, plumb, and level of the osteopath's highest or best skill and his well-trained mechanical genius, which should be of the highest mental standards of anatomical, physiological, and chemical knowledge. We believe that reason will bear us out that many, if not all, of the so-called liver diseases come from hurts, jars, jolts, temperature, and poisons. Should the hammock be cut loose at any point of its attachments, the liver would suffer. This can be illustrated by bringing forward the case of a lady who is comfortably resting in a summer hammock, when some additional weight is thrown upon the hammock, breaking the ropes of attachment and allowing the occupant to fall to the ground, a distance or one or many feet. She is shocked, bruised, and crippled the whole length of the spine, and probably suffers injury to the abdominal viscera. It is reasonable to know that the liver while in its hammock, doing the duties of its office, must be allowed to do its work without disturbance. The osteopath of average intelligence needs but little further explanation to comprehend the dangers and diseases liable to follow a disturbance of the liver while in this hammock, nest, basket, or resting-place, prepared by Nature to hold this organ while performing the duties which belong to it.

The Kidneys.

The diseases of the kidneys are as follows:

Congestion of the kidney,
Acute parenchymatous nephritis,
Chronic parenchymatous nephritis,
Interstitial nephritis,
Amyloid kidney,
Pyelitis,
Acute uræmia,
Renal calculi,
Cystitis,
Movable kidney.

Fighting Effects.

Before presenting the osteopathic opinion of the above list of kidney diseases, with the remote and active causes of their appearance as abnormalities, we will give the student the benefit of the best up-to-date theory and classification of diseases of the kidney. The very best authors on diseases of the kidneys seem to be satisfied to know and combat the effects of those diseases, and give only a little light on the cause. We see this is the case with many writers, who simply classify effects, such as changes of the urine from the normal to the various conditions as found and reported by urinalysis. We have an extensive description of the kidney, and know that congestion and inflammation produce many bad results, but we are not satisfied to proceed further without inquiring into the causes that produce the effects. The first question that arises according to the tenets of osteopathy is, Has the kidney been responsible for the production of the causes of its own destruction? If not, we must seek to discover a more satisfactory explanation. Leaving the kidney for a time, we will examine the structure and location of the ascending colon, carefully examine the mesentery or the meso-cæcum, and ascertain if the membrane or white muscle attached to the bowels is long enough or elastic enough to allow the cæcum to descend into the pelvis to the perineum. If so, the hardened fæcal matter will become the irritating cause of disease by pulling upon the spinal attachment of the mesentery just below the kidneys. If the cæcum has fallen into the pelvis, and the sigmoid colon thrown from left to right in this region, would it not compress the ileo-cæcal valve and stop the passage of fæcal matter from the small intestine into the colon? By the weight of this impacted fæcal matter that has accumulated in the ascending, the transverse, and descending colon, the ileo-cæcal valve is stopped and even the softer fluids are prevented from entering the colon. We have in this a cause for irritation of the pelvic organs and suspension of the flow of the fluids of the pelvis, and the whole lower division of the abdomen becomes filled up to the region of the renal system.

Our Basis.

We do not pretend to dispute the effects of the foregoing list of special named kidney diseases, but the cause that has produced those effects is what the osteopath must look for.

Without a good knowledge of the cause or causes producing those effects, we could not feel justified in offering any suggestion in the treatment of those diseases, because of the general failure in the treatment of kidney diseases by the best known medical authorities. The dependence of the medical doctor for the relief and recovery of his patient in renal diseases is all in one common channel—that is, drugs to suit such diseases as listed under each name, notwithstanding all known drugs have been a failure and the patient dies just as quickly with them, and often more quickly than without them. I have hinted at the possibility, the probability, and the certainty of the large intestine settling down into the lower part of the abdomen and pelvis, producing a partial or complete obstruction of the blood- and nerve-supply of that division of the body. I believe that the intelligent student will argree with me that ninety out of every hundred of the cases of renal diseases, stomach diseases, and pancreatic diseases can be proven by demonstration to have their origin in the condition of the mesentery of the ascending, transverse, and descending colon, allowing it to stretch down low enough to cause the large and small intestines to be responsible for the effects above enumerated. I think right here is where the M.D.s have shown the least sense of power of reasoning in relieving constipation, of the real causes of which they are ignorant. The effects that go on during this prolapsed condition of the bowels are plainly seen. Any man with a fairly good anatomical knowledge will decide, at once, that we have here a philosophy that is capable of being sustained by its application. I think here are facts that will make the advocates of medicine blush with shame because they have never solved the question, neither have they seen nor even thought of it, as shown by the best authors to this day.

The Stomach.

Gas is formed in great quantities in the stomach, in the small intestine, and in the colon. Gas is also formed in the lungs. The gas that forms in the stomach and bowels is formed from raw or crude materials that are taken into the stomach as nourishment. The fact that gas is generated in the whole alimentary canal is too well known to be questioned by anyone. We know it to be a fact. We also know that the whole canal from the mouth to the rectum is fully supplied with secretory ducts, and that they secrete such substances as are required for the metabolism of these parts. We know that the bowels contain fluids and gases in great abundance, and it is reasonable to suppose that Nature has an object in this work of generating or first converting food into gas. We have no evidence that an atom of flesh or bone that is found in the body has not been reduced to gas, either in the bowels or lungs, before it became blood. Our best microscopes fail to detect the smallest atoms of flesh or hair, bones, and teeth. We have such questions as this before us: Could the atoms of a hair be reduced to such fine condition in any other way than through the gaseous process? Astronomy claims that worlds are only gas condensed from vapor to solids. If so, we see the work of condensing done on a large scale to form a planet of eight, ten, or one hundred thousand miles in diameter. Another question arises: How is such a quantity of gas formed to make so large a planet as Jupiter, sixty thousand miles in diameter? or Arcturus, seventy-two million miles in diameter? Gas seems to be native to space, and how it is condensed is the question for astronomers to solve. We will limit our study to man's system only, and see how the gas-works in him form the fine substances found in his make-up. We speak of digestion, how various fluids are compounded and the changes brought about in the stomach and bowels, and how additions of pancreatic juice, gall, and so on produce a fluid that is taken up by the absorbents of the mesentery and called chyme, chyle, and lymph, and united with venous blood, and passed by way of the vessels of the liver and on to a successful landing in the lungs. There we find our eyes beholding this blood and lymph finished and divided into two hundred million parts, with that number of air-cells, to be converted into gas, the impurities separated from the pure, the bad cast out and the good condensed to blood and sent to the heart, to be sent out and appropriated as flesh, to take its place in the body and do all the duties incumbent on the economy of physical life. So far I think we are safe to say that all evidence is favorable to the fact that bones, teeth, muscles, tendons, nerves, blood-vessels, hair, and organs of the body have had their origin from gas, and are only condensed gas. Now, we as chemists of good health, to succeed in curing our patients, must keep the gas-making machinery in good mechanical condition to do laboratory work, or we surely will fail to cure or even relieve our patient.

The Philosophy of Digestion.

Digestion is food reduced to atoms of gas, both by chemical union and animal heat. The stomach is a finely constructed gas-retort. It begins the process of mixing food. At the time of swallowing the first morsel of food, it forms gas very fast, often faster than the secretions can take it up, and rifting of wind begins in order to relieve the oppression of the stomach. Evidently Nature would bring food to its highest purity to make blood. Thus the demand would be imperative for the reduction of all food to its lowest atoms, and as gas is that degree of the atom, it would be reasonable that the machinery to suit gas-making would be abundantly supplied in the body. The task for the wise man is to find and locate the machinery that does the work of converting the food into gas. As we have located the stomach and proven that it begins the process of gas-generating, we will follow the next step and begin at the duodenum, where the partially mixed food passes out of the stomach and receives gall, pancreatic juice, and other chemicals. Here more gas is formed by chemical action in the small intestine and passed into the mesentery from the bowels, clear on to the ileo-cæcal valve and on to the colon, the third and last division of the intestinal apparatus, which reduces substances to gas by stale fermentation and gives that gas to the great sheets of mesentery attached to the bowels and supplied with networks of lymphatics, whose work is to absorb the atoms of nourishment from the colon and pass them on to the thoracic duct and on to the liver, lungs, and heart. Thus we recognize the importance of keeping the gas-making machinery in good working order, by keeping out all kinks and twists in any part or division of the mesentery and small and large intestines. Is the machinery of the alimentary canal all that belongs to the process of refining food previous to its transformation into blood? No; we have another, and the greatest gas-works of all, when we get to the lungs, which receive the lymph almost in its pure state with the venous blood for its highest refining process before it can go to the heart as living blood. Thus we enter and close the whole process of forming blood through the gas process of digestion, the only reasonable method of getting bread into the condition of living blood.

THE PROCESS OF DIGESTION BY ELECTRICITY.

Take a halt, reason, and answer this one question: Has electricty any quality except force? Does it simply move worlds and such bodies as have form and motion? If a large tree is torn to atoms by electricity, does electriciy do that powerful work? Or does it cause an explosion of the elements found in the tree? Digestion is my object of inquiry. Man eats and drinks of almost all birds, beasts, and reptiles. He masticates until his teeth are all gone. He swallows hard chunks of beef and other diets without mastication, with but little change that is apparent in his health and strength. At this point I will say that I am not satisfied with the explanations of our physiologists on the subject of digestion. They tell us we chew, swallow, and our food goes through many changes in the stomach, and they stop after giving us a few Greek words, such as *osmosis*, *exosmosis*, *endosmosis*, motion, get out, get in. Back to my question: Have we not great reason to believe that digestion is Nature's process of reaching matter that is to be converted to the finest gaseous atoms before it can be formed into blood? If that be true, surely our diets must be combustible, and electricity causes the combustion and separation of the atoms of substances eaten by man and beast.

Constipation of the Bowels.

Gould says: "Constipation is a condition of the bowels in which the bowels evacuate at long periods apart." This gives the ordinary meaning of the word, but we must learn more of the causes that produce the effect known as constipation. As a disease it varies in degrees of severity. Some cases of constipation run from two to fourteen days, and are not then relieved without the use of purgatives, or the use of water with or without compounds to soften the hard and dry fæces. A halt has come; the bowels have failed in their function; the power to pass out fæcal matter is lost or overcome from some cause. Irritation from hard and bulky accumulation sets up and disturbs the nervous system, fever follows, backache, headache, and general abdominal disturbances come on, with various annoyances, such as piles, kidney troubles, bladder and womb diseases, womb, rectum, ovarian, and abdominal tumors, enlarged and cancerous liver, gall-stones, bladder-stones, sour stomach, loss of appetite, flatulency, congestion of the spleen and pancreas, stopping the normality in all organs of the abdomen and pelvis, until the heart and lungs are reached in the progressive effects of constipation. All these effects come with constipation. But the cause of all this trouble from the bowels not acting normally has not been shown to the student by the writers on disease. The fascia, mesentery, and peritoneum have not been reported on as causes, while being held in an irritable strain by the large bowels being out of their normal places, by having been forced into the pelvic cavity. This pressure across the abdomen when the bowels are full of fæcal matter pushes the cæcum down to the pelvic floor and forces it to stay there by the size and weight of the sigmoid colon. It closes the entry from the ileum to the cæcum, and cuts off the chances of the small intestine to supply the colon with water and other fluids, to keep the fæcal matter soft enough to be forced through the colon and out of the body.

The Treatment of Constipation.

The general understanding of constipation as taught and practiced through all these ages has been that there is much or some fæcal matter detained in the large intestine, beginning with the cæcum, ascending, transverse, and descending colon to the rectum. It also means that fæcal matter from some cause becomes hard and dry and accumulates in the large bowel because it is too dry; that the mucous membrane has lost its power of furnishing the fluids necessary to force the passage of the albuminous substances by removing friction between the fæcal body and the membranes of the inner surface of the bowels. It is a reasonable proposition that it would take more force to push a dry body over a dry place than it would to push a moist body over a well-lubricated surface. A question arises: From what part of the body does this fæcal lubricating substance come? If from the colon, evidently it would furnish this fluid, lubricate the fæcal matter, and peristaltic action would easily pass the substance on and out through the whole channel of the colon from the cæcum through to the rectum. We are told that the colon does not furnish enough lubricating fluid for this purpose; therefore we will seek for a more abundant supply from some other source, which would take us back, with our anatomical and physiological knowledge, to the pancreas. We will halt at the duodenum, to examine the gate through which this fluid passes. If an obstruction is at this point in the form of thickened membranes, gall-stones, or any other bulky substances that would shut off the pancreatic duct by stricture or interference, we should proceed at once to remove the obstructing cause that prohibits the free entry of the pancreatic juice. If constipation should resist all ordinary methods of relief, with a good supply of pancreatic juice in the small intestine, we should inspect every inch from the duodenum to the ileo-cæcal valve, with the view of finding the obstruction. At this point is the union or entry of the small intestine into the colon, a point about two or three inches above the rounded end of that part of the colon known as the cæcum. We are very likely to find the obstruction at the ileo-cæcal valve, the terminal of the small bowel, with the cæcum fallen and forced into the pelvis from the right iliac fossa. This would destroy the ability of the small intestine to pass this fluid to the colon and lubricate the large intestine with the pancreatic fluids. Then, as mechanics of osteopathy, we will take the knee-and-chest position, place the hands upon the abdomen, draw the cæcum out of the pelvis, and give exit to the pancreatic juice from the small to the large intestine, because we have found the cause of obstruction and know the remedy to be applied. When the cæcum is drawn from the pelvis and the ascending colon is brought back to its normal position in the right iliac fossa, with the rounded end about level with the symphysis, we can expect the ileo-cæcal valve to give passage to the fluids detained in the small intestine and discharge them freely. The fluids of the small intestine should be forwarded through the ileo-cæcal valve in order to keep the contents of the colon in a soft and movable condition, a condition in which peristaltic action is able to keep the fæcal matter in constant motion. We thus have a known cause for constipation, which is simply a failure of the fluids of the small intestine to enter the large. When the liquid substances have passed from the small to the large intestine through the ileo-cæcal valve, then we can expect a commotion, a colicky feeling throughout the whole extent of the colon, because of the addition of the fluids coming from the small bowel, which are forced into the large intestine and greatly increase the bulk already occupying the large intestine. This bulk is increased in size by the soft fluids dissolving the harder. In that condition there is need that the ascending colon be normal, that the transverse colon have its proper position, and that all parts to the point of descent and through the sigmoid division be absolutely normal.

In the treatment, carefully, while in the knee-and-chest position, with gentle pressure in the vicinity of the symphysis, give a gliding move up toward the left kidney, follow the transverse colon, raise any sagging that may be found in that division with a gentle upward move, without any gouging of the fingers, and raise the whole alimentary system up toward the umbilicus. Should there be very much colicky feeling, gently lift the bowels from the rectum back through the sigmoid division and descending division of the colon, clear back to the ileo-cæcal valve. Be careful not to let the cæcum fall back into the pelvis, to the condition that would shut off the ileo-cæcal valve and prohibit the continuous flow of the soft fluids into the colon. This is a successful method to unload the colon from the cæcum to the rectum if there be twists, kinks, telescoping, adhesions to the bowels, or stoppage at the ileo-cæcal valve by gall-stones or hard foreign substances that may have been swallowed. First raise the cæcum from the pelvis to its normal position, then the transverse colon that may have fallen; also correct the left division to the sigmoid, which becomes an obstruction when it falls into the pelvis. I say at this point that the folds of the meso-cæcum, meso-transversalis, and the meso-colon can generally be easily readjusted. Twists, kinks, and various obstructions to the passage of the fluids through the colon can be overcome and the obstruction cease to exist, and the normal action of the bowels brought about.

Skill Necessary.

I have given the student a general rule of procedure in cases of constipation, with the expectation that he will use some intellectual skill as he proceeds. The effects following the condition of the colon just described by the suspension of fluids from the small intestine, producing the class of mechanical irritations that accompany the impacted colon, will be given under the proper heading and place, diseases of the rectum, bladder, womb, kidneys, stomach, bowels, liver, pancreas, spleen, mesentery, and glands of the abdomen.

CHAPTER IX.

The Pelvis.

DISEASES OF THE BLADDER.

When we take up the diseases of an organ or vessel, such as the bladder, we must reason how such a part is made, by tracing out its nerve- and blood-supply. This being the case, we will go back to the first appearance of the bladder in the babe. We find the bladder to be a part of the peritoneum, or formed of the peritoneum. Then we go to the blood- and nerve-supply of the peritoneum, and look there for defects, because the failure to keep the system normal would naturally be found in the blood- and nerve-supply that give supply and force to the bladder. Thus the two supplies, blood and nerve, must be normal, or disease will show in the bladder, kidneys, and all organs of the body.

The nerve-supply of the bladder is from the third and fourth sacral, and also the hypogastric plexus of the sympathetic. The arteries are the superior and inferior vesical, and in the female the uterine artery also. The veins are the radicals of the internal iliac.

THE RECTUM.

It is my object at this point, in seeking further causes for the diseases of the abdomen, to make another beginning-point, with the rectum, which presents various kinds of diseases. We have congestion, inflammation, ulceration, cancer, prolapse, piles, constricture, inversion, and dilatation following an interference of the nerve-power of the muscles of the anus, which fail to contract with force sufficient to keep the bowels in their normal position. Outside of the effects of poisonous substances that have removed the mucous membrane either by injection of such substances into the bowels or administered by way of the mouth—I say, outside of the poisonous effects of the drugs, we have inflammation, ulceration, and so-called cancerous formations.

Blood- and Nerve-Supply.

We know from our anatomical knowledge that the lower bowel receives its blood-supply from the superior and inferior hemorrhoidal arteries. The nerve-supply governing arterial and venous circulation and lymphatics of this portion of the alimentary tract comes from the pelvic plexus. Neither the blood-supply nor nerve-force should be disturbed or suspended by mechanical or from other cause that would produce paralysis of the vessels or nerves while in receipt or discharge of the fluids intended to keep the rectum in a perfectly normal condition. When we investigate the blood- and nerve-force which has suffered a local suspension, we have two truths before us seeking our acquaintance. One is the blood- and nerve-supply, the other is the nerve-force and blood in return action. The one governs the arterial supply, the other the veins and excretories or drainage. We are not justified in saying or thinking that we have given a wisely constructed or judicious opinion, and omit the most careful inspection with the eye, to detect any and all variations from the perfect mechanical condition. Undisturbed relations must exist in this part of the machinery, whose business it is to receive blood and construct and purify to the last atom every muscle, vein, and artery, even of the nerve itself. As we have found an unhealthy condition of the rectum, or that part of the bowel whose location is confined to the pelvis, it is wisdom to seek an acquaintance with mechanical causes that obstruct the flow of blood- and nerve-forces to and from the lowest parts of the rectum. At this point of exploration, we will consider the pelvic chamber as a cup or tub-shaped chamber, larger at the top than at the bottom. We must see and know that no infringement on this territory exists by the unnatural occupancy of this tub-shaped vessel by the cæcum, which, as we have shown, is often driven into the pelvis by strains and jolts, and very often by the use of powerful purgatives, also following efforts to liberate the bowel from fæcal matter or any chemical or irritating substances. If we find the cæcum in a woman, by digital examination, occupying the pelvis, a condition easily discovered through the vaginal wall, we have discovered one cause of pressure. When the mesentery has been pulled down by cross-pressure of heavy weights on the abdomen, the cæcum can be, has been, and will be pushed clear down into the pelvic chamber to the perineum, which your knowedge of anatomy guarantees to be a correct conclusion as to the abnormal position of that division of the colon. This knowledge should be sought at all times and under all circumstances, when we have diseases of the rectum and their remote and immediate causes for consideration. Let us follow the fact that when the cæcum has descended into the pelvis, it pulls heavily on the transverse colon, and it also irritates the nervous system of the abdomen. In this condition, that division of the colon known as the sigmoid flexure can be thrown from its normal position in the left iliac fossa to the right, with the whole train ditched and piled up in the pelvis. A person of very superficial anatomical knowledge would know that the colon was badly ditched, when the wreck-train of inspection is put into active operation We use the very common and well-known term "ditched," because our patient's bowels are ditched, and badly ditched, and we are expected to straighten the track and replace every car; otherwise we are worse than failures. Our patient will die a death that should be charged to our anatomical stupidity when we pose as skillful osteopathic mechanics.

THE UTERUS.

We will introduce the subject of diseases peculiar to woman by drawing memory to her organs which become temporarily deranged before she feels that she must call in skilled help. Let us open the subject with a few questions of vital importance in the search for facts that will support a positively correct diagnosis, before we offer our services in her behalf with the hope of a cure, or before we will even make an effort to give her temporary or permanent relief. To assist the student in a cautious hunt and correct decision on the course to pursue to obtain such results, we will go to her abdominal house and see how it is furnished, and discover for what each part is intended, what it performs, and how, where, and through what blood-vessels supplies are delivered to keep each part normal in all particulars. Can an organ be normal and be starved? Can an organ be normal and be twisted, when it is naturally straight? Can an organ be normal and another organ prohibit the blood from coming to nourish that organ, to keep it strong and active, that it can do its own part and assist other organs when one depends much or little on the other for assistance? Can an organ do its part with other organs pressing on it too heavily? I have asked a few questions pertaining to organic action and life, because Nature is a school of questions and answers, which seems to be the only school in which man learns anything. This being true, we will make a list of woman's abdominal furniture and its location in the abdominal house. I need not give a list of the names, locations, and functions of the abdominal organs, because I think you know these; but I will give the list, or nearly so, to keep them before your eye and assist you in recognizing the confusion that would make a tumor, leucorrhœa, cancers, etc., targets for allopathy to shoot at with speculum, probe, and caustic. We will begin above or at the upper beginning of the abdominal wall, the diaphragm. It is the dividing sheet or strong muscular wall suspended across the body at the lower end of the chest, separating the chest organs above from the abdominal organs below. Above this wall, we find the lungs and heart. Below, we find the pancreas, spleen, liver, kidneys, uterus, bladder, the stomach, and bowels, both great and small. We find the aorta, vena cava, and their branches, running to and from each organ, all from the one artery. Then we see the organs drained by the vena cava and its tributaries. You see that the supply and drainage of all the organs below the diaphragm is a complete system, which shows great and perfect wisdom in the plan and purpose for which it was formed and placed in position, to do the separate and combined work of the abdominal host. When all do a perfect work, nothing but health can be shown as a result. No disease can possibly come to any of these organs while supply and drainage are absolutely perfect.

Effects of Wounds.

At this time we will change our point of observation and note a few effects of wounds inflicted upon any organ located in the abdomen. A congestion following changes of weather from hot to cold, dry to wet or damp, is a wound. The severity of the shock is shown by its effects on the organs, womb, bladder, and others, by soreness of the abdomen or tenderness, a feeling of weight in the pelvis followed sooner or later by bladder trouble, with a desire to pass water too often, followed by itching of the external parts of the vulva, and possibly hemorrhage. In young women, stopped flow, followed by monthly flooding, ulcers of the womb, polypi, headache, heart trouble, fits, insanity, cancer of the womb, prolapsus, and the growth of tumors, and so on to a long list of female troubles, any and all are possibilities from an injury to the womb that was hurt in-a fall, strain, jar, or shock produced by change of clothing or by atmospheric variations.

As this is not a medical school, it would not be supposed that we would follow old-school teachings in giving relief. When medical schools find a growth or ulcer, they hunt for knife and caustic, cut and burn. You see at once that the theory is to combat the effect, and not the cause. We cure these diseases by subduing the cause that has produced such alarming effects as angry ulcers, cancers, tumors, and all diseases that assail woman. We must apply our mental and physical energies to the place in the spine controlling the blood-supply sustaining the life and health of the womb, the bladder, kidneys, liver, spleen, pancreas, lymphatics, and all parts of abdominal life. Otherwise we are at sea, with no compass to guide us. We leave our patients in the clutches of the beasts of prey, to be cut and slain by the heads and hands that lack knowledge of cause and effect. Medical practitioners chop off and cut out tumors, burn ulcers, and kill by the rule of cut and try, and hope for good results when there is nothing good to hope for. When all kinks are straightened out, giving the strong arm of Nature full charge of the work of righting all wrongs and establishing the normal, beyond which man knows nothing, then we can reasonably hope for recovery.

TUMORS.

Tumors on the womb, by the old system, have been simply looked upon as dead weights that are injurious and of no use to the woman, and the sooner such growths are cut off or burnt out, the better for the woman. No doubt many growths, when first seen by the surgeon, have gone so far into decay that to remove is wise, and we, as osteopaths of good judgment, would proceed to operate and do the best we could to prolong life by removing any dead flesh whose fumes of decomposition would cause disease by their poisonous effects. But all diseases of the organs of the abdomen should have the wisest methods of osteopathy exhausted before the knife is invited to take a part in the effort to rescue the life of the patient. All have agreed long since that tumors and issues mark a cut-off in an artery, vein, or nerve. We are Americans, and have no time or patience to spend with theories that have no practical sense in them, that we cannot use beneficially. If we have a duty to perform, we want to know what that duty is. If it is to put the organs of the abdomen in position and form to act, we want to know it, and no "howevers" about it.

FROM HEALTH TO DISEASE.

I wish now to give a picture of a healthy woman from childhood to womanhood, full of blood and full of life, quick in motion, active in mind, able to answer and act to all the functions of life. You must know what a healthy woman is before you can think and act wisely with the woman who has lost her health, say of her sight, hearing, affecting mind, face, nose, jaw, mouth, tongue, throat, stomach, bowels, liver, kidneys, womb, bladder, vagina, heart, lungs, breasts, and all parts of a perfect woman. It is a perfect woman I want to present to your mind. The first thought of a successful osteopath is perfection, and he must place in mind perfection of form and function of the woman and keep that picture bright in his mind's eye all the time, or he will be a failure as a gynæcologist all his days. Now let us begin with a little girl of five summers. Generally at that age she is a perfect picture of health, perfect in form and action. She has rosy cheeks, sparkling eyes, and silken hair. She runs, jumps, climbs, laughs, sings, and talks from morn till night, sleeps, eats, and is a perfect little machine of human life and action. Now she takes her first change in life by entering the poorly ventilated schoolroom. She is exposed to cold and contagions, sits on benches from two to six hours each day, drags her feet through mud, snow, and ice from six to nine months out of each year. She has later added to her studies the changes from childhood to womanhood. Much of the exercise that gave her brilliancy as a child has been taken from her, and the active liberty that kept rosy her cheeks and gladdened her life changes to inaction, that weakens her whole body so much that she has lost the power to throw off a cold or the effect of changes from hot to cold, from wet to dry, and so on. Blood begins to circulate sluggishly in the brain. She has headache. The spine tires and she stoops forward, causing ribs to change position, closing intercostal arteries the whole length of the chest, and she has a heart under a great strain to force blood through the small arteries that run between the ribs from the aorta. Soon we hear of her as having heart trouble. With that organ disabled, she is a subject for other failures, such as lung diseases, spinal diseases, with all the resulting bad effects, as womb disease, and so on to the full list that follows. We have hastily passed through the life of the child to womanhood, and find that she has changed from a healthy child and girl full of life and vigor to a pitiable condition, sick and diseased all over. When we examined her as a child, we found a good and powerful brain, a healthy spinal cord, and all nerves full of life. As we stopped to view the throat, larynx, pharynx, trachea, and œsophagus, we found them perfectly healthy. A perfect glow of life was absolutely manifest We are so well pleased with the perfection of the form and workings of the parts of the machinery of a healthy girl that we conclude to stay in her body as an explorer. We will camp near the heart and lungs, to us two of the greatest wonders of the works of that unerring architect, God. I want to emphasize *God*, and give to Him the intelligence of a God, a God to be respected and followed to the letter by the doctors of my school. I am talking to the few or many who are not to be pitied for lack of brains to behold and comprehend perfection in the unabused machinery of life, let that abuse come from any causes whatsoever.

GYNÆCOLOGY.

For fear the student will think I have forgotten my subject, the heart and lungs, I will ask him to refresh his mind on those organs of life by a mental review of what he has been carefully and extensively taught of those organs in descriptive and demonstrative anatomy. Your grade-cards report that you have passed above 90 in both branches of anatomy, also in chemistry, urinalysis, histology, physiology, and the principles and practice of osteopathy. Honor bright, do you think you merit the high scale that appears upon all your cards? If you do, and have done your duty, you are ready to hear me upon one of the most important branches taught in the American School of Osteopathy—Gynæcology. Your studies thus far have taught you that the throat, heart, and lungs, with all their attachments with parts of the machinery of life, are and have been dependent on the brain for power, and on the spinal cord for nerve-distribution. I will invite you to go with me from the chest down through the diaphragm to this young lady's common organs of life and procreation. Let me ask you to kindly refresh your mind upon the blood- and nerve-supply of the diaphragm, that great, vital, active, and most important wall of separation, situated between the bony chest and fleshy abdomen. I say, " refresh your minds upon the blood-

and nerve-supply of the diaphragm," because of its uses and very important functional action upon the heart, lungs, and all organs above and below the separating line which it marks. It, too, with all the organs above, must be healthy in form and action; therefore all blood- and nerve-supply must be absolute. If upon this examination we find the diaphragm worthy and well qualified to do the duties incumbent upon it, we will pass on and again pitch our tents, establishing ourselves upon the highest pinnacle of mental observation possible, a philosopher's constant aim when beginning his observations of the harmonies of Nature in all its works. After thoroughly acquainting ourselves with the perfect works of Nature, we begin to fortify our reason by disturbing some part or many parts of the machine which has been doing perfect work. We will bend a shaft, slip a pulley, break a cog, slack a belt, throw dirt, sand, ashes, alkali, or any disturbing substance upon the journals, in the boxes, or any place that will produce a known variation from perfect normality of the machine. We set it to work again, and then compare the difference between the normal and abnormal. Thus his philosophy has given him an answer for both the normal and the abnormal, without which truth no philosopher can afford to commit philosophical suicide. Since we have seen the harmony that prevails below the diaphragm, we cannot do justice to the student and fail to examine the functions of those organs. We ask you at least to mentally run over the organs from your knowledge of anatomy. Now make yourself a child of inquiry and a student of Nature. Turn your eyes upon the pancreas, which lies just below the diaphragm, and rehearse mentally or aloud its blood-supply and its nerve-supply. Ask such questions as these: Why has all this deposit of fat been placed at so important a center? Is it possible that an oily compound is prepared in this little laboratory of animal chemistry and conducted to the liver to be mixed with chalk and other substances to prevent association of such substances to the dangerous degree of gall-stones? If so, a great duty falls upon us, to see to it that no disturbing causes appear that would damagingly affect the functioning of the pancreas. My eyes seem to settle next upon the liver, which is pointed out by my anatomical and physiological compass. Do you agree with me, or have you discovered greater truths by longer and deeper observation of the chemical laboratory beneath the diaphragm? Can we then afford to spend a few days and train our telescopes and microscopes of highest human skill upon the spleen, to observe the effect that would follow a crippling of the functions of that organ? Have we a functional derangement from nerve-disturbance that would cause the lymphatics to reverse their action of construction and throw albumin, fibrin, and watery fluids into the excretory ducts and destroy life by an exhausting drainage? Then we would be face to face with dyspepsia, dropsy, enlarged spleen, engorged liver, cancer, gall-stones, skin eruptions, change of color, constipation, inflammatory diseases, and ulceration of the stomach, bowels, kidneys, and the uterus. If we have observed the perfect, harmonious work of health, we are now prepared to adjust the machinery of life by taking all embarrassments from blood- and nerve-supply that are caused or could be caused by strains, jars, and nervous shocks or wounds that are produced by change of season, climate, and physical injuries of all kinds, be they great or small. Your work is completed when you have adjusted the human body to the degree of perfection in which the God of Nature left it. This is the limit of your usefulness; do your work well and you will get the results sought. Never grow weary in well-doing; we have proven that God is true. Drug systems have long since fallen in the minds of both men and women who have tested all the claims set forth and practiced by the medical schools of the world. If you have the ability to reason, you will be satisfied with the claims of osteopathy.

The Importance of a Healthy Womb.

The womb as a healthy organ would be classed as one of the most healthy organs of woman's system, because of the fact that there is perfect rest in its life from the time of babyhood until about the age of fourteen. Previous to that no action or growth in size or function is taking place, farther than the organ is kept in existence by a system of small arteries and nerves, microscopic in size until womanhood sets in. At the age of about twelve or fourteen years activity for maternal functioning begins to develop its size, with all the glands and appendages necessary for maternal uses. All the time previous to this period in her life, no growth has seemed to be necessary and no change in quality or quantity of blood has had an opportunity to cause disease. Thus no great changes could occur while neither the blood- nor nerve-supply was changing in quantity, motion, or quality. I have given a history of the womb in girl-life when it was in the best of health, in order to get a foundation from which to reason when we consider the womb in its many conditions of disease, as in abnormal discharges, ulcers, tumors, variations from its normal place in health, cancers, wounds caused in childbirth by forceps, retained monthlies, prolapse, sterility, menopause, inversion, procidentia, etc.

Diseases Peculiar to Woman.

What diseases does woman have that man does not have? Such diseases as belong to the womb and its appendages. Beginning with menses and on to pregnancy, delivery, care during and after labor, then variations in the position of the womb from normal, I wish to present her in both the healthy and the unhealthy condition. The osteopath, by his knowledge of her anatomical form and physiological functioning, can easily understand how and why she has changed from a healthy girl to a diseased woman. He can see how she becomes the mother of cancers, tumors, and deadly ulcers that spill her life-blood and cause her frame to yield in death. We must prepare ourselves for a very hard fight in her defense, or we will "lose out" and prove our inability to successfully combat the enemy. We must begin at her bones and know them, their uses and their places; then the binding ligaments of all the bones, and in particular her spine and pelvis. We must know them when normal, and qualify our hands, eyes, and reason to know when and how to detect any slip of bone or muscle or ligament. We must reason and search until we know what effect would be produced on any organ of the chest or abdomen by an anterior, posterior, or lateral change of the atlas, axis, or other bones of the neck; what effect on the heart would follow the changed position of a rib or vertebra from the first to the twelfth dorsal, the lumbar, sacrum, and innominates, because of a slip or change from the normal. Would it send more or less blood to the brain? The force would vary in proportion and allow the lungs to suffer loss of power in purifying the blood, and then a failure in the power of the heart would appear, and it would not be able to perform its functions; then a stagnation of blood would appear in the liver, spleen, pancreas, and so on *ad infinitum*. As a result, we would have disease from congestion and sluggish action in the organs upon which a healthy womb has to depend for its vitality and functioning in its part of the laboratory of animal life. To be diseased, then, would be a natural consequence. Since we have a weak heart to propel the blood, a weak set of lungs to purify the blood, and the liver, spleen, kidneys, and lymphatics filled with fluids other than healthy, and slow in action from a feeble heart, we can expect a process of active fermentation to set up and create from perverted fluids exciting substances that will annoy the nerves to abnormal activities, causing fits, hysteria, insanity, growths, tumors, sloughing and bleeding surfaces or ulcers of various cancerous natures that whip up all the nervous forces of the heart to drive the blood to repair the ulcerations; but when that blood arrives, it is poured out into space, because the blood-terminals are sloughed off. Cancers of the womb and bladder are found in their most malignant forms from causes above noted. The next thing to do is to set out to find the causes that produced those conditions. It matters not whether the cause is far remote or in close proximity to the uterus; we must find it, or we will be found in the antediluvian tribe of speculum cranks of all the blind female doctors' ages. We must stand true to the light and reason of anatomy or join the mourners who wail because their tricks are not now nor ever have been trumps when battling for a woman's health under the old tree that has nothing but woodpeckers' holes in its trunk and limbs.

Nature Our School.

To-day is our day, Nature is our school, and we must go by the pointings of the compass. We can never improve old theories to the degree of truths. They are not based upon facts. When we turn our eyes and look back for truths, back from Nature, we only behold the dark clouds of dying theories, without a single friend to mourn their loss. In osteopathy we have the tree of life, and the living man in it. Our science sees him, our science has proven him to be a living man, proven him to be the work of a living God, a wise God, whose works are alive and show wisdom in form and purposes. We must learn that Nature means wisdom, means mental ability, means business honesty, and we must not disobey its teachings. Nature never made a philosopher. He made the man to learn and act. Man can make of himself a philosopher or fool. The schools of Nature are all open and free to him. He can learn the lessons and become wise if he obeys the teachers; otherwise he learns little and his knowledge is of little use all his days. He has missed his opportunities; he is mentally unprepared for duties as a leader and as a teacher; he is only a slave to a theoretical life. In him there is nothing that is really useful, more than perhaps an ability to operate a bucksaw, and not even good at that, because there is more practice in that operation than theory. He fails for want of theories.

ANATOMICAL DIFFERENCES.

In this talk on the diseases of woman, I think about the best method would be to state or line up the diseases with which she is most liable to be afflicted. In general forms, the woman is just the same as man. They both have brains, spine, and limbs, the same in form, location, and use. Both have heart, lungs, diaphragm, pancreas, liver, spleen, stomach, bowels, and kidneys. They are both the same, so far, anatomically. At this point the explorer begins to notice a difference in the form of muscles, nerve-supply, shape, and the functions of the generative organs. At this time a mental halt is called. The mind finds that a new book opens to its view, and the student begins to ponder and question for light. What design could Nature have had in so wide a difference in the form and functions of these organs? He answers that question as best he may. With rapidity of thought and reason he then argues that as they differ in form and function, they will show the effect of diseases in a different manner from the organs common to both sexes, such as brain, heart, and lungs. The reader comes to the conclusion that woman would be affected just the same as man in all parts except in the generative system, which is different from the man's. In man we find more kidney diseases and inflammations of different kinds, the effects of strains, lifts, falls, overwork, heat, cold, fevers of climate and change of season. But we cannot reason that disease will show the same effect on the general system of woman that is shown in the man, when both are not alike in form and parts. Undoubtedly reason has claimed our attention and forced us to see and conclude that we must look for that which her make-up points us to when she is sick. We know that disease is an effect of some action that is abnormally producing it, and when the normal chain is broken, we know that the brain obeys the law of stimulants and narcotics. With no intention or expectation to make an apology for the cause I have undertaken to champion, I raise my flag in open view before the world with the inscription in the blackest letters, "No Quarter!" for any theory or practice that has no respect for a woman's modesty, no feeling whether she suffers much or little, is maimed for life, lives or dies, so she can be inveigled into a hospital to receive the torture of experimentation and death, or accidental recovery, by the hands of stupidity that are flourished by the present day gynæcologist, all for the amount of money that can be extorted from husband, father, or friends. I do object most emphatically to the every-day evidences of the bad teachings of the present-day medical institutions. Our school wants none of it. Our school has no use for its teachings. There is no osteopathy in it, and less truth. In behalf of the tortured, both living and dead, whose lives have been sacrificed boldly on the altar of the present-day teachings in gynæcology, on behalf of all womankind, I have raised the black flag of eternal vengeance upon the brutal system of obstetrics and the treatment of woman's afflictions, from the school-girl up to the oldest mothers and grandmothers. We want none of it taught, none of it practiced in this school. This school was not created for a slaughter-house, neither will it be tolerated as such by the scrutinizing eyes of the board of trustees. The suggestions of anatomy and physiology must be learned, must be taught, and must be practiced; then peace and harmony will prevail. My mother shall not be slaughtered; my wife shall not be butchered, nor my daughter stripped and exposed

Our Instruments.

An osteopath who knows his business has no use for a speculum, no use for a steel spindle or sound in the treatment of female diseases. Once in a thousand times the accoucheur's forceps may be admitted in case of pelvic deformity. Explorations and treatments by the osteopath who is worthy of the title D.O. should deliver nine hundred and ninety-nine children out of one thousand with no instrument but his hands; otherwise he is not fit to be trusted with birth of child and care of mother and offspring. It is not only a request and demand, but an order to be remembered, that osteopathy as a science is wholly independent of all other theories. Our works must show improvement or stop. Osteopathic truths can be taught, demonstrated, and practiced successfully and satisfactorily, and explained in words of the American language. Don't look for others. Remember that at the end of four hundred years we have had selected and compiled in our dictionaries upwards of one hundred and fourteen thousand choice words for our use. We contend that they have a place in our finest literature, equal to the best in the world. We can give the very best instruction with their use, and it is the object of our school to teach and practice the skilled arts of all branches with and through the words of our own language. We are not here to make a show of scholarship with words taken from the tongues of the antediluvian world. We are here to call a horse a horse, to demonstrate what we assert, and leave the results to be accepted or rejected by men and women who can and will think in the words of our own blessed language. An American should be proud of his country for having selected and compiled from the tongues of the world a sufficiency of words and phrases not equalled by any other tongue spoken now or in the days of the past. Cut out your Greek and Latin. "Talk United States."

THE MACHINE GIVES OUT.

Does the woman get sick? Yes. Why and how does she get sick? Because she is a machine made for life's purposes, and that machinery gives out by wear and abusive care, or lack of knowing how to care for it. What parts are the most liable to get out of good operative conditions? One part is no more liable to get out of working order than any other. Is the womb more liable to become disabled than other parts? No; because it was made to do its work and no more. It has, occasionally, long-time jobs to do, which it must stay with and superintend for nine or ten months. Other organs have to feed the womb to order and on time while in this service or contract job. It is like a vessel of the sea after returning from a long voyage; it has to report a very rough trip from start to return. When the ship goes in for inspection and repairs, she is dry-docked or raised out of the water, so that the master ship-builder can see her, learn how storms affected her hull, engine, boiler, and through a complete course of inspection, ocular, historical, and otherwise. He hands in his report: "She is not seaworthy. I find that all parts have suffered strains about equally, and it is a wonder that she has made the last trip when all parts have suffered almost to collapse. I have to report as inspector that a complete overhauling, leveling and plumbing, and rest for the crew is necessary, or another such voyage will mark a lost vessel."

EXAMINATION.

I have tried to tell the student that to do justice to gynæcological service, he must be a workhand in the navy-yard of life, and must examine the whole vessel when she comes to the dock for repairs. It is not necessary to look at the bottom of the ship all the time. Look at all parts with equal energy. Go over the hull and see if holes or cracks let water come into the hull. Don't do anything to her till the doctor says, "Endosmosis." Go to the boiler, and if you find a leakage of steam, lay down your hammer and rivets until the master mechanic says, "This is a bad case of exosmosis." Then be careful to wait until the chief boss says, "Osmosis" Then go to work, for osmosis or action is what is needed on the ship. You need Greek words, a Yankee hammer, a Dutch pipe, and sense enough to know that vessels get strained all over and all parts need careful attention, before you go to work to put all in good sea-worthy shape, previous to her discharge out of dry-dock for another voyage. All combinations for the purpose of giving motion to this vessel must first be known, with instructions of how much repair is needed, before the subordinate workman is supposed to proceed with the work of repairs. After this wise precaution, the skilled workman has no difficulty in knowing and doing the duties incumbent upon him. As no two vessels are likely to show the same effect from injuries received in storms, the important answer appears that no book of instructions can be writen by the wisest mechanic so perfectly as to reach the condition of any vessel that comes into the dock for inspection and repairs. One vessel may bump its bow against a large cake of ice, a stone, or another vessel, straining every bolt and the whole vessel from top to bottom, length and width, receiving a universal shock or strain. Another vessel may strike a reef in a quartering position or any other angle of contact. The result could not be expected to be the same. If a boiler should blow out, a man-head or a steam-chest explode, the result would be expected to be different from other causes. Thus we behold effects, proceed to hunt the cause, and repair according to the demands indicated by the discovery of the cause that has produced the abnormality.

I suppose we have no student who is worthy of a seat in the third or fourth term who is so stupid as not to be able to take up the woman and examine the surface of the body as an inspector would examine the spine or main beam of the vessel. He would see if that beam was stove up at either end from a shock or fall sufficient to slip any member of the spinal column from its true position, producing a bend or variation that would cause a suspension of healthy nerve- or blood-supply where force or nourishment were required to sustain the vital energy of organs of life, of muscle and motion. As a woman is the vessel that has come into port and gone into dry-dock for repairs, it is supposed that before we will commence any repairing we will carefully explore her spine, brain, lungs, heart, liver, and kidneys, omitting no part, and know that there is not complete harmony of action of all organs before we treat in a local way a prolapsed or diseased womb. It would be very unphilosophical to begin at the womb with our treatment and hope for good results, when the cause for its disability was at another point or place of nerve- and blood-supply. Right here I want to keep before you the arteries that nourish and supply the womb, and the nerves of sensation, motion, and nutrition of the organ, and the veins that convey the blood back to the heart. A short review of anatomy and physiology will refresh your minds on the important lessons on nerve- and blood-supply of the uterus and its appendages. As time is important to me and to you also, I will omit this minutiæ. With a clear comprehension of anatomy and physiology, abnormal growths with their causes are easily comprehended. Bloody and other wastings, with their causes, can easily be known and successfully relieved.

The Normal and Abnormal.

When we take up the diseases of woman as a subject of thought, we must confine them to her form, and that form in its most perfect condition. Then mentally we see a brain of perfect action in all its performances. We see a spinal cord with its army of life, all in motion, obeying all orders of a wonderful government, with every officer at the head of his division, repeating orders and having all work done to the finest rules of perfection. We must view her as perfection in all her form, her limbs all perfect for motion and their destined uses. Then take a stand for a bird's-eye view of all parts of her body. See that the liver, spleen, kidneys, and all internal organs are normal in size and place. Go to the bones of the spine and ribs, see them and behold all as truly perfect. Then take a physiological view and see the functioning of perfect life in the laboratory of a perfect woman. We will take up the subject of her abnormal condition with the view of discussing the causes that have produced the changed condition of brain, lungs, heart, liver, spleen, kidneys, pancreas, bowels, stomach, uterus, or nervous system. If her brain, heart, lungs, and all her organs have once been perfectly healthy and normal in all their functionings, why have they failed, one at a time, in so many places, that the body as a whole becomes a perfect wreck? Her brain was once perfectly healthy, ready to execute all duties that Nature required of it. The same was true of the lungs and all the other organs. Why has this great change given her abnormality in place of the harmony she at one time possessed? On examination, a slight disturbance is found in the lung, a tickling cough sets in and is continued with some gain in severity as months go on. There is a little quivering of the heart, and occasionally a lost beat in the pulse. Soon another disturbance appears; pain in the region of the liver, also on the left side in the region of the spleen. Then another break appears. An irregularity of the appetite is complained of, her stomach generates and throws off gas, and she looks pale and grows weakly. Finally she has added to these troubles misery and cutting pains in the region of the kidneys. After a few weeks or months in this condition, she reports that her monthlies are not acting on regulaar time; that she suffers a great amount of pain in the lower abdomen, with blood flowing until she can scarcely walk. She consults a medical doctor, and he very wisely tells her that she has a bad case of ovaritis; that the leukocytes of the epithelial tissue of the vulva must be examined *per vaginam* with a speculum at once, and that he must be quick about it. She is turned up in the Sims position, then on genupectoral position of exposure, and is told she must undergo an operation. She is sent off to some doctor who treats, cures, and kills, all for the dollars there are in it. The doctor who sends her in for the operation in nine cases out of ten gets one-half of the five hundred dollars. Then the minister gets ten dollars as her "sky pilot." It is not necessary to tell you this is true. You know that it is true. We want no such sins placed to our credit when Gabriel calls for our books.

Treatment.

The student asks the question, "How would you treat womb troubles?" The osteopath of skill can easily give the answer; he is trained to treat such troubles. The first step is to open the back door and throw out your speculum, probes, pessaries, syringes, dopes, and medicated cotton. Then begin at the nerves that caused her the first little hacking cough, and stay with an exploring eye and hand placed on the neck and upper dorsal until the cut-off is found that stopped the normal blood- and nerve-supply and caused constricture of the respiratory pipe from her mouth to her lungs. Make them take their places. Then you are ready to drop the lungs and look for the nerve- and blood-supply of the heart. Now you are ready to give her liver, spleen, pancreas, kidneys, and lymphatics a visit, as an explorer who has use for the most exacting and most thorough study of the true physiological perfection of the functions of the organs named. He has no business with her womb until he has stopped and booked practical knowledge at all points torn down by the disease that began at the lungs and prepared the womb to fail to perform its normal functions. I have just supposed a case, beginning at the lungs with only a slight cough, and followed its progressive effects from a simple cold through all the organs of the body, and found them giving way, one at a time, in quick or slow succession, until all were wounded or diseased, before the womb succumbed and became alarmingly diseased. I have tried to show you that the womb disease was only an effect, and the cause of its weakness was due to organs that it depended upon for health and strength. They had lost their power to keep the womb well nourished; the womb itself was not at fault in the cause of the disease. We have given you a case of womb disease, a dangerous ulceration of mucous membrane, to show the students how to hunt and find the beginning or remote causes that the doctor should always have in mind when he takes a case for treatment. Ever remember that ulcers, tumors, leucorrhœa, hemorrhages, and delayed or retained monthlies are all the results of preceding causes, that affect the womb by contracting its outlet by a constant irritation of the circular nerves of the os. This irritation may be caused in bony alteration in the spine between the eighth dorsal vertebra and the coccyx. Defects of the spine and sacrum in their articulations have caused strictures of the mouth of the womb. An M.D. will tell her to get on his table, give her Sims' or some other pet position, and then, after exploring her person, insert a speculum and push into the womb a pair of dilating tongs, tearing the womb open. We have no use for such indecent exposure or the stupid operator. We correct articulations in the spine, bones of the pelvis, and organs of the abdomen, and take away by that method all irritation from the constrictor nerves and the vaso-dilators We have no need for tongs to let monthly fluids flow easily from the womb. You must drop the tool idea. It is the breech-clout of the obsolete past, and is only kept up by ignorance of what a woman is.

WHITES, LEUCORRHŒA.

A few sensible Americanized questions and answers, such as. What is the disease you call leucorrhœa or whites? Why do you call it leucorrhœa? Does *leuco* mean something that is white? Why do you give nothing but big names and leave out causes? Why does she waste off or out that white compound? Our old authors have never told us a word that would point the student to the cause of such wasting of the bread and meat of a woman's life. Is not her blood the bread and meat that sustain her life? If so, what effect would be natural to take away her life support? How high up her back and how low down on her sacrum will the student find nodes or clusters of lymphatics, glands, blood-supply, fascia, muscles, membranes, cells, secretions, and excretions, venous drainage, and arterial supply? In a word, why are we summoned to learn how to cure an affliction on whose cause you can give us no light? As this is said to be a school of philosophers, where is the philosophy you have to offer the anxious seeker? When the pilot gets lost, then a committee of the whole is formed and suggestions are in order, from all or anyone. A new pilot is sought. Trouble is in the camp, a remedy is demanded. The life of the old pilot will pay the penalty. A mutiny is in all the camps. A Moses must be found to lead. No old field-notes will suit for guides. We have followed them to the letter. We are lost, and to follow farther will be suicidal. "Nature's compass must guide us," is the report of the committee of the whole. Now let Moses tell what leucorrhœa is, and its cure.

DROPSY.

The woman has dropsy to contend with. That does not come from her lungs (a dropsical condition often comes in consumption as a final wind-up). In case a patient with dropsical swelling of body and limbs should come to you for examination, I would advise a careful one, beginning with the atlas. Be very careful to know that it is true with the skull in all positions. A slip of the odontoid process over the transverse ligament would place the atlas on a lateral and downward pressure on the lymphatic nerves just below the axis. A failure of the cellular action would follow, and lymphatic and cellular membrane would retain water and other fluids in the lung muscles and the heart and pleura. Thus a beginning is established for general dropsy. Now follow up the process of crippling other nerves below, to the full extent of the body and limbs. A break of the articulations of the upper dorsal will cut off the powers of all nerves of supply and drainage below the point of broken perfection. Then you have a cause for enlargement of the liver, spleen, kidneys, and all organs below the diaphragm. The time to reason is the time when we are in prison, badly treated, and want to get out. The time has come for all fairly good thinkers to think themselves out of Osler, Byron Robinson, Shaley, and all prisons of torture.

In speaking to students on the subject of the uterus, giving its abnormal conditions, such as tumors, cancers, and other growths that change the uterus from the healthy to the unhealthy, we presented first the normal, healthy uterus as a guide to the knowledge of the differences between the healthy and the unhealthy womb. The object of the doctor is to relieve when employed to treat the abnormal uterus. He should at all times hold the picture of the normal uterus before his mind, as to form, size, and location, its blood- and nerve-supply. It would, as I consider it, be quite useless to consume your time on descriptive anatomy at this point, farther than to say that the blood-supply of this organ comes mainly from the ovarian, internal pudic, and uterine arteries. We will simply mention the sympathetic plexuses, with the lumbar, lower dorsal, and sacral nerves in their relation to the uterus, constituting its nerve-supply, and the importance of having the venous system perfectly undisturbed, that it can easily pass the venous blood, whose vitality has been exhausted while in the service, into the vena cava through its ordinary route to the heart, previous to being thrown into the lungs for final mixture with air and lymph, at which place it receives the nutriment for new blood, to be returned to the heart for general distribution. We are in full view of two channels that become obstructed previous to the growth of any tumor or malformation of the uterus, ovaries, Fallopian tubes, or any parts of this system. These two channels in which the venous blood and the lymph can be checked or stopped are known to us as the lymphatic and venous channels. How they are stopped in transit long enough to do mischief with and in the vicinity of these organs is the question that we must solve, or grope in the dark with no certainty of good results in banishing the oppressive causes of uterine deformities. We can reason that if we ligate a uterine artery, we have cut off nutrition and the organ becomes atrophied or shrunken. Then, on the other hand, if we stop the venous return by ligation, either with a cord or compress, and have left the arterial circulation undisturbed, the venous blood will accumulate and unite with the lymph and become a nucleus for tumors of various dimensions, which could not have had existence had the blood- and nerve-systems not been disturbed by being shut off

Cause of Uterine Disturbances.

With this knowledge of the form and functions of the uterus and all that belongs to it, we are prepared to seek and know the cause of uterine disturbances. A successful healing of the uterus and its appendages depends wholly upon the nutriment delivered by the artery, the drainage by the venous system, and the unobstructed nerve-force necessary to normal uterine health. Now let us proceed to hunt for the causes that would interfere with the harmony of the blood- and nerve-systems of the womb. Let us force the cæcum, which is two or three inches in diameter, into the pelvis down to the level with the perineum, and drag the uterus down by the side of the rectum in a position between the rectum and cæcum. Pile the small intestine and mesentery on top of the uterus when wedged down into the pelvis in this position; then from the left side bring the sigmoid colon with its contents on top of this heap; then have a dropping toward the pelvis of the transverse colon. You have a heavy strain on the mesentery of the descending colon and transverse and cæcum, all pointing and settling down with their contents upon the uterus. We see at once a system of ligation of all the uterine blood-vessels and nerves, excepting the uterine arteries, which continue to pump arterial blood into the muscles and membranes of the uterus. Thus we have a cause for unlimited growth, and we can expect tumors, and would be very much disappointed if we did not find them. If we wish to reduce the tumor, we must proceed to remove the obstructing causes, with the expectation of relieving and reducing the abnormal growths through natural channels of drainage. One would say, "How large a tumor can be reduced by the natural drainage?" I cannot answer that question. I have reduced a number whose diameter was from four to six inches, without the use of the surgeon's knife. I am satisfied that some tumors are not reducible, from the fact that they have passed the point of vital response before applying for a osteopathic treatment.

LESS HASTE WITH THE KNIFE.

Let me ask the surgeon of our gynæcological department not to be too hasty in the use of the knife, when a supposed tumor of the ovaries, uterus, or Fallopian tubes appears. Remember that life is very sacred and the responsibility is great, and that wisdom is often cautious procrastination. We want to know to a certainty that the only hope to save life is in the use of the knife before we use it. We should prove by skill, time, and patience that all the organs of the abdomen have been adjusted and kept in their normal places, to do their fullest and best work in carrying off all fluids that can be taken away from the tumor by the excretories of the uterus and all its appendages. The blood and lymph that is being delayed by any ligatory cause must move on, be that in the mesentery, omentum, or bowels, caused by having been twisted, folded, or fallen into the pelvis by lifts, strains, or irritable effects of drugs. We must remember that no tumor can form without a cause, and that the cause is surely a break in the action of one or more of the organ's nerves or blood-vessels. We know that no tumor can be made from nothing, and we also know that blood brings all the substances that are found in the make-up of all tumors. We will reason that if we do not want it to grow larger, we must know the blood-vessels that bring the blood by which it is being built will go on until the blood stops coming or passes away by the veins or excretories.

Make your diagnosis exhaustive before you are satisfied that there is an abnormal growth in the vicinity of or on the uterus We should be very careful about it, from the fact that fæcal deposits in some divisions of the colon have the appearance of a tumor, and these should be investigated before the diagnosis is announced of a uterine tumor. Preparatory to exploring for tumors of fleshy growths or deposits of fæcal matter in the colon, we recommend placing the patient in the knee-

and-chest position, with the chest for ease and comfort resting on a pillow, allowing the chin to hang over the head end of the table. Pass the right hand across the body in the lumbar region and under the abdomen to the right iliac fossa. Then place the right hand flat upon the bowels from the pelvis, with the left hand pressing gently on that part of the abdomen. Be slow and gentle in all movements, for fear of bruising the cæcum, ileo-cæcal valve, and the mesentery of that region. Make a gentle, strong pressure upward toward the ribs with the ascending colon. Follow across the abdomen from right to left, in order to straighten up the transverse colon to its normal position. Then lay the hand back toward the symphysis and gently press the sigmoid division toward the stomach, with a view to pulling that division of the colon and small intestine out of the pelvis. Then, with both hands gently and firmly pressed upon the anterior region of the abdomen, come up toward the stomach with this gliding motion, with a view to straightening the bowels, from the cæcum to the transverse, the descending and sigmoid division to the rectum. Also adjust the mesentery in all its attachments both to the large and small intestines, and give freedom to the ileo-cæcal valve, that the softening fluids may pass without delay into and through the colon. By so doing, we set at liberty and give freedom to the blood- and nerve-supply of the uterus, ovaries, and Fallopian tubes. We also take all pressure off the nerves which govern the uterus and venous motion of blood from the pelvis and through the whole uterine system of blood, nerves, and lymphatics, in the hope that proper reduction of uterine growths may be the result following excretory action of the uterus and its normal functioning process; also that the hardening fæces may be softened and passed out with the assistance of the fluids penetrating the colon after being set free from the small intestine after passing the ileo-cæcal valve in the colon. This treatment should be followed every two or three days until the abdominal viscera become normal in action and abnormal bulks have passed away through the universal excretory system of the abdomen, with all of which you are well acquainted by your knowledge of anatomy and physiology. Don't fail to persevere in well-doing.

Tumefaction.

Webster's definition of "tumefaction" is: "To swell by any fluids or solids being detained abnormally at any place in the body."

The location may be in or on any part of the system. No part is exempt. The brain, heart, lungs, liver, stomach and bowels, bladder, kidneys, uterus, lymphatics, glands, nerves, veins, arteries, skin, and all membranes are subject to swellings locally or generally, and with equal certainty they perish and shrink away. If either condition should exist, death to the parts or all of the body will occur from want of nutrition; for instance, in lung fever, which begins when swelling is established in the lymphatics of the lungs, trachea, nostrils, throat, and face. We find the nerve-fibers compressed to such a degree that they cannot operate the excretories of the lungs or any part of the pulmonary system. The blood in veins .is suspended by irritation of the nerves, and arteries are excited to fever heat with the increase of the tumefaction. A tumefying condition undoubtedly marks the beginning of all catarrhal diseases. Its ravages extend to diseases of the fall and winter seasons. They are so marked on examination that the most skeptical cannot dispute or doubt the truth of this position.

The medical doctor looks on, and treats winter diseases with powerful purgatives, sweats, blisters, and uses hot and cold applications with a view to removing congesting fluids. He is not very certain which team of medical power he can depend upon. He hitches up various kinds of drugs, hoping that a few of them may be able to carry the burden. He bridles his horses with opium, loads them down with purgative powders, and whips them through with castor oil, and for fear they will not travel fast enough, he uses as a spur a delicately formed instrument know as the hypodermic syringe. He punches and prods until his horses fall exhausted. Disease and death should give him a large pension for the assistance he has rendered in their service. All is guess-work, whose father and mother are "tradition and ignorance." It is ignorance of the kind that is wholly inexcusable to anyone but a medical doctor. An osteopath who does not understand the general law of tumefaction is a failure because of the fact that tumefaction, disease, and death are so plainly written on the face of all diseases that the blind need not have eyes to see, nor the philosopher any brain to enable him to know this foundation is the highest known truth of all man's intellectual possessions. Thus, by the law of tumefaction, death can and does succumb to its indomitable will. Observation will show any fair-minded person that tumefaction causes death in the majority of cases. But another power is equally as effective in destruction of life, which is just the reverse of tumefaction. It destroys by withholding nutrition and all of the fluids, and the effect is starvation, shrinkage, and death. Thus you see it is equally certain in results. In the one case death ensues from an overplus of unappropriated fluids of nutrition; in the other there is no appropriation to sustain animal life, and the patient dies from starvation. The same law holds good in any part as well as in the whole body.

CHAPTER X.

Fevers.

What Are Fevers?

Bilious fever, yellow fever, chills and fever, and every name and grade of fevers are effects of interrupted or perverted physiological functioning.

Drugs a Failure.

With my fifty years of experience in treating disease in its great multitude of forms, I feel that I am competent to speak of the weakness of drug medication theories and the drug medication training followed in the so-called "old schools of medicine." I was a disciple of the "old school" for many years and among its most faithful practitioners, until a better intelligence and a better understanding of God's provisions for the cure of human ills in the body mechanism itself led me to sever the ties that once held me blindly to drug medication.

Typhoid fever, bilious fever, yellow fever, scarlet fever, mountain fever, hectic fever, and all other fevers known by various names, are simply effects with different appearances; but to seek and to know the cause or causes that produced the effects has ever been lost sight of by the doctors of the "old school." No attention, or very little, if any, has ever been given to the parts of the body in a search for physical changes that have caused unnatural conditions in functions. They have been drilled in the faith that symptoms, well known, constitute a sufficient wisdom with which to open the fight. The drug physician finds some "heat" in the patient. He thinks that if he learns how "hot" his patient is, he then is in a position prepared to open the combat. He feels for his "pig-tail thermometer," and lo! he finds that it has slipped through a hole in his pocket and is lost. And the owner of the thermometer is just as totally lost.

The M. D.'s training is largely limited to observation of pulse and temperature. In the case of fever he has been loaded up with the importance of finding out how "hot" his patient is in the morning and how much hotter he gets at night, on through the days as the disease grows older in days and weeks. He is exhorted to keep a record of the degrees of heat, two, four, six, twelve, and twenty-four hours apart, and keep a similar tab on the pulse. He has been well drilled in the use of his unclean thermometer that goes into the rectum, the vagina, under the arm, and then into the mouth of a patient, but no thought is given to the physical changes of form or the functions of the affected organs of the body. Nor is the student of that school shown the causes of the change in temperature and pulse. His leading guides stick in their examinations and diagnosis to the pulse. He pulls out his watch and times the beats of the heart at 6 A. M., writes 83; at 6 P. M., 85; next day at 6 A. M., 84; at night, 87; and so the record of gains or losses goes on.

He has learned to tell what his patient's temperature is each day for a week; how much headache or limbache he has had; how body-tired and how sore he has been; how thirsty he was; how many times the bowels moved in twenty-four hours, how yellow, brown, red, or furrowed the tongue has been on the first, the fifth, seventh, ninth, and fifteenth days; but he has never been told by his school that these symptoms are only the effects and not the cause of disease.

"Now we have the symptoms, and we will put them all in a row and name the disease," says the medical doctor. "We will call it typhoid, bilious, or by some other name before we begin to treat it. Now that we have named it, we will run out our munitions of war and pour in hot shot and shell at each symptom." The command is given, "Throw into the enemy's camp a large shell of purgative, marked 'hydrargyri chloridum mite.'" Then the order comes to stop that groaning and those pains. "Fire a few shots into the arm with a hypodermic syringe loaded with a grain of morphine," is the next command. Then one might add, "Look at the pigtailum oftenum and note the temperum till it reaches 106." But he is given no idea of the cause of the trouble on which to reason.

An Array of Truths.

The above is given as an array of truths from start to finish. My object is to draw the mind of the student of osteopathy to the necessity of his thinking well as he reads books on diseases written by medical authors. One of the requirements of the old school, and one on which so much stress is laid, is the knowledge of symptomatology by which they are first to name the disease, the name to give them a foundation on which to build the course of treatment by drugs. Their books generally begin by telling us that fever is an abnormal heat that shows a degree of abnormality beginning at about 99 degrees Fahrenheit, and often running to 105 and 106 degrees. These effects are told and pointed out in detail, and if a certain amount of symptoms are found in a case, that case must be called typhoid fever and treated by the sacred rules laid down centuries ago for the treatment of that disease. Still they tell us that "they are self-limited diseases." Then they take up other fevers whose symptoms are similar in so many respects that one is puzzled to know what name to give the disease. He does not find quite enough symptoms to warrant him in calling it typhoid fever Then he is at sea without a compass and is left to do the best he can, even though boat and crew may be lost

We are in the beginning of the twentieth century, and the wisest doctors of all our schools and systems of the healing art have said that typhoid fever is "a self-limited" disease, in the treatment of which "drugs are a total failure." This, in substance is the conclusion of them all, excepting the most bigoted, and we believe that the conclusion is an honest and a wise one. The old-school physician is now saying, "Keep out the drugs and bring in the nurses." And I will say, that they give to the world no more light on any other fever, and no more hope to succeed with drugs in the treatment of any other fever. I believe that they have turned on their very best searchlights and ploughed through every possible sea in their hunt for the wise god of drugs, and all in vain.

I have been your leader for nearly thirty years, but I have had no books to guide me excepting those on descriptive and demonstrative anatomy, and those few in such crude form that they only suggest the wondrous provision that the God of Nature has placed in man with which to ward off or banish the cause of disease, if man were only studious and would only learn enough to detect the variations, and readjust the deviations back to the normal. I have long since believed that an engineer of the human body was the sick man's only hope, and to become a competent engineer the student must become masterly proficient in the knowledge of all the parts of that wonderful machine and the functions of all its parts. Not only to know the anatomical forms and positions of the parts, but to thoroughly know the entire system, the head, neck, chest, abdomen, pelvis, and limbs, with each separate function, and all functions in harmonious combination, free to perform their work as Nature had planned for man's health and comfort.

Begin with Facts.

When we reason for causes, we must begin with facts, and hold them constantly in line. It would be a good plan for you never to enter into a contest unless your saber is of the purest steel of reason. With the best only can you cut your way to the magazine of truth.

As we line up to learn something of the causes of fever, we are met by heat, a living fact. Does that put the machinery of your mind in motion? If not, what will arouse your mental energy? You see that heat is not like cold. It is not a horse with eyes, head, neck, body, limbs, and tail, but it is as much of a being as a horse. It is a being of heat. If cause made the horse and cause made the heat, why not devote energy in seeking the cause of both?

Who says heat is not a union of the human gases with oxygen and other substances as they pass out of the excretory system? By what force do parts of the engine of life move? If by the motor power of electricity, how fast must the heart or life-current run to ignite the gases of the body and set a person on fire to fever heat? If we know anything of the laws of electricity, we must know that velocity modulates its temperature. Thus heat and cold are the effects. If we understand anatomy as we should, we know man is the greatest engine ever produced, complete in form, an electro-magnet, a motor which would be incomplete if it could not burn its own gases.

On Fire.

When man is said to have fever, he is only "on fire" to burn out the deadly gases which a perverted, abnormal laboratory has allowed to accumulate by friction of the journals of his body or in the supply of vital fluids. We are only complete when normal in all parts; a true compass points to the normal only.

When reasoning on the fever subject, would it not be reasonable to suppose that the lowest perceptible grade of fever requires a less additional physical energy to remove the cause from the body, which at first would show a very light effect upon the system, with an effect of simply an itching sensation? Might not this effect come from obstructed gases that flow through and from the skin? If gas should be retained in the system by the excretory ducts, closing the porous system, it would cause irritation of nerves and increase the heart's action to such a degree that the temperature would be raised to a fever heat by the velocity with which electricity is brought into action. Electricity is the force that is naturally required to contract muscles and force gases from the body.

Let us advance higher in the scale until we arrive at the condition of steam, which is more dense than gas. Would it not take more force to discharge it? By the same rule of reasoning we find water to be much thicker as an element than either gas or steam.

Then we have lymph as another element, albumin, fibrin, with all the elements found in arterial and venous blood, all of which would require forces to circulate them, pass them through and out of the system. Therefore we are brought to the conclusion, that the different degrees of temperature mark the density of the fluids with which the motor engine has to contend. If gas produces an itching sensation, would it not be reasonable to suppose that the consistence of lymph would cause elevations on the skin, such as nettle-rash?

We Are Led On.

If this method of reasoning sustains us thus far, why not argue that albumin obstructed in the system of the fascia would require a much greater force to put it through the skin? The excretions of the body would cause a much greater heat to even throw the albumin as far as the cuticle. Why not grant this a cause of the disturbance of motor energy equal to measles? Let us add to this albumin a quantity of fibrin. Have we not cause to expect the energy hereby required to be equal to the nerve- and blood-energy found in smallpox? If this be true, have we not a foundation on which to base the conclusion that the difference in forces manifested is the resistance offered by the differences in the consistency of devitalized fluids which the nerves and fibers of the fascia are laboring to excrete?

By close observation the philosopher who is endeavoring to acquaint himself with the laws of cause and effect finds upon his voyage as an explorer that Nature acts for wise purposes, and shows as much wisdom in the construction and preparation of all bodies, beings, and worlds as the workings of those beings show when in action. As life, the highest known principle sent forth by Nature to vivify, construct, and govern all beings, it is expected to be the indweller and operator, and one of the greatest perceivable and universal laws of Nature. When it becomes necessary to break the friendly relation between life and matter, Nature closes up the channels of supply. It may begin its work near the heart, at the origin of the greatest blood-vessels, or do its work at any point. It may begin its closing process at the extremities of the veins, or anywhere that exhausted vital fluids may enter on their return to the heart for renewal by union with new material.

As Nature is never satisfied with incompleteness in anything, all interferences, from whatsoever cause, are sufficient for Nature to call a halt and bring the necessary fluids, already prepared in the chemical laboratory, to dissolve and wash away all obstructing deposits, previous to beginning the work of reconstruction and the repair of the injured parts of the machinery disabled by atmospheric changes, poisons, or otherwise.

Perfection in Nature.

When Nature renovates, it is never satisfied to leave any obstruction in any part of the body. All the powers of its batteries are brought into line for duty, and never stop short of the completeness that ends in perfection. All seasons of the year come and go, and we see, year in and year out, the perpetual processes of construction of one class of bodies and the passing away of others. Vegetation builds forests; cold builds mountains of ice, later to be dissolved and sent into the ocean to assist in purifying the water and keeping the brines from drying to salt.

All the processes of earth-life must be in perpetual motion to be kept in a healthy condition; otherwise the world would wither and die and go to the tombs of space to join the funeral procession of other dead worlds. All nature comes and goes by the fiat of wisely adjusted laws. Read all the authors from Æsculapius to this date, and leave the inquirers without a single fact as to the cause or causes of fever. One says fever may come from too much carbon; another says chemical defects may be the cause. I would like to agree with some of the good men of our day or the ancient theorists if I could, but they, both dead and alive, are a blank. Tons of paper have been covered with them by conjectures, and closed with the words "perhaps" and "however." All have explored for centuries for the cause of fevers, and on the return from their voyages say: "We hope some day to find the cause. We have done considerable killing, experimenting, but have failed to find the cause of fever."

Degrees of Heat.

To think of fever, we think of animal heat. By habit we want to know how great that heat is. We measure it with a thermometer until we find we have 100 degrees, 102, 104, to 106 degrees At this point we stop, as we find too much to suit life, which we think cannot consume more than 106 degrees of heat. We begin to ask for the substances that are more powerful than fire. We try all known fire compounds and fail.

The fire department has done faithful work, and has brought all it could bring to bear on the fire. It had used stream after stream of water, but the fire had ruined the house, with all its inside and outside usefulness and beauties. Another and another house gets on fire and burns as the first one did. All are content to look at the ruins and say that it is the will of the Lord, never thinking for a moment it was with the aid of the heart that the brain burned up the body.

Of what use is a knowledge of anatomy to a man if he overlooks cause and effect in the results obtained by the body machinery? He finds each part connected to all the others with the wisdom that has given a set of plans and specifications that are without a flaw or omission. The body generates its own heat and modulates it to suit the climate and season. It can generate heat through its electro-motor system far beyond the normal, to the highest known fever heat, and is capable of modulations far below the normal. A knowledge of osteopathy will prepare you to bring the system under the rulings of the physical laws of life. Fever is electric heat only.

Both Guess-Work.

Semeiology is defined as, "The science of the signs or symptoms of disease." Symptomatology is defined as, "The doctrine of symptoms; that part of the science of medicine which treats of the symptoms of disease. Semeiology." These definitions are from Webster's International Dictionary. Both words represent that system of guess-work which is now and has been used by medical practitioners as a method of ascertaining what disease is or might be. It is supposed to be the best method known to date to classify or name diseases, after which guessing begins in earnest. What kinds of poisons, how much and how often to use them, and then guess how much good or how much harm is being done to the sick person.

To illustrate more forcibly to the mind of the reader that such a system, though honored by age, is only worthy the term "guess-work," I will quote the following standard authority on fevers:

POTTER'S DEFINITION OF FEVER.

"Fever is a condition in which there are present the phenomena of rise of temperature, quickened circulation, marked tissue change, and disordered secretions.

"The primary cause of the fever phenomena is still a mooted question, and is either a disorder of the sympathetic nervous system giving rise to disturbances of the vaso-motor filaments, or a derangement of the nerve-centers located adjacent to the corpus striatum, which have been found, by experiment, to govern the processes of heat-production, distribution, and dissipation.

"Rise of temperature is the pre-eminent feature of all fevers, and can only be positively determined by the use of the clinical thermometer. The term 'feverishness' is used when the temperature ranges from 99° to 100° Fahrenheit; slight fever if 100° or 101°, moderate if 102° or 103°, high if 104° or 105°, and intense if it exceed the latter. The term 'hyperpyrexia' is used when the temperature shows a tendency to remain at 106° Fahrenheit and above.

"Quickened circulation is the rule in fevers, the frequency usually maintaining a fair ratio with the increase of the temperature. A rise of one degree Fahrenheit is usually attended with an increase of eight to ten beats of the pulse per minute.

"The following table gives a fair comparison between temperature and pulse:

Table of Degrees.

A temperature of	98°	Fahrenh. corresponds to a pulse of	60.
A temperature of	99°	Fahrenh. corresponds to a pulse of	70.
A temperature of	100°	Fahrenh. corresponds to a pulse of	80.
A temperature of	101°	Fahrenh. corresponds to a pulse of	90.
A temperature of	102°	Fahrenh. corresponds to a pulse of	100.
A temperature of	103°	Fahrenh. corresponds to a pulse of	110.
A temperature of	104°	Fahrenh. corresponds to a pulse of	120.
A temperature of	105°	Fahrenh. corresponds to a pulse of	130.
A temperature of	106°	Fahrenh. corresponds to a pulse of	140.

"The tissue waste is marked in proportion to the severity and duration of the febrile phenomena, being slight (or *nil*) in febricula, and excessive in typhoid fever.

"The disordered secretions are manifested by the deficiency in the salivary, gastric, intestinal, and nephritic secretions, the tongue being furred, the mouth clammy, and there occurring anorexia, thirst, constipation, and scanty, high-colored acid urine."

What has the student found by reading the above definition of this standard author and representative of present medical attainment but a labored effort to explain what that author does not even know?

Fevers Only Effects.

Fevers are effects only. The cause may be far from mental conclusions. If we have a house with one bell and ten wires, each fastened to a door and running to the center, all having connections and so arranged that to pull any one wire will set the bell in motion, without an indicator you cannot tell which wire is disturbed, producing the effect or ringing of the bell at the center. An electrician would know at once the cause, but to discriminate and locate the wire disturbed is the study.

Before a bell can be heard from any door, the general battery must be charged. Thus you see but one source of supply.

To better illustrate, we will take a house with eight rooms and all supplied by one battery. One apartment is a reception-room, one a parlor, one a sitting-room, one a bed-room, one a cloak-room, one a dining-room, one a kitchen, and one a basement room, all having wires and bells running to one bell in the clerk's office, which has an indicator for each room. If the machinery is in good order, he can call or answer correctly every ring and never make a mistake. But should he ring to the cook and her bell should keep on ringing and they could not stop it, they would summon an electrician. What would you think if he began at the parlor bell to adjust a trouble of the kitchen bell? Surely you would not have him treat the parlor bell first, because you know the trouble is with the kitchen bell. Now, to apply this illustration, we will say a system of bells and connecting wires run to all parts or rooms of the body, from the battery of power or the brain. These wires or nerves are connected with all active or vital parts of the body. Thus arranged, we see that blood is driven to any part of the system by the power that is sent over the nerves from the brain to the spinal cord, and from there to all nerves of each and all divisions of the body. Then blood that has done its work in constructing parts or all of the system enters veins to be returned to the heart for renewal. Each vein has nerves as servants of power to force blood back to the heart and constructed to suit the duties they have to perform in the process of life. If the blood travels to the heart too thick to suit the lungs, the great system of lymphatics pours in water to suit the demands, preparatory to having the blood enter the lungs to be purified and renewed. Nature has amply prepared all the machinery and power to prepare material and construct all parts, and when in normal condition the mind and wisdom of God is satisfied that the machine will go on and build and run according to the plans and specifications. If this be true, as Nature proves it to be at every point, what can man do farther than line things up and trust to Nature to get the results desired, "life and health"? Can we add or sugges any improvement? If not, what is left for us to do is to keep bells, batteries, and wires in their normal places and trust to normal laws as given by Nature to do the rest.

Result of Stoppage of Vein or Artery.

A few questions remain to be asked by the philosophical navigator when he sets sail to go to the cause of flux. Would he go to the blood-supply? Certainly, there must be supply previous to deposit. Reason would cause us to combine the fact that blood must be in perpetual motion from and to the heart during life, and that law is the fiat of all Nature, indispensable and absolute. Blood must not stop its motion nor be allowed to make abnormal deposits. The work of the heart is complete if it delivers blood into the arteries. Each division must then do its part fully as the normal heart does in health, and a normally formed heart is just as much interested in the blood that is running constantly for repairs and additions as the whole system is in the arteries of supply. You must have perfection in the heart first, and from it to all arteries. All hindrances must be kept away from the arteries, great and small. Health permits of no stoppage of blood in either the vein or artery. If an artery cannot unload its contents, a strain follows, and, as an artery must have room to deposit its supplies, it proceeds to build other vessels adjacent to the points of obstruction.

Fevers Are Fevers.

Fevers of the fall and summer season are neither hotter nor colder than the fevers of winter and spring. I speak thus to impress on the student's mind that heat is heat at any season of the year and is common to all diseases. In some diseases heat is higher than in other diseases. We speak of bilious fever, yellow fever, lung fever, and a long list of fevers, each one bearing a special name as measured out by the little books on symptomatology. All fail to show any difference between the fevers of eruptions and the fevers of any other disease, notwithstanding that much use is made of the hand-thermometer to ascertain just how hot the afflicted person gets. It matters little with an osteopath how hot or how cold a patient gets, his object of observation being in another direction, a direction that leads him to seek the cause of this fermentation and boiling of the fluids in the body. Fluids delayed in the blood-vessels, lymphatics, and excretories ferment, and during the process of fermentation the temperature naturally varies many degrees by the increased action of electricity. It is reasonable to suppose that before fermentation sets up its action it must have something to act upon, and, as it acts only on stagnant blood, it must find this stagnant deposit either in the veins, arteries, lymphatics, or cellular tissues of the organs, vessels, and other places for its temporary sojourn. We are ready to explore any organ in the thorax, abdomen, or pelvis, the lymphatics and glands of the fascia, superficial and deep, or any membrane of the body. In fevers we may expect to find congestion of the mesentery and of the peritoneum generally, also of the nerves, blood-vessels, and lymphatics of the fascia. We may expect and will find deposits and resulting chemical action that will show its energy by the degree of heat that is expressed by the touch of the hand or the register of a thermometer. All conspire to prove that heat is only an effect.

After being satisfied that there are no two kinds of heat, then we will take up the search and go at it in a systematic hunt, by exploring for abnormal variations in size and place of any organ, muscle, skin, fascia, lymphatics, and blood-vessels of the pelvis, abdomen, chest, and neck, caused by local or general congestion

GO TO THE SPINE.

A study of the nature of fevers leads us to the spine. We must see that all openings from the base of the skull to the lowest point of the sacrum are open and in good condition to allow free action of all nerves issuing from the spinal cord and giving force to membranes, organs, muscles, etc. If an organ has an area allotted to its use, we must reason that it can do no perfect work outside of that area. Each spine must be perfect in place and in articulation at each joint or a closure will appear, oppressing and hindering the action of the lymph, nerves, and blood-vessels. Thus we have blood and other substances stopped that should go on without delay to their proper destination and uses. By a careful study of the perfect spinal column and cord, and nerves and membranes holding organs and vessels in place, we will see that the system is perfect in bones, their shape, size, and place, with openings for passages of blood-vessels and nerves. The motion of the spine to all points is perfect and does not interfere with the blood- and nerve-supply. To know the spinal column from beginning to end is wisdom that we must have or fail. The student of anatomy knows that the flesh of the head, face, neck, and the whole system is united to the bones, and that this union means duties to be performed by the softer parts that are held in place or position by the harder parts, for the process of functioning to proceed. He also knows that the limit or space allotted to many organs is small, and that very little variation from this allotted position causes impingement upon other organs by confused nerve-action, blood-supply, and removal of waste matter through the excretory provisions. And the fact being known that muscles are attached to bones, and that bones articulate and have openings in them or between them for the passage of different substances, then a student need not be surprised, after the displacement of a bone occurs, to find thickenings appear in the air-passages of the nose or any part of the lining membranes of the mouth, the tonsils, the tongue, the throat, or the muscles, nerves, or glands of the windpipe, right back of which he will find membranes, fascia, ligaments, or mesentery to suit and complete the perfect attachment of the tongue or any organ, or the lining membranes of the mouth, tongue, or any membrane that has a bony attachment in the upper part of the system. We must not omit the importance that Nature has attached to the use of this great division in its work in the economy of life. The student must remember that he, at this point, enters an open door that will give him an opportunity to behold a part of the laboratory of life. He must know that all attachments in place must be perpetual; also they must not be bruised, strained, or misplaced; otherwise we have a diseased tongue, tonsil, epiglottis, thyroid glands, submaxillary or other glands of the face, loss of hair, sight, speech, the power of swallowing or hearing, and are left in a condition for the encouragement of abnormal growths, owing to perverted nerve- and blood-supply, which means, with us, the artery to feed and the vein and excretories to conduct away that which is of no more vital use to an organ and its territory. As the trachea, œsophagus, lungs, and heart all have membranous attachments to the spine, we must remember that the attachments must universally be undisturbed, absolutely. Strains, jars, jolts, partial or complete, and dislocations of spine or ribs may cause the heart and lungs by their own weight to pull down and cause a heavy straining upon the membranes that attach these organs to the spine, a fact undoubtedly producing great interference with the sympathetic nervous system and the spinal cord with its assisting nerve-fibers, governing and forcing the arterial blood from the aorta into the spinal openings.

CONGESTION, ETC.

Another cause that we will notice, other than surgical injuries that pull down the mesentery, causing much variation from the normal, is that of extremes in heat and cold, causing stoppage of blood, lymph, water, and other fluids, which are detained long enough to set up congestion, irritation, fermentation, inflammation, and sloughing into the thoracic, abdominal, and pelvic cavities, and which should have been conducted to the lungs or out of the body through the excretory system. It is my object at the present time to insist upon the attention of the student to the very important fact that the membranes which hold the organs of the body in place lengthen by heat and contract by cold. This membrane we call the mesentery, the peritoneum, the fascia, muscular attachment, or any other name we may select; but under all names these attachments will stretch, and stretch downwardly by the law of gravitation, causing irritation and death by strangulation. They will do this work of death by strangulation as certainly as the hangman's rope. You must remember that no unhealthy swing will be tolerated by the Master-Builder. I have endeavored to give you a cause that produces disease of the pancreas, spleen, stomach, liver, kidneys, bowels, and uterus, and it is done by the pendulous pulling of the loaded bowels upon the elastic membranous attachments to the spine You often will see dropping of the ascending colon from the right iliac fossa, which is the normal position of the base of the cæcum. You often have a lengthening of the mesentery that will allow this cæcum to fall from three to seven inches, disguise the ileocæcal valve, and conduct your patient to death by prohibiting the softer fluids from passing through the ileo-cæcal valve to save the life of the patient, who is dying from hardened fæcal matter in the colon, from the cæcum to any point above the anus. The bad effects are almost innumerable that follow malpositions of any organ, from the mouth to the anus, by their membranous attachments giving way, often resulting in the removal or change in position of organ after organ. This removal and new position taken by an organ would easily indicate the cause of many abnormal manifestations, such as are known by the name of typhoid fever, dysentery, flux, malposition of the uterus, malformation of the uterus, inflammation of the kidneys, liver, bladder, and so on, to an unlimited number of injurious effects that can all be reasoned out and traced to mesenteric disturbances.

LOOK FOR LESIONS.

I have spoken of the membranes that connect the tongue, trachea, œsophagus, lungs, and heart to the spine above the diaphragm; also of the whole list of membranes that hold the liver, spleen, and other organs of the abdomen in place. I have drawn the attention of the student to the blood-, nerve-, and lymph-supplies of the mesenteric systems of both the large and small bowels, with general remarks on the mesentery of all organs of the abdomen and their uses, in order that the student can have a direct method in seeking the causes that produce abnormal conditions of any organ of the chest, abdomen, and pelvis. Explore the spine for bony abnormalities at all points that any organ receives nerve-supply from the spinal nerves. Then pass to the abdomen for twists or folds of the mesentery or any change of position of any of the organs. You may find abnormalities in form and place of the bladder, uterus, bowels, kidneys, liver, spleen, and other organs below the diaphragm, that lead to disease and death by strangulation or suspension of the fluids of the meso-system, all the way from the tongue to the end of the sacrum. It is the connective tissue of the spine that directly connects the omentum and mesentery to the spine and other places of attachment to which we would like to point the attention of the student, because this connecting tissue is the bridge that conducts the nerve-forces to the great omentum and mesentery, generally, with their lymphatic vessels. To the connections with the stomach, bowels, spleen, and pancreas, we wish special attention given, and every point of organic connection, clear back to the tonsils and Eustachian tubes because we believe that inflammations of all membranes, organs, and glands of the thorax receive their irritating shock in the nerve-fibers as they pass from the sympathetic and spinal cord to the organs, blood, lymph, and nerves of the chest. Irritation by changes of temperature, shocks, jolts, and so on will set up contracture and confusion of the receipt and discharge of fluids or force designed to be passed through the membrane to and from any organ in the chest. This perpetual irritation causes congestion, inflammation, and decomposition of fluids, and can be accounted for by detention in the lymphatics of the chest. The remedy is self-suggesting. The demand for a perfect spine and ribs, with all their connections and articulations, is imperative, because the intercostal nerve- and blood-supply must be normal, or disease will follow from stagnation of fluids.

Summer and Winter Diseases.

I think one of the best methods to study acute diseases is by the seasons. We can not or do not have fall and winter diseases during the spring and summer months, nor spring and summer diseases during the fall and winter months. We will save time and grow wiser in comprehension and good results by cutting hay in the summer and killing hogs in the winter. Still there is much similarity in diseases that rage during the winter and spring to those of summer and fall. In the warm weather we find more diseases of the bowels, liver, kidneys, and brain. We have much congestion of brain, lungs, bowels, liver, and spleen, following long exposure to sun heat. We have very little summer diseases before July and August, when we get the direct rays of the sun with its full magnetic powers. We roast all day, work until we are afire with sun heat, and then throw cold water into our stomachs, chilling nerve and stopping blood-action by contracting arteries and veins. With cold drinks much blood is chilled to death, and we then have congestion of the circulation of all the abdominal organs, chest, and brain. Then the fire of Nature begins to start up to burn up or cremate its dead corpuscles. We say "fever" in place of "fire." We should look on all heat as electricity in motion. We should at all times, both winter and summer, remember that we are attending funerals of dead blood and other fluids. We are undertakers, and not life-makers. The funeral procession may have enough dead corpuscles on its train to leave the camp of life below self-defense.

Constriction and congestion govern and modify temperature. Cold universally causes stoppage of fluids by stricture of nerves and muscles. A fever of any kind is preceded by constricture, long enough to produce congestion and tumefaction about the neck to a degree of irritation of the motor nerves, which augments nerve-action to the degree of combustion, always an accompaniment of electric action. In all fevers we find the nerves and muscles of the neck very rigid, the blood-circulation much disturbed. Previous to a chill we have almost complete suspension of the venous flow from the brain, a temporary paralysis of the vaso-motor. Following this cold stage, action sets up in the motor nerves of the arterial circulation and becomes very powerful, throwing the blood with a velocity that indicates great friction all through the body from center to surface. Thus we have cause to suspect electric action to a very high degree, to a degree that would produce combustion by friction. On this foundation ever remember that heat and cold receive their orders from the neck.

PEDIGREE OF FEVERS.

Typhoid fever, bilious fever, and chronic dysentery all have their name. Each one of these fevers from an M D 's standpoint has a pedigree that is sacredly kept in a little book in the clerk's office. The name of this book is "Symptomatology." Each one of these fevers must have all the marks noted in the pedigree-book or you are not safe to label it. One is a Hereford, one is a Jersey, and one is a Polled Angus. Each one of these cows has a pedigree in which is described the size, weight, age, color, horns, eyes, udders, tails, legs, hoofs, spots, neck, and all marks but one, which is the chemical cause in the blood that makes the Polled Angus black, the Hereford red, and the Jersey yellow. The little book does not tell you that the Polled Angus, or typhoid fever of the winter, was caused by blood being held too long below the diaphragm so that it died, or that the Jersey, or summer disease, came from the same cause, but was born in warm weather, the blood being killed in the veins of the abdomen. Osteopathy knows this, and knows also that this truth is not in the old time-honored books of pedigree. The osteopath should not spend any time after the patient has given him the history of the disease, except to hunt for the cause, find it, and adjust the deformities, then wait a few days and note effects. If good, keep on, with an eye to guarding your patient against strains and jars that would cause bones and ligaments to fall back to the condition that caused the disease in the first place. Remember that the same cause will produce the same effect, and you will have to do your work over again unless care is taken long enough to let muscles get strong and normal

MOST DREADED.

Typhoid fever is a disease much dreaded by all, because it kills both young and old with equal certainty. It is dreaded by the doctor just as much or more so than by the patient. The best and oldest doctors have long since hung out a written failure. The M.D. has used his best skill. He has failed to cure or have any luck to encourage him in the thought that he is following a system that is trustworthy. He, too, must change his tactics or spend his days knowing that he is defeated in all engagements with typhoid fever.

TEMPERATURE.

As temperature surely has much or all to do with physical force, we think a little reasoning on the subject would be proper, at least as much as we can give it in the relations to animal life, motion of blood and muscles. The blood keeps in perpetual motion from and to the heart and through all organs and parts of the body. One says it is nerve-force or energy, and another says it is life-force that moves the blood, but how is this force generated, and when and where is it made to act as a blood-driving force? How is blood driven to the heart and returned to the place from whence it started? We know it leaves by the arteries and returns through the veins, but how do the arteries drive out and the veins drive or force the blood to return to the heart? What is the probable cause that gives this almost perpetual motion of the fluids of the body? We know by reason that the heart contracts at the center and forces the blood through the arteries to all divisions of the body. Also we know, just as well, that the veins contract at the greatest distance from the heart and force the blood to return to the heart through the veins by contraction of the veins, beginning at the capillaries and continuing the force by contracting the whole venous system from extremity to center. What causes the heart to forcibly contract and relax periodically? Why should the veins contract at all or dilate? Is it a shock on the nerves caused by the change of temperature of the atmosphere that causes this periodic tightening and relaxing of the blood-vessels? By periodically contracting and relaxing I mean the action of the heart and veins during the flow of blood. The heart contracts for a time, then relaxes for a time, periodically. This is the phenomenon that we will try to account for by atmospheric shocks on the nerves of the heart to drive the blood out, then irritation of the capillary nerves of veins, causing them to contract and return the blood to the heart.

Let us reason that with man's temperature above 90 degrees, an electric shock takes place with the action of the air taken into the lungs, and from action of lungs and chemical union of explosive substances while in the lungs. Thus an irritation of the nerves of the heart causes constriction of the muscles of the heart by atmospheric irritation of, first, the nerves of the lungs, then of the heart, and all the arterial system of nerves.

Temperature regulates the motion of the universe and all bodies therein. Life in motion is an effect of temperature just above 90 degrees Fahrenheit. Death is inaction, a lack of heat or motion. We cease to move, or are dead, as we say. When blood gets to 96 degrees, an explosive impulse forces it from the heart to the greatest distance, to awake a venous explosion among the nerves and cause the veins to contract and push blood back to the liver, lungs, and heart again. Thus by temperature we have explosion at the heart to drive out the blood, and at the capillary ends of veins and arteries we get another explosion that forces nerves to contract and drive the blood from the small veins to the large, keeping up perpetual motion by vital heat or temperature.

CHAPTER XI.

Biogen.

DEVELOPMENT AND PROGRESS.

Wonders are daily callers, and seem to have been greatly on the increase during the last century. As we read history we learn that no one hundred years of the past has produced wonders in such number and variety. Stupid systems of government have given place to better and wiser systems. Ocean trips have had months by sail reduced to days by steam. Journeys overland that would require six months by horse or ox are now accomplished in six days by rail. Our law, medical, and other schools have taken great strides in advance, the facilities for giving the pupil an education are so far superior, and the knowledge sought can be obtained in less time. Our schools are not intended for time-consumers. Our aim is to obtain useful knowledge in the quickest and most thorough way that it can be obtained. If there is any method by which arithmetic can be taught so that we can master it in thirty days instead of thirty months, let us have it. We want knowledge, and we are willing to pay for it. We want all we pay for, and we want our heads kept out of the sausage-mill of time-wasting. A great question stands before us: What are the possibilities of still further improving our methods of gaining knowledge, saving time, and getting greater and better results? I am free to say the question is too sweeping for me to give it an answer, as each day brings a new problem for the man or woman who reasons on cause and gives demonstrations by effects.

No one knows who the philosopher was that first asked the question, What is life? But all intelligent persons are interested in the solution of this problem, at least to know some tangible reason why it is called "life", whether life is personal, or so arranged that it might be called an individualized principle of Nature.

The Origin of Action.

If life in man has been formed to suit the size and duties of the being, if life has a living and separate personage, then we should be governed by such reasons as would give it the greatest chance to go on with its labors in the bodies of man and beast. We know by experience that a spark of fire will start the principles of powder into motion, which, were it not stimulated by the positive principle of Father Nature, which finds this germ lying quietly in the womb of space, would be silently inactive for all ages, without being able to move or help itself, save for the motor principle of life given by the Father of all motion.

Right here we should ask the question, Is action produced by electricity put in motion, or is it the active principle that comes as spiritual man? If the latter, it is useless to try or hope to know what life is in its minutiæ. But we do know that life can only display its natural forces by the visible action of the forms it produces. If we inspect man as a machine, we find a complete building, a machine that courts inspection and criticism. It demands a full exploration of all its parts, with their uses. Then the mind is asked to find the connection between the physical and the spirituual. By Nature you can reason that the powers of life are arranged to suit its system of motion. If life is an individualized personage, as we might express that mysterious something, it must have definite arrangements by which it can be united and act with matter.

Then we should acquaint ourselves with the arrangements of those natural connections, the one or many, in all parts of the completed being. As motion is the first and only evidence of life, by this thought we are conducted to the machinery through which life works to accomplish the results as witnessed in "motion."

If the brain be that division in which force is generated or stored, you must at all hazards acquaint yourself with the structure of this machine; trace the connections from the brain to the heart, from heart to lungs, and other organs that can be acted upon by the brain, whose duty may be to construct the fleshy and bony parts of the body. Trace these connections from the brain to the chemical laboratories, and note the results as they unite and prepare blood and other fluids that are used in the economy of this vital, self-constructing and self-moving wonder known as man, wherein life and matter unite and express their friendly relation one with the other. While this relation exists we have the living man only, expressing and proving the relation that can exist between life and matter, from the lowest living atom to the greatest worlds. They can only express form and action by this law. Harmony only dwells where obstructions do not exist.

The osteopath finds here the field in which he can dwell forever. His duties as a philosopher admonish him that life and matter can be united, and that that union cannot continue with any hindrance to free and absolute motion. Therefore his duty is to keep away from the track all that will hinder the complete passage of the forces of the nervous system, that by that power the blood may be delivered and adjusted to keep the system in a normal condition. Here is your duty. Do it well, if you wish to succeed.

FORCES COMBINED.

We see the form of each world, and call the united action biogenic life. All material bodies have life terrestrial and all space has life, ethereal or spiritual life. The two, when united, form man. Life terrestrial has motion and power; the celestial bodies have knowledge or wisdom. Biogen is the lives of the two in united action, that give motion and growth to all things. Thus we have life terrestrial, or the power to move, and the wisdom from the celestial to govern all motions of worlds and beings, by union of the life of space and the life of matter. The force and wisdom of both by that union is driven into motion by temperature from the ethereal life, to form and control the universe and all worlds and beings of each planet. If a seed is planted in the earth and it obeys both the terrestrial and the celestial forces, then the result is a tree. A man, biogenic force, means both lives in united action to construct all bodies in form, with wisdom to govern their actions. Thus endowed, two beings or worlds, when in contact, give wisdom and force to work out greater problems than either could accomplish alone. As both have been formed by terrestrial forces aided by celestial wisdom, then greater results can be hoped for, and in friendly unison in action such results will appear as the effects of that harmonious union of two great causes. Thus biogen or material life of the two obeys the wisdom of the celestial mind or life. The result is faultless perfection, because the earth-life shows in material forms the wisdom of the God of the celestial. Thus we say biogen or dual life, that life means eternal reciprocity that permeates all nature. The celestial worlds of space or ether-life give forms wisely constructed in exchange for the use of the material substances. Reciprocity through the governments of the celestial and terrestrial worlds is ever the same, and human life, in form and motion, is the result of conception by the terrestrial mother from the celestial father. Thus we have a union of mind, matter, and life, or man.

To bring this subject within the comprehension of the student, that he may know why the arterial or celestial force should be brought to act with full force upon the terrestrial or the substances of the body, he has only to think for a moment that man contains in his physical organization all chemical substances that belong to the earth, and that these substances are put into growing motion, first by the living force or nourishment obtained from the soil. So far no growth could appear without the assistance of the celestial, heavenly, or atmospheric forces, such as dews, rains, light, darkness, and temperature to suit the vital action of vegetation. He has only to think a moment to see that the laws governing the growth of vegetation govern animal bodies in a similar way. The earth substance has its biogen peculiar to giving strength to vegetation, and the body of man, which is composed of material substances taken from the earth, has its equivalent to the biogen necessary to vegetable growth. This biogen is peculiar in its nature to the growth of animal bodies. The kinds of substances consumed in vegetable growths are very different from those used in the growths of animal bodies or forms. The circulation of the fluid substances is very similar, both being obliged to pass through arterial channels suited to the requirements of each, so we see that the law of assimilation, appropriation, and growth is very much alike. It is just as important for the healthy growth of the tree that the plentiful supply of sap and substances necessary to the growth of the tree should be undisturbed, as it is necessary that the blood or sap of human life meet with no hindrances if successful growth of a bone or muscle is to be expected. Since the purest of blood is required to do physical work in the human body through the whole system in the best of shape, we will offer as a substitute some impure or inferior quality of blood to be appropriated in the economy of life, and ask what can be expected but bad results in all organs supplied or fed by such low nutritious diet. As a little leaven leaveneth the whole loaf, would not a little diseased blood disease the whole viscera? By way of illustration, let us wound the liver, omentum, pancreas, spleen, kidneys, or bowels, or cause blood to die and decompose in one of the organs. Have we not made a nucleus for an increase in the quantity and quality of the poisonous blood that will extend with its poisons through the whole sysetm? If so, we have no other question to ask. We know the cause and should well understand and relieve the sufferer by opening up drainage, forwarding the best of blood for the repair of damages done by stagnant impurities. To illustrate this thought, we will begin the preparation of diseased blood by deranging the colon from the rectum through the descending, sigmoid, transverse, and ascending colon or the cæcum, which contains the gate of exit through which the fluids must pass to keep the fæcal matter in a soft, digestible, and movable condition. We will bruise, poison, ligate, kink, or twist the colon from the cæcum to the descending curve on the left side. If we stop the blood, we have stagnation, congestion, fermentation, death of fluids, and poisonous blood to be absorbed by the lymphatics and other members of the secretory family, and to be conveyed to the liver through the venous system. This diseased blood becomes the nourishment for the liver, which is expected to be healthy and act as a purifying laboratory, preparing substances through purification for blood—the blood of life, and not the blood of death, with poisonous impurities. A physiologist with even a moderate degree of anatomical knowledge knows just what arteries supply the liver and what veins keep the organ pure. He also knows just as well that the drainage of the whole abdomen passes directly to the liver, through which blood passes on its journey to the heart and lungs for further purification. He knows that diseased blood returned from the rectum or colon becomes poor food for a healthy liver. He knows that diseased blood from the bladder, the uterus, or any membrane or gland of the pelvis is thrown into the channels and conducted to the liver without regard to its purity. The venous system and the liver itself must report and deposit fluids, good or bad, in the liver. The man of our school knows, if he has the brains to be a successful osteopath, that this diseased blood becomes a fire to the hepatic laboratory, and that fire of disease circumnavigates the whole system, bone, brain, nerve, and muscle. Thus, you see, if the liver is diseased, the body is diseased, and the cause of this deadly compound has had its origin in the rectum, low down, by displaced members of the abdominal viscera. We see the process of generating poisons by cutting off or disturbing the venous flow of blood in the rectum long enough to allow it to lose its vitality and decompose and do the deadly work of forming poisonous gases and deposits.

Matter in the Atom.

When matter is reduced to its greatest degree of atomic fineness, then it can submit to any bodily form, because all substances contain in kind that of all other kinds by nature, and can easily take the form of man, beast, bird, or reptile, because this fineness is equal to that of spiritual food or the motor powers of life. An atom is the limit of inaction, the point at which life rests in matter, because of its crudity. When matter passes beyond the degree of being atomized farther, then it is life, and it acts and forms itself to suit the body of any being or the world. When matter ceases to be divisible, it then becomes a fluid of life and easily unites with other atoms, and is a mass or body of living matter and recrystallizes into the form given by the parent causes. Thus man's body is a form given by celestial life to the terrestrial life that is reduced back from the living matter to a man, world, or being, with form of a being given by the celestial forces acting on living matter whilst in the living state of matter, so fine that the atoms blend and become a unit, or melt and become one being or body of living matter, with quality equal to all qualities of life, wisdom, and material substances, never to return to their original state, either as matter or life. In man's body have been prepared and united the two kinds of life, the celestial and terrestrial, and the result is man and beast. "All matter," says one, "is living substance." We know life only by the motion of material bodies. That self-moving principle which we see in all animal bodies we call life, because we see them move independent of other bodies or forces. That life acts and moves in that being of its own force. Life is individualized and has its limit of action, which extends no further than the man or beast governed by that individual power known as the life of man or beast. Then we behold a living body, and we say, "That body is all alive; every atom moves." How long have the atoms moved as man, all united in form? If but a few years in that form of associated atoms, and the atoms were living when they first met, how long have they been alive, and when and how did they become living atoms, or is life eternally the same in the atoms?

The Material and Immaterial.

It matters very little to man where mind, motion, and matter came from, the one place or the other. They are all in his make-up, and he is interested in keeping them all healthy. If he is a doctor, he is interested in quick cures, because his living depends on his success. The doctor does not have to furnish his patients mind, matter, or motion. His work is to keep the body adjusted so it can supply itself with brain and muscle; then mind and motion will appear and keep the laboratory full of the choicest chemicals and free from disease. Healthy organs and food are what keeps a man healthy. The doctor can aid in keeping the organs in place. This he can do if he knows the forms and functionings of the different parts of the body. If not, he is of but little use or benefit to the sick.

The Visible and Invisible.

All visible matter is life retired from labor to rest. All motion is matter in action. An explosive is matter at rest, and an explosion is matter in motion; so of motion in man. Life begins to unfold by explosions of lower orders of material life in matter. Thus all action marks the amount and quality of explosives used by the body that moves. What we call life is matter at labor; death is matter *minus* explosive ability and at rest. The velocity of the union of the two forces doubles the explosive powers of either. Animal life appears on the stage of action. We see "motionless matter, earth, stone, and on to all visible bodies." And we see moving matter; we say "living matter." When we see dead bodies that do not move, we say "dead matter." But is it dead, or is it in a state of inaction or rest only, and waiting its time to fall in line as living active matter that is rested and ready to take up the line of march and give its energies to the orders of Nature? We speak of life, but know of it only as we see bodies move by life back of the visible matter Does Nature have a finer matter that is invisible and that moves all that is visible to us? Life surely is a very finely prepared substance, which is the all-moving force of Nature, or that force that moves all nature from worlds to atoms. It seems to be a substance that contains all the principles of construction and motion, with the power to endow that which it constructs with the attributes necessary to the object it has formulated from matter and sent forth as a living being. We think it is not unreasonable to conclude that life is matter in motion, with ability to carry its kind and impart the same to other bodies. To illustrate, we would say that smallpox is the effect of living matter that permeates all systems in which it may dwell, and consumes to partial or complete destruction. The same law is true with other contagious substances. They are materials reduced to the degree of living fineness. They proceed to take possession of the human body and inflict their wounds and cause disease and death. These are effects—not of dead matter, but of living matter, that seeks to live and destroys organic bodies by subsisting on the substances that should sustain the life of man. Thus one dies of starvation and a new creature lives, takes his flight in search of nourishment, and keeps up a perpetual journeying as one of the finest principles and efforts of Nature, which is matter refined to the condition known as life.

Thus far we see nothing in matter but life at rest. Even the human body that we see every day is matter called to a halt and at rest. This is life of a lower order submitting to the edicts of the higher life, which life keeps up motion by the combustion of the terrestrial substances within the body. This combustion is conducted, prepared, and brought into action by the refining laboratory that issues nothing but the active substance known as life. That life substance, when conducted to a higher condition of unfoldment, is ready to take its place and send forth the wondrous action of the principle known as mind, when prepared by Nature to that degree of incomprehensible refinement known as mind, whose existence feasts and flourishes upon the waters of the ocean of universal intelligence, which speaks and proves the intelligence of God as the wisest of all chemists, who has united the necessary substances at His command to produce a union of matter endowed with action and the power of continuing the refining process until mind, the incomprehensible, appears with man as the crowning effort of the wisdom of an all-wise chemist, be he known as God, Nature, the Unknowable, or the ever-living Genius of the universe.

We have given a few thoughts on this line of life, hoping the osteopath will take up the subject and travel a few miles farther toward the fountain of this great source of knowledge and apply the results to the relief and comfort of the afflicted who come for counsel and advice.

Man Is Eternal.

Human life is eternal. We have no proof otherwise. Life enters the forest of flesh as man. It carries constructing wisdom and ability. It begins with the atoms of flesh, adds by ones to countless millions, and carefully adjusts each to suit the form of the plans and specifications to make a physical habitation to suit the union of mind and matter. Thus we see the form, material man. It, man, begins work as a wise and great builder. It plans as it goes. All requirements are known and are well finished with perfect skill throughout. All parts fit to suit all other parts, he qualifying and preparing each atom of matter to the greatest gauge of purity of each kind, with forms to suit each atom, previous to being placed in its required position to harmonize with all other atoms entering into the form of bone or muscle. All work is so nicely done that we are forced as critics in the fine arts to conclude, from the work and skill shown in man's physical being, that man began as a skillful life, led on and on by perfect wisdom, each stroke in unison from start to finish. We must conclude that he is a builder guided by wisdom to the fullest and most satisfactory proof that life is the essence of wisdom in action in all nature, and man is life and mind without beginning of days or end of time. Man could not be man and not be a wise builder when he dwells in worlds of matter whose powers to select and build have no limit short of perfection. He came to the forest of matter a master builder, and used such material as perfect wisdom only could select. In him we find no assistance given, nor was any necessary. He alone builded his own house, with all thereunto belonging. Where he got his power and wisdom is the question whose correct answer we do not know. His work is the silent witness of his abilities to do perfect work. When he picked up the first atom of matter and placed it, he added others to countless millions as his work progressed to the finished man. He did not come as a living germ, but as man, who was able to prove that he was master of matter and was perfection as a building genius, and only asked the skeptic to contradict his word or prove that it was not true by bringing forward the builder who made man, if he, man himself, did not handle the first, last, and all the other atoms in his form. He borrowed timber from the maternal forest and bore all the burdens of the required labor in building the house in which he lives. If he partakes of the nature of the universe, then, by that quality, he has constructiveness to perfection as a natural quality of his animal perfection. Thus, by nature, he not only proves to be perfection as a builder, but endowed also with power to reason, to care for and conduct his house of life and locomotion through its journey of physical union. In him nothing is imperfect excepting his reason. There seems to be greater wisdom shown in his construction than in his reasoning powers. We find him a skilled workman, and not "*an atom of life, a living germ of protoplasm.*" Man. Who made him? One says, "God made him." Another thinks that if God had anything to do with man-making, that He, God, or the universal law under which man comes, put into his life-compound the essence of perfect constructive ability, which quality pervades the whole universe in the construction of worlds and beings of animal forms. Thus, to construct wisely is natural to all things.

THE ADVENT OF MAN.

No record shows the exact time when man's foot first appeared on the earth. A knowledge of his advent might be profitable. The unwritten history of the human races, if we had it, might to us be a book of great knowledge. It is not supposed that the mind of man has become observingly active only in the last few centuries. Absolute evidence of purer and deeper reason than we have been able to present stands recorded on the faces of many valuable "lost arts" which we have never been able to equal. Is it not reasonable to suppose that the powers of mind have also degenerated from some cause?

The stock-raiser carefully chooses the best and most healthy of the males and females of his flocks and herds for breeding purposes, that their offspring may be healthy and well developed for the purposes for which he raises them. As a result, he raises from year to year stock with marked improvement in form, strength, and usefulness. Should he be foolish enough to kill off the healthy and well-developed males as they appeared in his stock, for one or two generations, would anyone with average intelligence suppose that the standards would or could be kept up? If for breeding purposes he would save calves, colts, lambs, pigs, goats, or any other young males that had had legs frozen off, one or both eyes plucked out, necks and ears torn by panthers, what would you think of the man's sanity?

THE SURVIVAL OF THE WEAKEST.

On this line we would ask, What has been the procedure in human life? Has it not been to select the strong and healthy males and drive them out to the field of battle to destroy a million or more of other strong men? Our war of the sixties illustrates this. Since that war closed, the fathers of our children have been mainly crippled, worn-out, and degenerated physical wrecks, and the "refused," who, for lack of physical ability, were barred from entering the service of the United States. Many of these physical and mental wrecks have been the fathers of children born during the last thirty-five years. Every healthy young lady who married and became a mother after the early sixties had to select a husband from a war or hereditary wreck. From that degenerated stock of human beings our asylums are filled and the beams of the gallows pulled down by the weight of the bodies of those mental dwarfs. Run this train of reason back for a few hundreds or thousands of years. This degenerating force has been bearing upon the offspring, and is it a wonder that we have physical and mental wrecks all over the country?

Now if we have been mentally degenerating, killing our best men for a few thousand years' time, and still have a few left who are fairly good reasoners, what were the mental powers ages ago as compared with now? They could think from native ability; we only through acquired ability by our methods of education. Should an original thinker occasionally appear from among the crippled and maimed, he will have much that is unpleasant to contend with, unless he is generous enough to credit the cause to an effect produced by the lack of mental and physical forces in the sires just described. A man who is able to reason cannot afford to wear out his physical and mental forces by spending time in tiresome discussions with such blank masses, who are fortunate if they have intelligence enough to make a living under the methods that require the least mental action It would not be unwise for him to allow a feeling of combativeness to arise and to spend his forces on such persons. Prenatal causes have dropped them where they are, and a philosopher is sorrowful instead of combative. All that is left for him to do is to trim his lamps and let the lights defend themselves.

The ancients did much thinking. Great minds existed then, as is evidenced by the architecture displayed in the building of temples and pyramids. In philosophy, chemistry, and mathematics we have living facts of their intelligence. In some ways we are equal and even surpass them, but in the establishment of religious and political governments, national and tribal creeds, powerful minds and bodies of thousands and millions have been slain and their wise counsels lost by death. Reason says that under the circumstances we must make and do the best we can for our day and generation.

METHODS OF HEALING.

Some evidence crops out now and then that ancient methods of healing were natural and wisely applied, and crowned with good results. As far as history speaks of the ancient healing arts, they were logical, philosophical, good in results, and harmless. It is true we have great systems of chemistry that are useful in the mechanical arts, but they are very limited in their uses in the healing arts. In fact, a great percentage of the gray-haired philosophers of the medical schools unhesitatingly assert that the world would be better off without them. These conclusions are sent forth by competent and honest investigators, who have tested all known combinations of chemicals and drugs and carefully observed the results attained in the science of drugs from a quarter to a half a century. Let us call it "a trade," as the use of drugs is not a science. The drug practitioner in a majority of cases, when he administers drugs, gives one dose for health and nine for the dollar.

As it becomes necessary to throw off oppressive governments, it becomes just as necessary to throw off other useless practices and customs. Drugs have had their day. Their fate is sealed just as surely as the millions of their human victims.

Allopathy, a school of medicine known and fostered for these many years, attempted to find the real cause and cure of diseases, but gave up the search and went into camp and constructed temples to the god who purged, puked, perspired, opiated, and drank whisky and other stimulants. Allopathy has destroyed its thousands, ruined nations, established whisky saloons, opium dens, insane asylums, naked mothers, and hungry babies, and still cries aloud, and says: "Come unto me, and I will give you rest. I have opium, morphine, and whisky by the barrel. I am the god of all healing knowledge, and want to be so recognized by people and statute. I do not wish to be annoyed by eclecticism, homœopathy, Christian science, massage, Swedish movements, nor osteopathy. I do not like osteopathy any better than I do a tiger. It scratches me and tears away all my disciples. I cannot destroy it. It uses neither opium nor whisky, and it is impossible to catch it asleep. It has scratched our power out of seventeen States, and there is no telling where it will scratch next. We must prepare for more war. I have heard from my scouts that on osteopathy's flag the inscription reads thus: 'No quarter for allopathy in particular, and none at all for any schools of medicine farther than surgery, and war to the hilt on three-fourths of that as practiced in the present day. The use of the knife in everything and for everything must be stopped; not by statute law, but through a higher education of the masses, which will give them more confidence in Nature's ability to heal.'"

Primitive Man.

It is reasonable to suppose that the Mind that constructed man was fully competent to undertake and complete the being to suit the purposes for which he was designed. After giving him physical perfection in every limb, organ, or part of his body, it is reasonable to suppose that at that time He gave him all the mental powers necessary for all purposes during the life of his race. With perfection in the physical, it is supposable he approached very near to intellectual perfection. Primitive man was a mathematician, not by collegiate process, but by native ability. He did not have to take a course in a university to study chemistry, because of the fact that he was a chemist when he was born. Possibly he could speak or understand all languages spoken by the human tongue from the powers of his mind, which occupied a pure and healthy physique. In a word, he was well made and fully endowed with all the physical and mental forces necessary for the whole journey of his life. Now a question arises, When did he begin to degenerate physically and mentally? Let us reason a little along this line. History is young and has had imperfectly recorded only such events as have transpired during a few centuries, and with records imperfectly preserved.

We see evidences all along of prehistoric man's life, though the being and his bones have been mostly obliterated. We see close to his bony remains the stone axe and the flint dart. We find acres of ground in many places close to mounds and caves with countless millions of slivers that have been scaled from flints and formed to suit war's purposes. Bones found in caves and in buried heaps indicate that many thousands fell in mortal combat here and there. Possibly they were old in the skilled arts of war at that day. Great and powerful men, who should have been parents of the coming generations, were slain and destroyed, and the conquered became the captives and slaves of the conquerors, with all opportunities for mental development suppressed. Other nations and tribes entered the bloody fields of battle, and have nothing to report excepting the death of their best physically formed men, leaving the propagation of the race or races to those who were left behind as physically unfit for battle, owing to lack of strength of either body or mind.

This process of destroying the mentally and physically great has been kept up to the limits of our history's record.

We must go to school about one-half of our time, in order to cultivate and stimulate our mental energies sufficiently well to follow the ordinary business pursuits of life.

Mental Dwarfs.

Without worrying the patience of the reader, we will ask him if it is not reasonable to believe that during all the past thousands of years that men have fought over their gods and governments, there has resulted a mental dwarfage? Our professional men are only imitators of one another. They spend many years in school because of a lack of native ability. This is our condition, and we must make the best we can of it. Most of our so-called learned men of to-day stand upon heaps of mental rubbish. You seldom see in an editor's columns any evidence of originality and mental greatness. He clips, quotes, and sells his "wisdom." He takes up some hobby, religious or scientific. He lauds his own religious views. His scientific ideas he wishes embalmed for the use of future generations. His law is *the* law. His medicine is God's pills, notwithstanding he is the laughing-stock of all who know him. I want to be good to these fellows. I expect to be good to them, as they are suffering from the effects of prenatal causes thrown upon them by their ancestors for thousands of years. By those causes they possibly have been wounded worse than I have, and I do not expect to spend any time in combats with mental dwarfs, be they political, religious, or scientific bigots. If I can successfully run my boat over the riffles of time, I shall credit it to good luck, not native ability; for I, too, feel what they should—the deep plowings of mental dwarfage, the result of the slaughter of all the great and good men for ages before us.

The Appearance of Œdema

Œdema is one word that appears at the first showing of life and death in animal forms. Previous to death there is a general swelling of the system, a watery swelling of fascia and lymphatics, even to those of nerve-fibers. If a disease should destroy life by withholding all fluids, we can trace such cause to a time when there was a watery swelling of the centers of the nerves of nutrition to such an extent as to cut off nerve-supply until sensation ceased to renovate and keep off accumulating fluids as long as fermentation did the work of heating till all fluids had dried up, and the channels of supply had closed by adhesive inflammation, and death followed by the law of general atrophy.

To make the assertion that all diseases have their beginning in œdema may be wide in its range, but we often find one principle ruling over much territory Mind is the supreme ruler of all beings, from the mites of life to the monsters of the land and sea. There we see a ruling principle without limit. The same of numbers. By heat all metals melt. Acids must have oxygen to make them solvents of metals. We only speak imperfectly of a few common laws to prepare the student to think along the line of probabilities as I hold them out for consideration. Suppose we begin at the atoms of fluids, such as enter the construction of animal or vegetable forms, and have them held up until decomposition begins. In a delay like that, does not Nature call a halt and refuse to obey the laws of construction and let all other supplies pile up even unto death? Is not all this the result of œdema? Œdema surely begins with the first tardy atom of matter. Pneumonia begins by œdematous accumulations of dead atoms, even to the death of the whole body, all having found a start in atoms only.

We will now propound a few questions which the osteopath should keep in mind:

Are animal forms complete as working machines?

Has Nature furnished man with powers to make his bones and give them the necessary form?

Does a section in Nature's law provide fastenings to hold these to one another?

How will this body move, and where and how is the force applied?

Where and how is this force obtained?

How is it generated and supplied to these parts of motion?

What makes these muscles, ligaments, nerves, veins, and arteries?

Are they self-forming, or has Nature prepared machinery to make them?

Does animal life contain knowledge and force for the construction of all the parts of man?

Can it run the machine after it has finished it?

By what power does it move?

Is there a blood-vessel running to every part of this body to supply all these demands?

If it has a battery of force, where is it?

What does it use for force?

Is it electricity? If so, how does it collect and use this substance?

How does it convey its powers?

How does man keep warm without a fire?

How does he build and lose flesh all the time?

Where and how is the supply made and delivered to proper places?

How is it applied and what holds it to its place when adjusted?

What makes it build the house of life?

Do demand and supply govern the work? If not, what does?

Are the laws of animal life sufficient to do all this work of building and repairing wastes and keeping it in running condition?

If they are, what can man do or suggest to help them?

Is this machine capable of being run fast or slow if need be?

Does man have in him some kind of chemical laboratory that can turn out such products as he needs to fill all his physical demands?

If by heat, exercise, or any other cause he gets warm, can that chemistry cool him to normal?

If too cold, can it warm him? Can it adjust him to heat and cold?

If so, how is it done? Is the law of life and longevity fully vindicated in man's make-up?

CHAPTER XII.

Smallpox.

The History of Smallpox.

The subject of smallpox is a serious one for the minds, bodies, and pens of the doctors of this century, as it has been for those of many centuries of the past, if records are true, as we believe they are. We have learned nothing of the origin, nothing of the action of the deadly poison which it contains, and when we sum up all that has been written for thousands of years, we only learn that the doctor does not know what it is nor what it does, more than that it has the power to kill the human race by the millions. Judging from their writings, our wisest doctors know nothing more than does the savage, so in the twentieth century we need not look back to them for knowledge. The field is just as cloudy to-day for the doctor as at any period of the remotest days of man's history, when he thought God had sent smallpox as one of His choicest plagues to punish the nations for some sin of disobedience to His holy ordinance. Man has tried many ways to stop its deadly work. He has prayed, sacrificed, and dosed, but all to no effect up to the hour of the coming in of the twentieth century. I think the doctors of the medical schools have done the best they could to combat and stop its eternal fire, where the "worm" hath not died by the hands of the most skilled authors or doctors of medicine. The medical doctors, with all they know of cause or cure, are just as afraid of smallpox as the commons. I claim it is the privilege and duty of the American School of Osteopathy to take a hand in this fight and do what it can to stop the ravages of the filthy curse, smallpox. Many things have been tried, but all have failed. Vaccination and inoculation have both been well tried, but the smallpox is here, there, and all over the earth, and as defiant to-day as at the close of each day or century of the historic past.

Our school charter reads: "To improve on our present systems of surgery, obstetrics, and treatment of diseases generally." I will confine myself to that charter. We claim to use any means that are better than any known method of the past, as used in surgery, as used in obstetrics, and the treatment of diseases generally. It will not be my object to speak of the improvements made by osteopathy in surgery and obstetrics, nor in treating diseases of climate or diseases of the different seasons of the year, but to give my reason for a change in our method of treating smallpox and other contagious diseases.

Smallpox is the most dreadful disease known to the human family. It has killed its countless millions, and has been a deadly terror for thousands of years. It visits and slays men, women, and children of all nations, civilized and savage. It has no mercy on any human. It lives on human flesh only; nothing but human blood has been found or known that will appease its wrath. All of this the people of the earth have learned by sad experience, but have been powerless to combat it. If we would prevent the ravages of the disease, it is first necessary for me to make an inquiry into its nature.

Does the virus, the seed, or the substance of smallpox act so as to corrode the albumin, blood, and fat? Does it cause the magnetic battery of man to call into the system such gases as ammonia and phosphorus and set them on fire by electricity, exploding the nitrogen that is stored so abundantly in the cellular system of the body? Smallpox does something. What is it? Surely some vital shock causes this awful confusion.

Have all the doors of the excretories been shut? Does the introduction of the germ of smallpox into the lungs cause a contracture of its cellular system, by means of which the virus is retained in the system until the eruption is developed? To the writer this is reasonable. Has not man gone far enough with his abortive method of reasoning to halt and think on other lines? We should learn what the physical change is, and combat it accordingly. Do substances, beings, animals, trees, and stones throw off an incubating vitality of their own? Can their life-substance be conveyed to another body over a conducting wire, or is it conveyed by the atmosphere? Is there not a life-giving force common to all nature, and when that force passes from a diseased human to another, does it not show by its action that it is a living substance?

The Origin of Contagious Diseases.

Do contagions or contagious diseases come from seeds of matter, or from changes of the powers of life, life-activities being modified by force of compounds that have been driven from natural channels, and creating new or abnormal activities that unite substances into other compounds that are poisonous to the healthy fluid of animal life? Thus a snake-bite or its virus only causes an explosive shock to the cells of different gases, whose union, when disturbed by other additions, causes universal explosion and spills substances that are poisonous to the contents of other cells. Explosion and death take place when union with the fluids of other cells or different kinds occurs. Not a germ, but an electric condition, shock, or change in natural functioning, causes changes of the corpuscles in blood, and this changed blood, when ejected into mucous membranes, is mistaken for foreign germs.

Do contagions pass from the diseased person to the healthy person by emigrating bugs? If by emigrating from one to the other, where do they camp to enter this new physiological field? Do they camp or locate in the ears, on our heads or our backs, or do those germs wisely select the lungs, where there is an abundant supply of food, water, and air? If each air-cell of the five lobes is a house that would accommodate a couple of germs, male and female, which fertilize the nerve-cells with the seed of smallpox, how many houses would be filled when all had an occupant? We have reason to believe that all contagious diseases seek the lungs to pasture and deposit their germs.

In the neck will be found the nerves that rally all forces which convey contagious vapors or seeds into the air-cells where the nerve-terminals open the mouths of secretion and take up the life-gases of smallpox and other contagions and convey that substance to the nerve-cells for development through all stages to perfect eruption of measles, chickenpox, or any other rash on to smallpox. Thus we see that the vital vapor enters the body by way of the lungs, first entering the air-cells, and then being taken up by the mouths of the nerves at the periphery, and conveyed to the nerve-cells or cavities for development and general distribution to the whole cellular system of the body, beginning with the fascia and ending with the skin I think by this time the student of Nature will seek to know the cause of the great physiological changes that we see in eruptive fevers, such as smallpox, measles, chickenpox, and all glandular changes as found in mumps, typhoid fever, syphilis, tuberculosis, and chronic dysentery I think I have pointed out just how smallpox and many other diseases enter the system of nutrition, construction, and renovation, leaving deposits in blood-vessels, lymphatics and the membranous and cellular systems, whose decomposition feeds and sustains the deadly diseases of consumption, chronic dysentery, diphtheria, cancer, Bright's disease, scrofula, and many others equally destructive. With the knowledge of how and where the germ is deposited, how it is fed and grows to universal occupancy of the system, we have but little to seek, except to know how to work the machinery and cause it to unload.

Jenner, of the seventeenth century, reasoned that man could ward off the disease by the use of vaccine matter, which is only localized, modified smallpox. We feel proud of his energy as shown in his effort to modify the ravages of smallpox. We know that his object was good, and that if one infectious poison was in possession of the body, it would hold it immune to other infections. I say, I believe that his object was good, but I do believe other substances will do the warding off of disease by possession just as well as or better than vaccine matter, and have no bad effects follow their use. I chose cantharides as a substitute for vaccine, and I will give my reasons for looking for something better than the vaccine matter that is taken from a sick cow with an eruption that appears on her teats or bag. This was originally taken into the milkmaid's hands in any place that the skin had a fresh crack or broken surface in which the virus could enter the skin for development to the rash.

The following definition of "vaccine" is taken from Dunglison: "The cowpox is a disease of the cow arising spontaneously or perhaps from the smallpox contagion of man, or from the matter of grease in horses conveyed by the milkers, which, if transmitted to man by means of inoculation, may preserve him from smallpox contagion. The promulgation of this valuable property of the vaccine virus is due to Dr. Jenner, who, after many experiments, extending over twenty years, made a definite announcement in 1798 regarding the nature of the virus."

In Dunglison's definition he speaks of spontaneous production in the cowpox; he is not positive that it is spontaneous. Neither Dr. Jenner nor Dunglison has told us any more of the origin of the cowpox than that it comes on the cow spontaneously, or from grease-heel of the horse, or it is smallpox caught by inoculation from a milkhand who had smallpox while he handled the cow's teats. You see, they are "supposed-sos." They both guess and suppose to a finish. From what both have said, I will guess that both have failed to find or know anything of the cause of the cowpox. Neither have left any light for the reader.

USE OF VACCINE.

Now we will take up the subject of immunity from smallpox by the use of vaccine. I will not dispute that smallpox cannot enter the system during the time that vaccine is acting on the system as an eruptive fever. It is reasonable to conclude that the eruptive fever that goes with vaccine will hold the fort of life against any other eruptive substances and prevent it from being taken up and receiving vitality. Suppose it will hold the system immune by occupancy until the system has washed itself to purity from the old before a new virus will take effect and develop to any rash. Then we see that all safety from smallpox lies in the fact that the system is full of cow-rot, and that there is no place for smallpox nor the rot or seed of any other contagious disease. Cantharides is a safer preventive than vaccine, and why? First, the cow is subject to lung diseases, tuberculosis, and pneumonia; so much so that for safety from diseased milk very stringent laws have been enacted to prevent its use. The cow has about as many diseases as man, or more: cancer, blackleg, erysipelas of the mouth, pink-eye, and many other diseases; she has lockjaw, and she has poison in her system that will and does kill human beings when put into their systems. Then, if Jenner's philosophy is true, that one animal poison while in the body will keep out others by occupancy, we should select from the species that are not known to be diseased. We do know the cow to be a very much diseased beast, and, since her blood has been inserted into man's system, that man's death-ratio from cancer, scrofula, and consumption has asked for and received from two to four hundred thousand humans each year in America alone. Smallpox doctors have been in the Jenner rut since the year 1798. Jenner reasoned from the cowpox and the grease-heel of the horse, or, as we say in America, "scratches." He and all the M.D.s of Europe have been good men and have kept their feet in the rut of tradition, particularly in fighting smallpox, and as the English did in fighting the Boers. The Englishmen fought well without reason, but the Boers "licked" them every time until all their resources were exhausted and they had to submit to a so-called surrender. What did the Boers do? They moved out of the old English and German ruts of war, and fought and thought with power to suit the occasion and with consummate skill. We read reports of all their battles, following Johnny Bull and the Dutch, with Johnny repeatedly getting thrashed and sending for another general, who would come in and fight just as the officer did whom he succeeded. He walked out bravely as a lion, and also got whipped. My blood is English, Scotch, and German, but it has been in America for four generations, and I feel free to say that I hate a hen that sits on a nest that has no eggs in it just because her grandmother sat there. If she sits on nothing but rotten eggs, what will she get but rotten chickens, like the rotten virus that Jenner put under his hen of reason one hundred years ago? But his work was good, but *minus* the reasoning that one rotten substance was all the system could combat at one time, and if the patient was kept full of horse- and cow-rot, that the seeds of smallpox could not push out the cow-rot and get possession of the system. I believe we are on safe ground to cut a more extended system of experimenting with smallpox and its abatement by the cantharides or any substance that would create an infectious fever. When we have an infectious fever, that fever has possession of the whole body, and, by all rules of reason, will hold possession until it has completed its work. Then other infections may take possession of the body and proceed to plant that seed of another eruptive fever and hold the body immune to all others. "Stop that!" The people have commenced to say, "Stop that!" for many hosts are so uselessly murdered daily by poisons forced into their systems by hypodermic syringes.

Jenner's Command Not Heeded.

It is claimed that Jenner commanded the sun (smallpox) to stand. It did not stand. Others before and since his day have tried cowpox and grease-heel of the horse, but both have failed. Isolation reports a hopeless failure. Pest-houses are in all cities, and so is smallpox. People are afraid of it. The doctor is the first to run. It is a fight he will not go into. He claims that it is better to run than to get whipped. I believe that the philosophy of Jenner, the groomsman and the milk-maid, is good, but it gives nothing to the world excepting the accidental cure or supposed preventive to smallpox. No reason was given why one poison would immune the person from another poison. Jenner simply accepted, tried, and adopted the supposed remedial powers of cowpox and sore or cankered heels of the horse. He and his disciples gave us no caution nor hint that the grease-heel of the horse might be a venereal disease peculiar to the horse only. They told us nothing of the cowpox, whether or not it was venereal in nature, or whether, like the adoption of most medical "remedies" the doctor uses or has used, it came to notice by accident. I do not wish in the least to antagonize the effort of Jenner. I think it was good, but I do think that more effective and less dangerous substances can be used than the putrid compounds of variola. I believe that this philosophy which I present can and will be found as protective against leprosy, measles, and syphilis as against smallpox and other infectious contagions. This is the twentieth century. Our school was created to improve on the past. Let us keep step with the music of progress.

CREDIT WHERE CREDIT IS DUE.

We should be thankful to our ancestors, and give them credit for all their various methods of combating smallpox. Give them praise and love. They thought that they had found a remedy that could modify the death-dealing scourge, smallpox. The popular opinion of the world is that smallpox has been greatly reduced in its destruction of human life all over the world since the introduction of vaccination by Jenner. To him is due the credit of rescue from the unmerciful slaughter of all races of men. That belief is shared in and practiced now by all nations and people on earth. It is not my object to dig up his bones and abuse him. I believe the philosophy of fighting one infection with another infectious substance that could hold the body immune by long and continuous possession is good and was good. Like any benefactor, he perhaps did not select the best material to bring his thoughts to their best and most defiant proofs. Many persons have died who have been vaccinated with the blood of the cow or horse. Many have gone into decay, consumption, cancerous ulcers, and lost both limbs and life from diseases latent in the cow and horse, many of them supposed to be syphilitic and gonorrhœal. The cow and horse have many diseases loathsome in effect which, through lack of caution, had not been seen or known of when the virus was taken from the animal for man's use and protection. This has been the danger in using dead pus from the cow and horse that had glanders, gleet, farcy, and other deadly diseases. I think Jenner was right in his object, but he made a bad choice of germifuge to ward off infections. Reason at once brings us to conclude that, as the horse and cow are both very subject to many diseases equally as dangerous as smallpox itself, to choose their blood, let it decompose and rot, and then insert that blood into the human body, would be dangerously unwise, and it should go out of use as soon as a safe and better substitute is found. I have chosen the cantharides, and will give the reasons why I have chosen it as a better substance than that of the cow or horse.

DANGERS OF VACCINATION.

When we read of the diseases to which the cow and horse are subject, we find them to be very numerous. They are almost equal to those that attack the human race in variety, and are just as deadly. Our oldest and youngest authors all talk much about smallpox. They talk in Latin, Greek, Hebrew, Sanskrit, German, and in all known and unknown tongues about the disease and its mysterious workings; but when they are weighed by an American who only wants to know the "how" and "why" of anything, he is forced to say that he is no wiser when he has read one thousand authors than he was before he had read a single work on smallpox. They all talk much, but make no point that is positively sure to be depended on by him who wants an up-to-date truth proven by the facts of demonstration. One says vaccination immunes. Another says it does not. Vaccination may prevent one-half from the contagion, but does not prevent the virus from killing thousands with lockjaw, syphilis, gonorrhœa, and syphilitic tuberculosis. I would like at this time to report that I had found some light on the mysterious disease, smallpox. So far I am only able to report, "Hold out your arm and take your poison." The doctor wants fifty cents. I believe that if the fifty cents were taken out of vaccination that the doctor gets and lives on, the practice would die out. The doctor knows that he is as afraid of smallpox after his arm has been filled with cow-rot as he was before. He fears that his immunity will not stand up to him when he gets in the ring and boxes with smallpox.

When all the good has been said in favor of vaccination, the world only learns that for years it has been a hopeless failure and so confirmed. If you go into towns and cities where the most rigid systems to compel people to become vaccinated exist, you will find just as much smallpox or more than where than has been no vaccination at all. To-day, with all the police force and cow-rot that has been forced into men, women, and children, there is no less smallpox. I believe the time is close at hand when forcible vaccination will not be necessary, as a better method, and one that will do the work and leave no bad effects as in the case of vaccination with the cow, horse, and other animal poisons, has been found. The dread of disease and death by vaccination causes people to hesitate to allow vaccine matter to be put into the arms of children and older persons by military force. When they learn that a fly blister as large as a fifty-cent piece on the arm will keep off smallpox in all cases, there will be no fear nor trouble about smallpox or vaccination.

Stand Ready for the Fight.

I have followed the history of the ravages of smallpox as presented by the most learned historians of all ages as far back as the pen of man has given any record of the malady. All have said they do not know what it is nor how to stop its eternal progress, knowing that it is in possession of the whole globe. I am asked by students and graduates of the American School of Osteopathy what I would advise them to do in case smallpox should break out; would I advise them to stand, or "skip out" and leave their patients, many or few, who did not have the smallpox, to suffer and die? I advised them to agree with facts already proven: that smallpox is an infectious disease, also contagious; also that the statutes in many parts of the world obliged both old and young to be vaccinated that the body might be disinfected, and force all houses in which there had been smallpox to be disinfected Then the thought came that the laws would be enforced to "prevent the spread" of the disease, and that vaccination was believed to be a reliable disinfectant to the body, and there was no choice but to show an arm with marks of effective vaccination or of having taken a dope of vaccine matter into the system, with syphilis, tuberculosis, leprosy, and all other diseases of man and beast which are attributes of vaccine, killing nearly a million each year from syphilitic and other diseases transmitted from diseased persons and glandered horses and cattle from which the vaccine is taken. A legal rot, and legally put in your arm and that of your wife and child, to eat out your lungs with syphilis and your brain with glanders. I say to all sensible persons: Wake up and seek a deadly germicide to smallpox, and when you find anything better than the rotten flesh of the horse or cow, I say, use it, if you find it to be better than the old, or you are an osteopathic coward. Our school was chartered and built to improve on the old theories for man's good, and you must show it by your works. Read the charter of your school every night before you go to bed. It says "improve" on old theories.

A few words on germifuge, which, according to Dunglison, means "to expel or drive away germs; any agent that will destroy germs or micro-organisms or their spores, on which contagious diseases may depend; mercury chlorid, iodid, aluminium acetate, sulfurous acid, heat at continuous temperature of 230 degrees and over." To find a successful germifuge for smallpox has been the anxious study of the whole world for all time. Prayer has been tried—no good, no life saved. Jenner sought to insert into the body a modified poison that would stay in the system as a perpetual germifuge for smallpox. His idea was good, but there is a doubt as to his choice of substances being the best. A failure of all systems to meet and banish smallpox stands recorded to-day. The osteopath is in the contest, and to him the world looks for light and hopes for relief from smallpox.

Victory in a New Germicide.

A successful hunt for an innocent and trustworthy germicide for smallpox I felt confident would be successful early in the twentieth century if we would expel the vaccine and do some reasoning. Should an osteopathic doctor come in contact with a case of smallpox, with the rash just breaking out, would you recommend any medicines, palliatives in the drug line, in the treatment? I would not. His remedies would be confined to the nerves of the excretory system, which have proven to be all that is necessary. Our success without drugs has been very satisfactory in all cases treated and reported. In all cases of smallpox that I met in my practice in the sixties and treated with medicine, I could give only temporary relief by opiates. I then believed that there was danger in stopping the fluids in the system by sedatives. Diuretics alone seemed the best of all. Fermentation of fluids seemed to be the dangerous condition to be avoided by a doctor of medicine or in any other system of relief. I often think that death comes from poison absorbed from diseased gases generated in the system. When the fluids of the body are formed, they are chemically pure, full of life, and should pass out and on for uses for which they are designed. No delays can be tolerated after they are prepared for use. It is only reasonable to look for fermentation of fluids if delayed too long in the cellular system of nerves, of fascia, or other parts or organs of the system. Thus death follows shocks to the cellular system from any cause. A closing of cells with their fluids holds their contents, and this is followed by fermentation. To ferment any substance will cost the life of all substances that are fermented, their organic life as such giving place to the gases that are produced by fermentation. Thus a complete vital change appears in all substances that ferment. A collapse of cells comes with fermentation, which fills cells to the point of rupture and deposits gas in the fascia to be passed out by the porous system. A failure to exit through the skin is followed by eruptive inflammation—thus a pock. I think we can reason fairly correctly when we begin with the lungs and trace the poisonous seeds, fumes, or gases of smallpox as they are inhaled by the lungs, taken into the air-cells of the lungs, where the nerve-terminals in the mucous membrane, with open mouths, receive and convey nutrition to the nerve-cells for their action and uses. If the terminals receive pure food, good work will naturally follow; but if food has poisons instead, then Nature would not be true to itself if it did not build diseased conditions of diseased matter. Thus we know how and why the pock is builded of diseased matter. A little leaven leaveneth the whole lump. This leaven was conceived in the lungs and became the champion over life by distributing the leaven through the whole system or lump, beginning with the air-cells of the lungs and ending with the cells of gas, fat-cells, and lymphatic cells of the system, the nerves, blood-supply of the superficial fascia, and the cellular system of blood- and nerve- supply of the skin that covers the entire body. Thus we see a little yeast has been magnified and added to The system has gone through its deadly ferment.

What Smallpox Does.

Smallpox does its deadly work by closing the cystic and lymphatic ducts. The reader will see that if a cylinder is closed at both ends whilst that tube is filled with animal fluids, death to the fluids will occur. Then fermentation will set up and inflate both tube and cyst, which will cause a rupture and collapse of lymphatic ducts and force the contents into the cellular membranes of the fascia, which form pus from dead fluids of the adjacent region. The fumes or vital ether, when inhaled by the lungs, would naturally be taken up as nourishment by the nerve-terminals of the lungs and conveyed directly to the nerve-cells. Thus the seeds of smallpox are soon conveyed to the cells of the fascia, then by the lymphatics to the whole glandular system, so that the places of entry are easily reached by the living virus of variola. Then its vital action has the aid of the whole system of nerves, including the motor, the sensory, and the nutritive, to continue the process to completion of all the work from conception to the complete smallpox. All this we know before we understand how to treat the disease successfully. If we know where the cut-off is, then we are at ease as to what to do to let out dead fluids, even after the eruption has appeared, and know how to do it. All fluids are conveyed through the body by arteries, veins, lymphatics, and excretory and secretory ducts. Let us take a case for reason and relief—a case that has gone on to the eruptive stage. Can we do any good? Had we better leave the patient and make no effort to relieve the sufferer? Before you can give an honest answer to this grave question, you must know the body in all its parts and functions. You must be correct on the lymphatic and cellular systems. You must reason that the lymphatics must never stop action by closure of tubes. Remember that a lymphatic duct is full of lymph that must be taken to the nerves for constructive purposes, and delayed lymph or chyle in any tube or cell dies, ferments, inflames, and forms pus, which process is death to the surrounding flesh, all being the effect of the shock given to the system from virus poison taken up by peripheries and conveyed to the nerve-cells. We should look out for free action of cellular and lymphatic systems; we are combating constriction in all cases of variola. The constriction of nerves and muscles is the force that shuts down circulation and retains fluids to deadly decay.

Treatment of Smallpox.

As all evidences obtainable by human reason point directly to the lungs and to the womb-like cells as the place in which the virus of smallpox deposits its seed for growth, from conception to fully developed smallpox, to combat this malady successfully we must philosophize and select the nerves that deal with sensation, motion, nutrition, and the voluntary and involuntary forces of the lungs. Because of the demand that is on the excretory nerves to disgorge the lymphatics and cells of the system, the same nerve-cells may be strengthened by nourishing food, taken up by the peripheral system of nerves of the lungs and conveyed to the nerve-cells of the lungs and on to the whole system. Then we have force to take up vitality in place of the poisonous compound that is being generated by the deadly fluids as the vital fumes of smallpox form and throw off and are taken up by the absorbent vessels. Thus we have given Nature a chance to strengthen its energies to purify the body by casting out the dead substances, after which nutrition is in full possession, with power and pure material to repair the injurious work following constriction, congestion, inflammation, and pus-formation. Let us examine the neck carefully, and see if it is constricted. If so, we have a disease of constriction, and are warranted in addressing our attention to the vaso-constrictors. We must modify that constriction by adjusting the bones of the neck, that the famishing nerves may be quieted by arterial nutritious blood. We must also address our attention to the dilators, which control the quantity of blood that should or does pass through them, and relieve the fascia of impacted lymphatic cells and increase the circulation of blood through the fascia of the whole system. Thus we are applying our remedies to the neck, where the mischief is being done by the abnormal condition of the vaso-constrictor and vaso-dilator nerves. As the constrictor nerves of the neck are the most important in treating smallpox, and as the reason why has just been given, we will continue the exploration to the dorsal, lumbar, and sacral nerves. Give much attention to the upper dorsal system for the relief of the lungs from the constriction that exists to a powerful degree, during the process from gestation to the period of convalescence and complete recovery. When the vital fumes of smallpox are conveyed from the periphery to the maternal nerve-cells of the lungs, they cause a shock by irritation, which causes constricture of the sphincter system of cells, and retains this vital ether for the purpose of adding to the germ of smallpox nutriment which develops a sufficient quantity of this vital gas to supply the whole system with the yeast of development to all fluid cells from lymph to chyle. Thus it is ready to enter and proceed successfully with its deadly war with all that is vital in the human system. As it lives upon vitality and must be deposited in the most vital parts of the system for development, we see as a result that it consumes this vitality in the whole system, and the effect is what we call death. There is no doubt about the fact that if the excretory system of cells, glands, and lymphatics is greatly impeded in throwing waste fluids of the body, accumulation follows, then fermentation, with inflammation added to congestion and fermentation. By this time all the cells are filled with dead matter, fluids, and gases. All glands of the body become loaded with inflamed fluids and are burning with fever; then all lymphatics and nerves of the superficial fascia and its blood-vessels and porous systems are overcome by irritation and pressure by the bulky deposits in the superficial fascia; then follows the preparation to get this dead pus out of the fascia. To do this, the excretory ducts must be enlarged. Boils form in the skin and rot out holes to drain the fascia where the great mischief of smallpox is done.

Good Nursing.

After the rash appears, the doctor can do but little more than nurse, feed, and look to comfortable rooms, dress boils, and such other work as the condition may suggest to his judgment and experience. Look after the nerves of motion of the lower dorsal, the nerves of the neck, and also the lumbar nerves. The renal nerves keep the veins free to drain in fullest flow. Let the patient smell for a few full breaths a handkerchief with ten or twelve drops of cantharidin. Never take more than three full breaths from the handkerchief at a time, and not oftener than twice a day, and not more than three days in succession, for fear of irritating the lungs too much by the cantharides that is in the tincture. A few breaths of tincture of cantharidin dropped on a handkerchief will act on the breath and start the kidneys to active draining, and also cause the lymphatics of the fascia to throw out their contents. Before the doctor of osteopathy enters a room of smallpox, he must take time to allow a blister as large as a dollar to draw on the outside of his arm about three inches above the elbow. I would not have any fear of even confluent smallpox after my arm had a well-drawn blister. It will hold you immune to all danger. I believe I am perfectly safe in so advising osteopaths—or all people, for that matter. Why does man take smallpox, and why is his dog immune to the disease, both having been exposed at the same time? Because all animals below the man have musks of immunity that are more powerful than the fumes or germs of smallpox, measles, mumps, cholera, yellow fever, and so on to the general list of human ills. Nature has furnished the flesh-eating birds, animals, and reptiles with protective musks or germifuge. Many can be smelled one mile or more. Any wild beast or bird can eat the most putrid flesh of the dead mad-dog, smallpox, or leper with perfect safety. They would be failures in nature if they would take smallpox or hydrophobia and get wild and die. We would soon be without the buzzard or any other scavenger to clean the earth of putrescence. But, as man's germicidal powers cannot resist the smallpox, he must try to arm himself with an artificial substitute, which I believe we can do and have done with wonderful success in the use of the cantharidin as now reported in hundreds of cases. It creates an infectious fever that is innocent in after-effects, and will hold full possession of the body and defend it from all other infections whilst it has possession, and be a perfect immunity to smallpox at last.

I believe all immunities are based on the philosophy or law of possession. "Possession is nine points of the law," and is just as good in contagious infections as in governments or any forceful possession of property or power.

An Application of This Principle.

If you have measles in your body, it will hold the body and defy all contagions to enter while it has possession. We have no report from history of any person taking the mumps, measles, chicken-pox, or any contagion during the time that smallpox has possession of the body and is doing its work as an infectious disease. I believe we have a reasonable philosophy in the use of cantharidin. Start an infectious and innocent fever that will defy the entry of variolus poisons and hold man, woman, and child perfctly safe amidst smallpox, mumps, measles, and other contagions. This treatise of the subject of smallpox is given for you to ponder on it. I believe the days of smallpox are numbered in the minds of osteopaths who can and do reason.

MEASLES.

Let me ask, What is the measles? How does it get in and out of the body? Well, it is some kind of poison that comes out of the lungs of another person, who has poison in his system that has gotten strong enough to poison two people. That poisoned air was breathed from No. 1 by No. 2. When the poisoned air was taken into the lungs of No. 2, the nerve-terminals of the lungs took in the poison by the periphery and carried it to the nerve-cells. Then the work of growth of the poison began in the cells, and, multiplying, carried on its poison to the nerve-cells of the lymphatics of the deep and suoerficial fascia, which did the rest of the work by fermentation.

If disease is so highly attenuated, so ethereal, and penetrable in quality, and multiple in atoms, and a breath of air, two quarts or more, are taken into the lungs fully charged with contagion, how many thousand air-cells could be impregnated by one single breath? Say we take a case of measles into a schoolroom of sixty pupils, in a warm and poorly oxygenized atmosphere all day, would not the living gas thrown off from active measles enter and irritate the air-cells and close the most irritable cells with the poisonous gas retained for active development in those womb-like departments in the lungs?

Now you have the seeds in thousands of cells, which are as vital and well supplied by nerves and blood as the womb itself. Would not reason see the development of millions more of the vital beings who get their nourishment from the vitality found in the human fascia, which comes nearer to the surface in the lungs than in any other part of the system, except it be the womb?

In proof of the certainty of measles being taken up by the lungs at one breath and caught by the secretions and conveyed to the universal system of fascia to develop the contagion, I will give the case of one of my boys who was sick with a cold, as I supposed. The symptoms were watering of eyes, cough, fever, and headache. He was in the country about eight miles from home, and on our return he stopped to get his books at a small school-house. He ran in, picked up his books that were lying upon the desk, walked the length of the room, which was about forty feet, was not there over half a minute, and in just nine days forty-two children broke out with measles. So certain is contagion to be taken up by the nerves and vitalizing fluids of the fascia.

It seems that all the fascia needs to develop anything is to have the substance planted in its arms for construction; the work will be done, labeled, and handed out for inspection by the inspectors of all works.

A Comparison.

In smallpox the motor energy must be equal to the force that would convey albumin through all tissues. In measles it would be less, and so on according to the thickness of the fluids present. The power to drive dead fluids from fascia must be much greater in smallpox than in cases of measles. We see why the pulse of smallpox is so powerful during development of the pox. After killing the fluids by retention in the fascia of the skin, a still greater force is created by injury to the nerve-fibers of the fascia. Then the motor energy appears, and all the powers of life combine to help the arteries force the fluids through the skin and push them to the fascia of the skin to be eliminated. In some parts elimination fails; such places are called pocks. They suppurate and drop out, leaving a pit, the pock-mark. Now had the nerves of the skin and fascia not been irritated, contracting the skin in opposition to the fascia passing its dead fluids through the excretory ducts of the skin, we probably would have had no eruption. Is it not quite reasonable to conclude that after the heart overloads the fascia and the nerves lose their control by pressure of fluids, all that is left is chemical action to the production of pus, which throws it out of the fascia in intervening spaces? Then, should the fascia have greater destruction of its substances, we have one spot running into others, and we have "confluent smallpox."

Scarlet Fever.

As defined by allopathy: "Scarlet fever begins with a short period of tired feeling. A short period of chilly sensation, fullness of eyes, and sore throat. In a few hours fever begins with great heat in back of head. It soon extends all over the body. Sick stomach and vomiting generally accompany the disease. Rash of a red color begins on the back, and extends to the throat and limbs. About the second or third day the fever is very high, from 100° to 104°, and generally lasts to the fifth or seventh day, at which time fever begins to diminish, with itching over the body. The skin at this time throws off all the dead scales that had been red rash in the fore part of the disease. Often the lining membranes of the mouth, throat, and tonsils slough and bleed. Also pus is often formed just under the skin in front of the throat. Such cases usually die." The latter is very true if treated by a drug practitioner.

Scarlet fever, as defined by osteopathy, is a disease generally of the early spring and late fall seasons. Generally it comes with cold and damp weather during east winds. It begins with sore throat, chilly and tired feelings, followed with headache and vomiting. In a few hours the chilly feeling leaves and a high fever sets in. The patient is rounded in chest, abdomen, face, and limbs by congestion of the fascia and all of the lymphatic glands. This stagnation will soon begin its work of fermentation of the fluids of fascia, then you see the rash. If you do not want to see the rash and sloughing of throat, with a dead patient, I would advise you to train your guns on the blood, nerves, and lymphatics of the fascia and stop the cause at once, or quit.

CHAPTER XIII.

Obesity.

When Reason Begins.

When we eat and drink, we do so because we get hungry. We do that for many years before we try to reason why we grow from small to large-sized bodies, of bone and muscle. We get too fat or too lean, we gain or lose in flesh. We are sometimes with tolerably good strength, but usually strength is lost. We know we are not what we have been; we are much larger, but have little strength. So much we know and stop. We are fat or lean, but we do not know why. We eat and drink about the same kind of diet. Now we want to lose the surplus fat, or add enough to get back to our old standard of size and strength.

A Dyspeptic Condition.

In trying to reason on the cause of these conditions, I am forced, in conclusion, to believe that these deposits of fat are the effect of a dyspeptic condition of the nerves of nutrition of the fascia, which should consume such fluids, and digest and appropriate the same to the energies and strength of the body. That failure to take up, digest, and use as fast as the supplies come is the cause of the filling up of oily fluids in the spongy tissues under the skin and through the body. I believe the maternal process is cut off from the spinal cord at the place where such energies issue from the cord. We must learn just where such interference is located, and treat for the renewal of the forces; then we can reasonably hope to see the fat consumed and corpulency reduced by the process of normal consumption.

Now we have arrived at the point to locate and establish our observations. We want a clear and unobstructed view of the subject that we are about to explore, that we may arrive at a satisfactory and philosophical conclusion. We must have facts to build upon or our foundation will surely give way. We must have two persons of unnatural conditions, the one abnormally fat, the other abnormally lean. One is too great in size, the other with a very dwarfed condition of the whole system. The first thing necessary to a foundation to a philosophical observatory is knowledge on the "hows" and "whys" of animal construction; of supplies, how consumed and appropriated, and what dispositon is made of this material after being appropriated. We should carefully inspect the machinery of digestion, the machinery of construction, the machinery of renovation, and must thoroughly know these three processes. Then we are confronted with the question, Why is it that two persons eating at the same table, one will take up and deposit flesh-making substances to burdensome abnormality, while the other takes on no flesh at all. Is not this surplus amount of fat an evidence of a dyspeptic condition of the nerves of force and action? Have not the nerves failed to drink this fatty fluid and convert it into motor energy, and when done with such substances, to convert them into gaseous fluids and expel them from the body? Certainly the far-reaching telescope of a well-trained philosopher can readily behold the cause, and he can form his conclusion that both variations are dyspeptics The one should be treated to take up more of the substances, and the other should be treated in such a manner as to cause him to burn up in the furnace of life all fuel sent there by Nature to keep it hot and in motion. Now we are ready to apply and exhibit with judgment the skill of a physiological engineer. If we understand the physiological processes of the preparation of substances, which when prepared are taken up and delivered to their proper places, and if we understand when those substances have supplied the natural energies and when they are placed into excretory ducts and carried away, then we are on the right line of reason, as engineers of the human body, to keep down unnatural deposits.

SUPPLY AND DEMAND.

As we proceed with our mental labor in discussion of why the system does not use the fat-substances as fast as delivered, we will be wise to confine our mental powers more carefully to inspect for better acquaintance just what power at the place of delivery fails to work up the fluid before it hardens to the degree of flesh. As we reason, such questions as these naturally arise: Do the nerves of the fascia have anything to do in constructing muscle or any other physical forms? If so, do they connect directly with the spinal cord? Do they become obstructed so as to suspend their functional action? How much suspension of nerve-power will drop life so low that it will not receive, prepare, and appropriate this fat-substance and prevent bulky accumulation? Then another question: How low a degree of nerve-vibration marks or would mark on the scale of nerve-action just when the body can no longer receive this crude material and go on with its process of taking up, digesting, and qualifying this fluid to enter the higher degrees of functional action? The doctors of past ages have been failures because of their inability or simple failure to prosecute an acquaintance with the functions of physical action along the line which the foregoing has indicated. If you have given close attention and made yourself thoroughly acquainted with anatomy, physiology, and the suggestions they present, you will need no further explanation to know the cause and cure of obesity and atrophy.

CHAPTER XIV.

Ear-Wax and Its Uses.

NATURE MAKES NOTHING IN VAIN.

That Nature makes nothing in vain is an established truth in the minds of all persons whose observation has created in them a desire to reason. That having been my faith for many years, I tried to discover why Nature had made and placed in man's head so much fine machinery just to make a little ear-wax. If "nothing is made in vain," what is that bitter stuff made for? It is always there. I have read many authors on ear-wax, and about the best the wise or unwise have said is that it would keep bugs and other insects out of our heads. I thought if that was all that it was made for, that Nature had done a great deal to "shoo" off the bugs. The idea that it was made bitter to the taste just to make bugs sick was, in my opinion, a weak philosophy, if Nature has never done any useless work or made anything in vain. At this time I saw the doors open and a good chance for the loaded mind to become unloaded and give us other uses for ear-wax than as a bug food and a lubricant for auditory nerves. In my search to find some more reasonable use or object that Nature had in forming so much delicate machinery for this product, I reasoned that this dry, hard wax was once in a gaseous or fluid state.

I had, previous to this, about concluded to sit down with the rest of the doctors and say that wax was wax, when I was called to attend a fat boy of two summers who was reported to me to be dying with croup. I began to think more about the dry wax that is always found in cases of croup, sore throat, tonsillitis, pneumonia, and all diseases of the lungs, nose, and head. On examination, I found the ear-wax dried up. So I put a few drops of glycerine, and after a minute's time a few drops of warm water, in the child's head, and kept a wet rag corked into its ear at intervals for twelve hours, and gave it osteopathic treatment. At the end of twelve hours all signs of croup had disappeared. To soften the wax, I used the glycerine, which, combining with the water, formed a harmless soap, better qualified for washing the ear and retaining the wax in solution than anything I have tried; for it is my opinion that the ear-wax should be kept in a fluid state. When in that state, the cells can more readily take it up and use it in the economy of life.

An Experiment.

The same day two ladies came to my house, sore in lungs, necks tied up, sore throats, fevers, and headache. As an experiment, in addition to osteopathic treatment, I put a few drops of glycerine into their ears, and followed it with water with which to soften and moisten the wax, which was hard and dry. Both were relieved of their sore lungs and throats in a short time, and in twenty-four hours they were about well, and the lungs were coughing out phlegm easily.

From this I think that the cause of croup is largely the result of abnormality of the cerumen system. As the question of the uses of ear-wax has been before man for ages without an answer given that passes the line of conjecture, I think there can be no reason why a few looks through the field-glass of inquiry should not be given in a limited way on that great plane of fertility. As far as the writer can learn from reading and from other methods of inquiry, the power and use of ear-wax has never been known, looked for, or thought of as one of life's agents for good or bad health. Some one asks this question, "Why are you talking about ear-wax—the filthy stuff?" In answer, I ask, "What do you know about ear-wax?" The answer comes, "I don't know or care anything about the stuff." As my spleen is my organ of mirth, I let it bounce against my side a few times at such ignorance, and decide to give the wax subject more study than ever. I began to read all the books I could find on anatomy, physiology, and histology, for knowledge of the machinery that the wise Architect of that greatest of all temples had made to generate wax. A conviction came to me to be sure of its uses before I gave an opinion. We find the center of nerve-supply of the ears located at the base of the brain and side of the head, in front of the cerebellum, just below and near the center of the brain, a little above the foramen magnum, close to and behind the carotid arteries, deep and superficial, just above the entry of the spinal cord to the brain. Thus it is situated directly in communication with all nerves to and from the brain to every part of the body. Another question came, and another, only to come and go without an answer, such as: How and where is this wax made? Of what use is it? Why so bitter? Has it any living principle? Is it produced in the brain, lymphatics, fascia, heart, lungs, nerves, or where? How much of it would kill a man? Would it kill at all? What is it made for? Is it used by the nerves as food, or used by lungs, heart, or any organ as an active principle in the magnetic or electric forces? So far all authors are silent, not even offering a speculative opinion on how it is made and its uses. So far we have received nothing that would cause a man to think that the Creator had any great design when He made so wisely constructed machinery and gave it such a prominent place.

MAKE HASTE SLOWLY.

By this time the reader begins to mentally ask, "What does this wax evangelist know about the wax and its uses?" I wish to observe and respect all nature, and never be too hasty. My aim is to carefully explore all, and never leave until I find the cause and use that Nature's hand has placed in its workings, never overlooking small packages, as they often contain precious gems. I am sure no man of brilliant mind can pass this milepost and not hitch his team and do some precious loading. At this point my pen will give notice to all anatomists, histologists, chemists, and physiologists, that I will give "no sleep or slumber to their eyes" until I hear from them an answer, yes or no, to these questions: For what purpose did God make ear-wax? Is it food or refuse? If food, what is nourished by it? And how do you know your position is true and undebatable?

Life means existence. Existence means subsistence Subsistence means something to subsist upon, and of the degree of refinement to suit the skilled work which is found marked on the trestleboard of the wisest of all builders, Whose work is absolutely correct in form and action, and beautiful to behold. It calls out the admiration of man and God·himself, Who did say of man: "Not only good, but very good."

A Great Problem.

I consider ear-wax one of the most important questions before the minds of our physiologists. The first and only knowledge of this substance begins with the observer's eye, when he beholds the dry wax as it is excreted and dropped into the cavities of the ear. A question arises, and stands without answer: Is this substance which is commonly called ear-wax, technically called cerumen, dead, or is it alive while in this visible form? If dead, why and how did it loose its life? Why has it not been consumed if once a living substance? When alive, is it in the gaseous or fluid state? And when alive and consumed as nutriment by the system, what does it nourish? These are questions for the philosopher's attention; not his superficial, but his deepest thought. Why is it deposited in the center of the brain, if not to impart its vital principle to all nerves interested in life and nutrition, both physical and vital? Its location, in itself, would indicate its importance. Another thought is, that no better place could be selected in which to establish and locate a universal supply office for the laborers of all parts of the whole superstructure. Another question arises: When we examine a person paralyzed on one side, why do we find this bread of life in such great quantities and not consumed? Have not one-half of the brain and the nerves of that whole side, limbs and all, lost their power of digestion? Is hemiplegia a dyspepsia of the nerves of nutriment of the brain and organs of that side? If so, we have some foundation on which to build an answer why this wax is not consumed and is dried up in the ears of the paralytic. The answer would be, that nutrition is suspended.

DIFFERENCES IN SEVERITY.

Let us take croup, diphtheria, scarlet fever, la grippe, and all classes of colds on to pneumonia. They present about the same symptoms, differing more in degrees of severity than of place. All affect the tonsils, nostrils, membranous air-passages, and lungs in about the same way. Croup exceeds, by contracting the trachea enough to impede the passing of air to the lungs. Diphtheria has more swelling of the tonsils, throat, and glands of the neck, but all depend upon the same blood- and nerve-supply, or a general law of blood-supply beginning with the arteries to the veins, lymphatics, glands, and ducts, to supply and take away all fluids that are of no farther use for vital and material support. As all authors have agreed that the brain furnishes the propelling forces to the nerves, it would be proper to inquire how the brain is nourished. The great cerebral system of arteries supplies the brain, to which it gives materials of all fluids and electric and magnetic forces, which must be generated in the brain. Then a question arises: If the heart, lungs, liver, pancreas, lymphatics, kidneys, and all parts of the body depend upon the brain for power, what do they give in return? If they give back anything, it must be of the kind of material of the organ from whence it comes. Each must help to keep up the universal harmony by furnishing its mite of its own kind. Suppose lung fever is the effect of lack of renal salts; where would be a better place from which to dispatch to renal organs than the ears, to reach the brain and touch the nerve that connects with the sympathetic ganglion?

Suppose we take the cerumen, in its fluid state, from the ears, by secretions to the lungs, and see the action of air and other substances on it, and it on them. We may safely look for a general action of some kind. If it be magnetic food, we will see the magnetic power shown in the lungs and through the whole system, vitalizing all organs and functions of life. Thus the lymphatics will be moved to wash out impurities and the nutritive nerves will rebuild lost energy. As but little is known or said of how or where the cerumen is formed, we will guess it is formed under the skin in the fascia and conveyed to the ears by the secretory ducts. Its place and how it is manufactured are not questions of as great importance as its use in disease and health. I have reason to believe I have found a reliable pointer for the cause of croup, diphtheria, and pneumonia; also a rational cure which any mother can appropriate, and thus save her babe from choking to death in her arms. Having witnessed croup in all its deadly work for fifty years, and seen the best skill of each year and generation fail to save, or even give relief, I lost all hope, and began to believe there was no help, and that the doctor was only one more witness to the scene of death and carnage found along the mysterious road that croup travels in its destruction of the babes of the earth. Of late days we have new and different names for the disease; but, alas! it kills the babes just as it did before it was called diphtheria, la grippe, and so on.

Written for the Home

I write this more for the mothers than for the critics. I say to you mothers, as you are not osteopaths, you are perfectly safe in putting glycerine in a child's ears. It is made from oils and fats. I believe when the wax is not consumed it clogs up the excretories with dead matter, and the irritation of the nerves of the throat, neck, lungs, and lymphatics give cause for the swelling of the tonsils and glands of the neck. I see wisdom in treating croup from the nerve-centers of the brain. The uses and importance of healthy ear-wax as a cure for disease has not had the attention of any author on disease or physiology, so far as I can find. I hope time and attention may lead us to a better knowledge of cures for diphtheria, croup, scarlet fever, and all diseases of the throat and lungs. My experience up to date with such diseases, when treated as indicated, by keeping the ear-wax in a fluid state, has been very encouraging. Though it has been but a short time since I began treatment by this method, it has proven successful with both the young and old

As all authors so far seem silent, even on the subject of when or how the wax is formed, we must resort to careful investigation to find the relation of the cerumen system to health. To intelligently acquaint the mother with this treatment, who does not understand anatomy sufficiently to give osteopathic treatment for croup, diphtheria, and so on, I will say: Take a soft cloth, wet, and wash the child's neck and rub gently down from the ears to the breast and shoulders; keep the ears moistened, frequently dropping glycerine into them. Use glycerine, because it will mix with the water and dissolve the wax, while sweet oil and other oils will not do so.

No Time for Debate.

On one occasion I was called to see a babe having malignant croup in its worst form. I examined its ears to see the condition of the wax. I had noticed in consumptives that some cases had great quantities of dry wax in one or both ears, but up to this time I had not thought of such deposits as being an evidence of lost or suspended action of the nerves that manufactured cerumen and sustained vitality. In this case I found the wax dry and very hard, with considerable swelling and hardness in the region of the ears, Eustachian tubes, and tonsils. I reasoned that the excretory duct had become clogged, and that by the wax being retained in ducts and glands an irritation of the nerves of the cervical lymphatics had caused contraction near the head, and had produced congestion of the lymphatics, of the pneumogastric, and cut off the nerve-supply from the lungs. Believing this to be very likely, I concluded to act on the above line of reasoning and see if I could give some relief. I did not stop to debate why the wax was hard and dry, but how to soften the wax was the question of importance to me then. So I proceeded. I reasoned that soap and water would be the best treatment to clean the ears and soften the wax. At this point the selection of the best make of soap was desired, so I took pure glycerine and water, dropped in a few drops, and took a small roll of cloth moistened in warm water and pushed it into the ears to keep them wet. In a few minutes I dampened and inserted soft cloth corks into the child's ears. I twisted the corks around in the ears to mix the water and wax to a softened condition. In a few minutes I got the wax softened, and the child coughed up phlegm easily, and when came the dreaded hour, ten o'clock at night, all danger had passed.

CHAPTER XV.

Convulsions.

Old Systems Unreliable.

I have been trying to unfold, and feel I have succeeded in unfolding to a better understanding, natural laws; laws which should be our guide and action in treating all diseases that mar the peace and happiness of the human race by misery and death. Old systems, with their unreliable suggestions to guide the doctor in treating diseases, have proven unworthy of respect, if merit is to be the rule of the weights and measures of intelligence. I have become so disgusted with the verbiage and nonsense that follow the pens on treatises on disease that I have concluded, for the time being, to give names that may appear novel to the reader, as I draw his attention to a knowledge of the mysteries hitherto unsolved and unexplained. We have panned and washed along the suggestions of the medical authorities, and have obtained no gold.

There are two very large and powerful rivers passing fluids in opposite directions over a territory that I will call the Klondike of life. This territory is bounded on the east by a great wall, which, according to the old books, is called the diaphragm. Through this wall courses a great river of life that spreads all over the plains of the anterior lumbar region. On that plain we find a great system of perfect irrigation of cities, villages, and fertile soils of life. This region of country covers one of the greatest and most fertile fields of life-producing elements, and places its products on the thoroughfares, and sends them back over the great central railroad, the thoracic duct, from lymphatics of the abdomen, to the heart and lungs, to be converted into a higher order of living matter. When refined there, it is called blood, and is used to sustain its own machinery, and all other machines of the body. What would be the effect on life and health if we should cut off, dam up, or suspend the flow of the aorta as it descends close to the vena cava and thoracic duct as they return with their contents through the diaphragm on their journey to the heart and lungs? And after having supplied the plain, what would be the effect if the vena cava and its system of drainage, and the thoracic duct, should be dammed up so that chyle and blood could not be carried to the heart and lungs for renewal and purification and changes? How much thought would it require to see that by stopping the arterial flow or that of the vena cava, an irritating and famishing condition would ensue, with congested veins, lymphatics, and all organs of the abdomen, causing fermentation, congestion, and inflammation, which in time cause confusion and conditions that have long been a mystery, and have been called typhoid fever, dysentery, bilious fever, periodical spasms, and so on through the whole list of general and special diseases.

Panning for Gold.

I would advise the practicing osteopath to do some very carêful panning up and down the rivers of the Klondike, for if you fail to find gold, and much of it, you would better spend the remainder of your life where reason dwelleth not. Ever remember that ignorance of the geography and customs of this country is the wet powder of success.

Fits.

We often see persons afflicted with fits or falling sickness, which the doctor has failed to cure. What is a fit? For want of better knowledge, we have an established theory that "hysteria" is purely a woman's imagination, and, as we must respect old theories, we will call it a fit of meanness. This and other theories we have had for breakfast, dinner, and supper, year in and year out, and we are asked to respect such trash because of "established theories." We are instructed by the universal "all" of the various medical schools to proceed to punish her with a wet towel, well twisted and administered freely, more comprehensively expressed by the term "spanker," and spank her very much. The American School of Osteopathy has made a departure, however, and has issued orders to "wallop," and "wallop" very freely, the empty-headed schools and theories that have no more sense than to torture a sick person, and do so only to disguise their ignorance of the cause of her disease. This ignorance is shown by the name of the spasmodic effect that has been given by the little book of guesswork, generally called and known as "symptomatology."

Not a single author has hinted or in any way intimated that the cause of her disease is a failure of the passing of the blood, chyle, and other substances to and from the abdomen to nourish and renovate the abdominal viscera, that are diseased owing to a lapsed diaphragm, which would cause resistance to the blood-flow in the aorta, through which passes the arterial blood, and the vena cava, through which the venous blood returns. There must also be interference with the flow from the receptaculum chyli.

The afflicted one is intoxicated. Here is where she gets a poisonous alcohol, and will never be relieved permanently until the "wet towel" of reason has been slapped on both sides of the attending physician's head, so he can hear the squeezing and rattling of regurgitation, and the straining and creaking of the fluids in their effort to pass through the diaphragm. Until he learns this, I would apply the "wet towel" of reason to the doctor, for fear he might become lukewarm in his studies and give his patient a hypodermic injection of morphine, which is the advice given at one of the recent conventions of medical men, who practice "old established" theories rather than be honest enough to say, "The woman is sick and I know it, but I do not know the cause of her trouble."

What Is a Fit?

If God's judgment is to be respected, a fit is the life-saving step and move, perfectly natural, perfectly reasonable, and it should be respected and received as divinely wise, because on that natural action which is thus produced on the constrictor nerves first, then the muscles, veins, nerves, and arteries with all their centers. It appears that the vital fluids have all been used up or consumed by the sensory system, and in order to be temporarily replenished, this convulsion shows its natural use by squeezing vital fluids from all parts of the body to nourish and sustain the sensory system, which has been emptied by mental and vital action, until death would have been inevitable without this convulsing element to supply the sensory system, though it may be but for a short time.

The oftener fits come the oftener the nutrient part of the sensory system cries aloud in its own though unmistakable language, that it must have nourishment that it may run the machinery of life, or it must give up the ghost and die. In this dire extremity and struggle for life, it has asked the motor system to suspend its action, use its power, and squeeze out of any part of the whole body, though it be the brain itself, a few drops of cerebro-spinal fluid, or anything higher or lower, so it may live

Those of you who are acquainted with the fertile fields which we have here referred to will be enabled to furnish the sensory system with such nutriment as will not make it necessary to appeal to you through the language used by the unconscious convulsions with all their horrible contortions.

You surely see with the microscope of reason that the sensory nerves must be constantly nourished, and that all nutriment for the nerves must be obtained from the abdomen, though its propelling force should come directly from the brain. The nerve-course from the brain must be unobstructed from the cerebrum, cerebellum, medulla oblongata, and on through the whole spinal cord. We must have a normal neck, a normal back, and normal ribs, which means to an osteopath careful work, with a power to know and a mind to reason that the work is done wisely to a finish. I hope that with these suggestions you will go on with the investigation to a satisfactory degree of success.

Rib Dislocations.

I wish to insert a short paragraph on a few effects following a downward, forward, and outward dislocation of the four upper ribs on either side. We have been familiar with asthma, goitre, pen paralysis, shaking palsy, spasms, and heart diseases of various kinds. We have been as familiar with the existence of those abnormal variations as we are with the rising and the setting of the sun. Our best philosophers on diseases and causes have elaborately compiled and published their conclusions, and the world has carefully perused with deep interest what they have said of all these diseases and of diseases of the lungs. We are left, however, in total darkenss as to the cause of those diseases, as well as of fits, insanity, loss of voice, brachial agitans, and many other diseases of the chest, neck, and head. As the field is open for any philosopher to make known the results of his observations, I will avail myself of this opportunity and say in a very few words that I have found no one of these diseases to have an existence without some variation of the first few of the upper ribs of the chest. With this I will leave farther exploration in the hands of other persons, and await the reports of their observations *pro* and *con.*

CHAPTER XVI.

Obstetrics.

Morning Sickness.

When a woman disregards the laws of Nature to such an extent as to overload the stomach beyond its powers and limits, distending it so that it occupies so much space as to cripple the laws of digestion and retain the food, decomposition will set up an irritation of the nerves of the mucous membranes to such an extent as to cause sickness and vomiting. When the nerves cannot take up nutrition, they will take up destruction and other elements which are detrimental to the process of nutrition, and there is no other chance for relief except in "unloading." The stomach itself is a sac. When filled to its greatest capacity, it irritates all the surroundings, and in return they irritate the stomach. Thus it unloads naturally for relief. Now we wish to treat of another vessel similar in size, similar in all its actions, which receives nourishment for a being, which nourishment is contained in the blood, and conveyed from the channels commonly known as uterine arteries. To all intents and purposes, this nourishment is taken there to sustain animal life. After having constructed the machinery, it appropriates the blood to the growth and existence of a human being. This is the womb. The placenta in the womb is provided with all the machinery necessary to the preparation of blood that is used for all purposes in the formation and development of a child. Both the stomach and womb receive and distribute nourishment to sustain animal life. Both get sick; both vomit when irritated, and discharge their load by the natural law of "throw up" and "throw down." Now note the difference and govern yourselves accordingly. The one is the upper stomach that takes coarser material and refines the unrefined substances, and keeps the outer man in form and being. The other contains the inner man or child, and by the law of ejection, when it becomes an irritant, it is thrown out by the nerves that govern the muscles of ejection.

Cause.

Diseases of the nerves of the pelvis come from pressure of the bowels and other organs of the abdomen and osseous disturbances. Thus we have a cause for morning sickness in pregnancy. All the nerves of the pelvis are pressed down upon from above by the weight of the large and small intestines and the weight of the womb pressing down upon the nerves of the sacrum and pelvis. Thus morning sickness seems to be natural. We would conclude, from the relation of arteries and nerves which at this time begin an active upbuilding for the development of the fœtus, that any disturbance from the normal would be a cause for this sickness.

Treatment.

To relieve such conditions, having the patient in the knee-and-chest position will place the abdomen in the proper form for unloading the pelvis of any impacted condition. Then place the hands low down on the abdomen and draw the contents of the pelvis forward toward the umbilicus and up from the pelvis, to give free passage of blood and other fluids circulating in the lower part of the abdomen. Often the bowels are filled with dry fæcal matter and press upon the uterus, rectum, and bladder, causing irritation of nerves of the organs of the abdomen, also pressing on the blood- and lymph-vessels, stopping healthy action in the economy of life in the whole viscera. Thus to be sick at the stomach would be natural. We reason that to confuse the normal flow of the fluids that enter into the formation of urine would cause these fluids to be taken up by other secretory ducts and conveyed to nerve-peripheries and cells, causing sickness at the stomach. We find, by any method of reasoning, that morning sickness is the result of poisonous fluids being taken up by the solar system, and that it is the effort to get such poisons out of the system that makes vomiting necessary.

To assist the young operator, we would suggest that he refresh his mind, previous to proceeding with operations to relieve the stomach of this irritable condition, by looking over the nerve- and blood-supply of the uterus and other abdominal organs. Know the nerve-supply of the uterus; know the ovarian plexus and the inferior hypogastric and sacral nerves, with which you are no doubt familiar. The blood-supply of the uterus comes from the ovarian, vaginal, and uterine arteries, with which the student should also be familiar.

Development of the Fœtus.

Just as long as digestion and assimilation keep in harmony and the mother generates good blood in abundance, the child grows, and by nature the womb is willing to let the work of building the body of the child go on indefinitely. But Nature has placed all the functions of animal life under laws that are absolute and must be obeyed. We are asked to note the similarity of the stomach and womb, as both receive and pass nutriment to a body for assimilation and growth. When a stomach gets overloaded, sickness begins, because digestion and assimilation have stopped; then the decaying matter is taken up by the terminal nerves and conveyed to the solar plexus, causing the nerves of ejection to throw the dying matter out of the stomach. Try your reason and see the stomach below sicken and unload its burden. Is this sickness natural and wisely caused? If this is not the philosophy of midwifery, what is? As soon as a being takes possession of its room, the commissary of supplies begins to furnish rations for that being, which has to build for itself a dwelling-place. The house must be built strictly to the letter of the specifications. Much bone and flesh must be put into the house, and some of all elements known to the chemist must be used and wisely blended to give strength. All material to be used in the house must be exact in form and of given strength, sufficient to furnish the forces that may be necessary to execute the hard and continued labors of the machinery that is used in all these transactions and motions of mind and body. Now we must go to the manufacturing chief and have him, through the quartermaster, deliver and keep a full supply of all kinds of material for the work, and when the engine is done, put it on an inclined plane and cut the stay-chains and let it run out of the shop. Be careful not to let the engine deface or tear the door as it comes out. A question is asked: On what road does the quartermaster send the supplies? As there is but one system over which the engine can bring supplies, we will call that road the uterine system of arteries. The machinist replies that he will open the door of this great manufacturing shop and let the engine roll out by the power and methods prepared to run out finished work. First you see a door open because the lock is taken off by a key that opens all mysteries. The great ropes that have been far inferior to the power of resistance that has held the door shut are all-sufficient in power. By getting sick, muscles become convulsed with force enough to easily push the new engine of life out into open space, by Nature's team that never fails to deliver all goods entrusted to its care.

PREPARATION

A student of midwifery can only learn a few general principles before he gets into the field of experience. Actual contact with labor teaches him that much that he has read is of but little use to him at the bedside. What he needs to know is what he will have to do after he gets there. He must know the form and size of the bones of a woman and how large a hole the three bones of the pelvis make, for the reason that the child's head will soon come through that space. He must know a normal head cannot come through a pelvis that has been crushed in so much as to bring the pubes within 1½ to 2½ inches of the sacrum. He must examine and know these conditions soon after he is called, for the reason that he will have to use instruments in such deformities, and may wish the counsel of an older and more experienced doctor. This precaution will give him time to be ready for any emergency.

More than 90 per cent of all cases, however, are of a very simple nature. The mother is warned by pains in the back and womb at repeated intervals of one-half hour or less. When by the finger the doctor can tell the mouth of the womb has opened to the size of a quarter or half-dollar, he then may know that labor will soon start, and at this time it is well to call for twine and prepare two strings about a foot long to tie around the navel-cord.

CAUTION.

The first duty of the obstetrician is to carefully examine the bones of the pelvis and spine of the mother, to ascertain if they are normal in shape and position. If there is any doubt about the spine and pelvis being in good condition for the passage of the head through the bones, and you find the pelvic deformity enough to prohibit the passage of the head, notify the parties of the danger in the case at once, and that you do not wish to take the responsibility alone, as it may require instruments to deliver the child and there is danger of death to the child and to the mother also, but less danger to the mother than to the child. Now you have done that which is a safeguard against all troubles following criminal ignorance.

First Examination.

I will give you a condensed rule of procedure in all normal cases of obstetrics. With the index finger, examine the os uteri; if closed and only backache, have the patient turn on her right side, and press the hand on the abdomen above the pelvis, and gently press or lift the belly up just enough to allow the blood to pass down and up the pelvis and limbs. Relax all nerves of the pelvis at the pubes.

Second Examination.

Wait a few hours and examine the os again. If still closed and no periodical pains are present, you are safe to leave the case in the hands of the nurse, instructed to send for you if regular pains return at intervals. On your return, explore the os again, and if it is found to open as large as a dime, you are notified that labor has begun its work of delivery. You now place the patient on her back, propped to an easy angle of nearly 30 degrees, with a rubber blanket in place. After you find the os dilated to nearly the size of a dollar, then relax the nerves at the pubes. Soon you will find in the mouth of the womb an egg-shaped pouch of water, which you must not press with the fingers until very late in labor, for fear of stopping labor for perhaps many hours. Remember the head can and does turn in the pelvis to suit the easiest passage through the bones, while in the fluids of the amniotic sac. Now, as you know why not to rupture the sac and spill the fluids, you are prepared to proceed to other duties, which are to prevent rupture of the perineum. Place the left hand on the belly, about two inches above the symphysis, and push the soft parts down with the left hand; support the perineum with the right hand until the head passes over. This is necessary to prevent rupture of the perineum. If you follow this law of Nature, laceration may occur in one out of a thousand cases, and you will be to blame for that one, and may be censured for criminal ignorance.

Now you have conducted the head safely through the pelvis and vagina to the world. You will find the pains stop right short off for about a minute, and that is the time to learn whether the navel-cord is wrapped around the child's neck. If it is found twisted around the neck once or more, you must slip a finger around the neck and loosen the cord, to let blood pass through the cord until the next pain comes, in order to ward off asphyxia of the child.

Care of the Cord.

When the next pain comes, gently pull the child's head down toward the bed. There is no danger of hurting the perineum now that the head has passed the soft parts. At this time the danger is suffocation of the child. Never draw the child too far away from mother's birth-place by force, as you may tear the navel-string from the child and cause it to bleed to death. If you value the life of the child, then you must be careful not to place the navel end of the string in any danger of being torn off. Now you have done good work for both mother and child. The child is in the world, and you want to show the mother a living baby for her labor and suffering of the past nine months. The baby is born, and the mother is not torn. But the baby has not yet cried. Turn it on its side, face down, run your finger in its mouth, and draw out all fluids, thick or thin, to allow air into the lungs. Then blow cold breath on its face and breast to stimulate the lungs into action.

Severing the Cord.

The baby cries and all is safe. Baby is born and cries nicely, but still has the cord fastened to the afterbirth. It has no further use for the cord, as life does not depend on blood from the afterbirth any longer. Take the cord about three inches from the child's belly, between your thumb and finger, and strip toward the child to push the bowels out of the cord if there should be any in it, as a safeguard for the bowels; then tie a strong string around the cord—first, three inches from the child's belly, and second, four inches; take the cord in your hand and attend carefully to what you are doing. If the baby's hand should fall back to the cord, you might cut off one or two fingers, or wound the hand or arm very seriously. Cut the cord between the two strings just tied around the navel-string, and look out for your scissors; then pass the child over to the nurse to be washed and dressed, while you deliver the afterbirth from the pelvis or womb.

Dressing the Cord.

As the child is cared for, cut a hole the size of your thumb in a doubled piece of cloth, five inches long by four wide, put the hole two inches from one end, and run the cord through the hole. Lay the cloth aross the child's belly; then fold the cloth lengthwise over the cord, which must lie across the child so it will not stretch the cord by handling or straightening the child out. Now you are ready to finish the delivery of the afterbirth. You have a plug of soft and tender flesh to get out of the womb and vagina.

Delivery of the Afterbirth.

As the afterbirth has grown tight to the womb during all the days of the mother's pregnancy, furnishing all the blood to build and keep the child alive in the womb for nine months, it has done all it can do for the child and is now ready to leave the womb. You are there to assist it to get out of the place it has occupied so long. You must begin to rotate or roll the placenta, first one way and then another, up, down, and across the vagina, by gently pulling the cord. Look out, or you will pull the cord loose from the placenta, and then you will have made your first blunder, with no cord with which to pull the placenta out, and the mother bleeding and faint from loss of blood. Now is the time and place to save life. Pass your hand forward into the soft parts to get your fingers behind the placenta; now give a rolling pull and bring it out with the hand. You will find it an easy matter to get your hand into the vagina and womb after the birth of the child. Get all the placenta out; then take a wad of cloth as large as the child's head and press it under the cross-bone of the pelvis; push the cloth under and up, so as to completely plug the pelvis. Now pull the hair gently over the symphysis, which will cause the womb to contract by irritation.

Care of the Mother.

All is now done excepting provision for the mother's comfort, which is your next duty. Draw her chemise down her back and legs until it is straight; then, with safety-pins, pin the chemise on the inner side of the thighs, so that the chemise will go around each thigh separately. Now you have the shirt fast to keep it from sliding upward, and you are ready to make a band of the chemise to support the womb and abdomen. Bring the chemise tightly together for two or three inches above the pelvis to form a band. Previous to pinning, draw the womb, which you feel above the symphysis, up; then pin, and the belt you have made of the chemise will support the womb. All is safe now, but you must not leave for two hours. You may have delivered a child from a feeble woman who may flood to death after the delivery of the child, if you do not leave her safe. I have in mind one case who flooded all of two quarts at a single dash. The first symptom was a pain in the head.

Post-Delivery Hemorrhage.

I know of only two causes that would produce hemorrhage or bleeding after the child is delivered. One is when the afterbirth, the placenta, is separated from its attachment to the womb and still retained in the womb or vagina, or when a part is separated and still lies in the womb. That retention of placenta preventing the natural circular contraction of the womb to close on itself and retain it, with force enough to prevent the further discharge of blood, would give a chance for a continued stream. Then, should the patient bleed profusely after the placenta has been removed, another cause would be in pulling away the afterbirth, as part of the upper portion of the womb may be pulled to an inverted position, which would be like a hat if you should press the top down with the hand. Then there is a chance for leakage because of this unnatural fold made in the womb.

Treatment.

My method of relief is to insert the hand and with the backs of the fingers smooth out all folds. Before you draw the right hand from the womb, place the left hand on the abdomen, catch the womb between the thumb and finger, and withdraw the hand. With the left hand pull the hair above the symphysis or scratch the flesh just above and across the region of the symphysis, just enough to make an irritation. After the hand is out of the vagina, pass a small bundle of cloths as far under the symphysis as would be necessary to hold everything up, and then fasten the chemise, beginning at the symphysis and drawing it tight about two inches above the symphysis, fastening it with strong pins. Be sure you keep the garment tight by pulling it down between the thighs. The coarser the chemise the better, as you want to make a strong bandage at that point, so as not to push the womb down into the pelvis. If the patient's general health is fairly good, allow her to tell you what she wants to eat and give it to her. Let her diet be in line with her usual custom. You must remember that she has just left the condition of a full abdomen. Lace her up, fill her up, and make her comfortable for six hours; then change her bedding.

Diet.

Remember this, that if you stop digestion for some hours with teas, soups, and shadows to eat, you carry her to a condition where it would be dangerous to give her a hearty meal. My experience and custom for forty years has been crowned with good success. I never lost a case in confinement. I have universally told the cook to give her plenty to eat.

Treatment of the Breast.

If your patient begins to have fever, followed by chilly sensations, with swelling of one or both breasts, I relieve that by laying her arm ranging with her body. Let someone hold the arm down to the bed; then I place both of my hands under the arm and pull it up with considerable force till I get it as high or higher than the normal position of the shoulder. Then pull her shoulder straight out from the body, a fairly good pull; then pull the arm up on a straight line with the face, and be sure that you have let loose the axillary and mammary veins, nerve, and artery, which have been cramped by pulling the arm down during delivery. No breast should become caked in the hands of an osteopath. Do not bother about the bowels for two or three days. It may be necessary to use the catheter if the water should fail to pass off after inhibiting the pubic system.

This is straight midwifery, and will guide you through in at least 90 per cent of the cases you will meet in normally formed women.

Right here I wish to say one word. I think it is very wrong to teach, talk, and spend so much time with pictures, cuts, talks, and lectures, and hold up constantly to the view of the student births coming from the worst possible deformities, and call that a knowledge of midwifery. It is normal midwifery you want to know and be well skilled in. The abnormal formations are few and far between, and when a case of that kind does appear, it is your knowledge of the normal that guides you through the variations. You will very likely never find two abnormal conditions presenting the same form of bone. As this is intended only to present to students natural delivery, I will let the subject drop with one word about the sore tongue of the mother. Adjust her neck, and relieve constrictor and other muscles that would impede any blood-vessel that should drain the mouth and tongue. Remember this, that a horse that is always hunting bugbears never finds a smooth road.

CPSIA information can be obtained at www.ICGtesting.com
Printed in the USA
LVOW111933140912

298880LV00013B/124/P

9 781176 930681